Women Confront Cancer

Making Medical

History by

Women

Confront

Cancer

Choosing Alternative and

Complementary Therapies

Margaret J. Wooddell
and David J. Hess

Foreword by Barbara Joseph, M.D.

NEW YORK UNIVERSITY PRESS
New York and London

NEW YORK UNIVERSITY PRESS
New York and London

Library of Congress Cataloging-in-Publication Data
Women confront cancer : twenty-one leaders making medical history by
choosing alternative and complementary therapies / [edited by]
Margaret J. Wooddell and David J. Hess ; foreword by Barbara Joseph.
p.   cm.
Includes index.
ISBN 0-8147-3586-X (cloth : acid-free paper)
ISBN 0-8147-3587-8 (pbk. : acid-free paper)
1. Breast—Cancer—Alternative treatment—Case studies. I.
Wooddell, Margaret J., 1961–   II. Hess, David J.
RC280.B8 W665   1998
616.99'44906—dc21   98-19752
                            CIP

New York University Press books are printed on acid-free paper,
and their binding materials are chosen for strength and durability.

Manufactured in the United States of America

10 9 8 7 6 5 4 3 2 1

And now, men and women of America, is this a thing to be trifled with, apologized for, and passed over in silence?

—Harriet Beecher Stowe

Contents

Foreword

Women Confront Cancer drives home a powerful, deeply resonant message: Women can and are changing the realities of their cancer diagnoses and treatment. And as we create these new realities, we are healing on deeper levels. Our healing involves the emotional and spiritual, not only the physical dimension. The healing journeys documented herein involve personal changes that cannot fail to have sweeping consequences.

In our struggle to overcome cancer, we must continually confront the strict limitations of conventional cancer treatment modalities—surgery, chemotherapy, radiation. While these treatments may benefit, they may also harm. While they kill cancer cells, they undoubtedly weaken and undermine our immune response. We have had to make choices—whether to rely on conventional therapies, which ones to embrace and how best to combine them with a host of alternative/complementary treatments—all without enough information. As we strive to know as much as we can—to understand pathology reports, to grasp the applicability of various treatments and procedures to our individual cases, to take into account long-term effects of treatments, to discern recurrence from survival data, and to look at the probabilities and procedures from all angles, making use of all available data—we also acknowledge that not only is our information limited, but that each of us is a unique individual with unpredictable responses, walking a path that is ours alone.

"First, do no harm." But how to define "harm"? Most of us believe women have a right to be informed of all available treatments and to have appropriate access to them. Yet, the lack of knowledge and interest of conventional M.D.'s in nutrition and other alternate cancer treatments is obvious. While it is profoundly intimidating to go up against the medical establishment when we are newly diagnosed and vulnerable, at a time when we are especially in need of reassurance in the form of a skilled physician's recommendations, sometimes we must do exactly that. We must beware of opinion masquerading as fact; we must demand a more humane medical profession that does not lay claim to information that it does not possess, one that does not put undue pressure on women to choose conventional treatments of questionable benefit, that does not misinform or obfuscate with confusing terminologies, that does not use fear to motivate choices in therapies, that validates a woman's decision-making process, and that, first, does no harm.

It is a question not only of raising more money for research but of steering the research in the right direction. Attention must be given to treatment trials comparing conventional treatments with nontoxic treatments. The effects of nutrition, supplements, mind-body techniques, acupuncture, homeopathy, and chiropractics must be further explored. We need to recognize the powerful effects of environmental toxins and psychological stress, in its various forms, on the development of cancer. And we must be attentive to the existence of a powerful cancer industry that profits more from cancer treatment than from cancer prevention and cancer cures.

Despite all these difficulties, many of us talk about cancer as a journey of empowerment. To choose is to exercise power, and this volume rings with the voices of the sick and powerful, the healing and the whole. These voices speak of the therapeutic effects of hope, of personal responsibility, of community, support systems, intuitive guidance, and dream work, and of finding the rituals that give us pleasure. Susan Moss says that she always gets a second opinion, and "the second opinion is always my opinion."

Healing from cancer requires a tremendous commitment, and I am inspired by the spirit that moves the women who have contributed to this volume. We all face cancer together, and together we can weave straw into gold. We are courageous women, each in our own way venturing to go where no one has traveled before.

Read our stories and feel our power.

Barbara Joseph, M.D.
author of *My Healing from Breast Cancer*
February 1998

Acknowledgments

This material is based upon work supported by the National Science Foundation under Grant No. SBR-9511543, "Public Understanding of Science," for which Hess was the principal investigator and Wooddell was the research assistant. Any opinions, findings, and conclusions or recommendations expressed in this material are those of the authors or the interviewees and do not necessarily reflect the views of the NSF.

The current volume is part of a larger research project that involves interviewing sixty people who in some way can be said to be opinion leaders in the alternative cancer therapy field. About two dozen interviews involve clinicians, researchers, and the heads of referral organizations; those results will be published in the companion volume to this one, *Evaluating Alternative Cancer Therapies* (1999). The remaining interviews involve discussions with women patients who have used alternative therapies, primarily for breast cancer (this book), and men patients who have used alternative therapies for prostate cancer (another planned volume).

This book does not recommend any therapies, doctors, or institutions, and under no circumstances is the information presented here intended as medical advice for individual patients. It is dangerous to attempt to self-medicate, even with food supplements, herbs, or dietary programs. Readers are urged to consult a qualified health care professional for any medical problem and to make decisions under medical supervision. This is particularly true for cancer, which ideally requires individualized treatment programs. Some of the therapeutic modalities mentioned herein may be contraindicated for some individuals in some programs of treatment.

Introduction

The women in this book are current or former cancer patients. Their stories are gripping. Much more important, however, is the biopolitical message they convey. This group stands out from the millions of other women in North America who are living with cancer or the fear of its recurrence. These women are opinion leaders in the movement to open up conventional medicine to the possibilities of nontoxic alternatives. They have assumed an active role as authors of books, support persons for other cancer patients, or public speakers and community resource leaders. Together they represent a selection of the women leaders who are exploring potential therapies beyond the limitations of conventional treatments.

The women have faced a range of different cancers and different experiences, and they maintain different opinions. Some, such as Sharon Batt, are very cautious about the use of alternative and complementary cancer therapies (ACCTs). Others are strongly opposed to chemotherapy, radiation, and, in a few cases, surgery as well. Many of the women are vocal advocates of ACCTs. Most of them advocate a middle ground where patients have the right to make choices from both conventional therapies and ACCTs. If there is a common ground among all the women in this book, it is the recognition that cancer patients need to have better information and more options than are currently offered.

We interpret the interviews of these women not as medical case studies but as political documents in the struggle for women's increased control over their bodies and the availability of diagnostic and therapeutic options. By far one of the dominant political issues involving women and cancer is breast cancer politics. Although some of the women in this book were not diagnosed with breast cancer, we believe that the experiences of all the women point to valuable lessons for breast cancer activism as well as women's health care activism in general. Women have been quite suc-

1

cessful in moving the political and charitable machinery toward the dedication of more funding for the health care concerns of women. For example, in 1996 the *New York Times* labeled breast cancer the "charity of the year." Breast cancer activists have changed the spending priorities of the National Institutes of Health, where only AIDS tops the total spending that is now going into breast cancer (Walker 1997).

Nevertheless, political activism for breast cancer—as well as for cancer in general—has tended to remain within the confines of patients' demands for increased spending and more testing. Historically there has been very little questioning of the fundamental premises of cancer research and the resulting new therapies. We believe that the interviews in this book carry valuable lessons for the politics of breast cancer, cancer in general, and women's health issues. They suggest a different political agenda than that of demanding more spending. These interviews point to fundamental policy matters such as providing sufficient funds to evaluate nontoxic (or less toxic) alternatives that might provide some answers that seem to have eluded cancer researchers for decades.

We suggest that as patients continue to learn more about both conventional and alternative/complementary therapies for chronic disease, the ethics of medical practice will necessarily change. For example, the principle of informed consent will expand beyond its current limitations. Nowhere is this change more likely to occur than in the intersecting worlds of cancer treatment, alternative medicine, and the feminist movement. Once women thoroughly understand the limitations of many conventional cancer therapies and diagnostic procedures, and once they learn about the possibilities of less toxic and less invasive alternatives, the research agendas of publicly funded organizations will come into question. Cancer organizations and women's health organizations will move beyond demanding more funding: the key political question will shift to reforming the research agenda, in particular to promoting a thorough and fair evaluation of less toxic and less invasive alternatives that women patients, along with a few far-sighted clinicians, have begun to discover.

This book is based on the premise that there is now a critical mass of women who can provide the necessary leadership to reform the cancer agenda. These women have had the courage and determination to question the recommendations of surgeons, radiologists, and oncologists, and to examine alternative or complementary approaches. Far from rejecting conventional medicine or their doctor's care, in many cases these women have put together treatment programs that combine the best of both worlds. This approach is now gaining recognition among some oncologists in the United States, such as Keith Block in his program of integrative therapy (Block 1997). In some cases the women have overcome the survival expectations of conventional medicine. A few women have even achieved long-term survival without the use of any conventional therapies. Some of them have also had very difficult experiences in the world of alternative and complementary therapies. Several have encountered excessive claims for alternative/complementary therapies that did not work for them personally. In other words, they have a variety of experiences to share, but overall they convey lessons for negotiating among conventional and unconventional approaches to cancer.

The overwhelming message of the women whom you will meet in this book is a call for better information about both conventional and alternative/complementary therapies, for the right of each woman to choose a mix of modalities that suits her disease and life circumstances, and for women to be able to make those decisions without being afraid that their doctors, family, and friends will reject them. Although some women have very strong opinions about the toxicities of conventional therapies and diagnostic procedures, the message is not antidoctor, nor is it even anticonventional medicine. Rather, it is a message about patients' rights. Those rights involve much more than informed consent or even medical freedom of choice. Beyond those concerns, the patients' rights issue gradually weaves into a broader right (and duty) of citizens to challenge spending priorities for publicly funded research programs.

It is important to underscore that the case histories presented here are not designed to be medical case histories; we view them more as case histories in the tradition of medical sociology and anthropology. We draw no medical conclusions from the case histories; our goal is to document the decision processes, choices, and dilemmas that women face when they consider alternative and complementary cancer therapies. Our hope is to contribute to a better understanding of the policy changes that need to be made in order to provide women the opportunity for true informed consent, medical freedom of choice, and valuable, valid information about the safety and efficacy of both conventional therapies and ACCTs.

It is worth pausing to clarify the terms *alternative* and *complementary*. Some women and many doctors now prefer the word *complementary* to *alternative*, because they use the therapies along with conventional therapies rather than instead of them. We prefer Susan Holloran's use of the terms. She suggested that the same therapy can be alternative or complementary depending on how it is used. When women turn to visualization, meditation, vitamin supplements, dietary changes, herbs, exercise, and immune system–stimulating products in their health care programs, they may use them to back up a conventional treatment program and therefore as complementary therapies, or they may use the same therapies as alternatives: to replace parts of a conventional program (such as instead of adjuvant radiotherapy after a lumpectomy) or as complete substitutes. As for most of the women you'll meet in this book, we do not think of the choice between alternative and complementary uses as an issue that can be settled across the board. Rather, the point is that the use of an alternative/complementary therapy is a question of informed consent and patients' rights. In other words, we support individualized protocols in which decisions are made between patients and open-minded health care practitioners.

In order to have true informed consent, patients need information about therapeutic and diagnostic efficacy. Which alternative procedures work, and which do not? The question returns us to the issue of cancer funding priorities. Congress has not mandated that the National Cancer Institute (NCI) perform a series of well-controlled, fair, clinical trials of nontoxic cancer therapies such as dietary, herbal, and nutritional programs. In the few cases where public pressure has prodded the NCI and other organizations to test such therapies, the experimental protocols appear to have been altered in ways that introduce biases against the therapies. The scientific politics are well known and carefully documented in books such as those of Ralph Moss (1995, 1996). Given the controversies surrounding previous attempts to get the NCI and other organizations to test alternative and complementary cancer therapies, patients and their representatives in Congress need to think through the goals of evaluating ACCTs. The Office of Alternative Medicine within the National Institutes of Health is a good start, but to date it has neither the funding nor the bureaucratic mandate to sponsor controlled trials or even outcomes analyses of alternative cancer therapies. Part of the problem of evaluation also rests with clinicians and hospitals associated with ACCTs. In general they have not provided a great deal of research. There are some substantial exceptions, such as the work of the Gerson Research Organization in San Diego (Hildenbrand et al. 1995, 1996) and the work of Helen Coley Nauts (1975, 1980).

The women in this book will, we believe, help to crystallize the will that is needed to provide the public funds to test alternative cancer therapies. These women represent the opinion leaders in the intersecting worlds of cancer advocacy, the women's health movement, and alternative/complementary medicine. As opinion leaders, activists, or resource persons in the vast personal networks of patients and cancer care, their ideas are important and will be increasingly influential, if our assumptions are correct. They deserve to be heard, and their experiences and recommendations deserve to be incorporated into national policy.

Our interviews were informal and open-ended, but they were not random conversations. We asked each woman a uniform series of questions: what their experiences were, how they made their decisions, what role science or other factors played in the decisions, what advice they want to share with other women, and what their opinions are of cancer research and publicly supported cancer organizations. Wooddell, a doctoral student in Science and Technology Studies at Rensselaer Polytechnic Institute, interviewed the majority of the women. Hess, a professor there, did some interviews, wrote the first drafts of the introduction and conclusion, assisted Wooddell in the write-ups and editing of the interviews, and shepherded the manuscript through the publication process. Because the telephone interviews generally lasted from one to three hours, we edited them to the current length with the hope of capturing the main points. We then contacted the women with the write-ups and asked them if they wanted to make any changes. We offered all the women the option to remain anonymous; most of them are public or semipublic figures, and the women included here were all comfortable with having their names revealed.

The women who were chosen for the interviews are from North America, have been diagnosed with cancer, have utilized some ACCTs, and have some public profile and therefore can be counted as leaders. Many of the women have written books, some have appeared on radio or television programs, and others are active in organizations. We included three patients of Stanislaw Burzynski, M.D., Ph.D., because their stories were so powerful and because they raised political issues. The Houston-based doctor is known for his discovery of antineoplastons, a therapy for cancer that is similar to immunotherapies, and he has been in the news because of the controversies surrounding attempts to stop him from treating patients with antineoplastons. The Burzynski patients in this book have been active in the demonstrations, trials, and various other activities in support of Dr. Burzynski, or in the support networks for his patients. The struggle to allow him to continue to practice in the face of continued suppression represents only the most recent skirmish in the long-standing battle for medical freedom for cancer patients.

The stories of the women are gripping. They are strong women who have inspired us to continually question health care options. Let us also hope that they can help lead us to better health care in the next century.

References

Block, Keith
    1997 "The Role of the Self in Healthy Cancer Survivorship: A View from the Front Lines of Treating Cancer." *Advances* 13 (1): 6–26.
Hess, David J.
    1999 *Evaluating Alternative Cancer Therapies: A Guide to the Science and Politics of an Emerging Medical Field.* New Brunswick, N.J.: Rutgers University Press.
Hildenbrand, Gar, L. Christeene Hildenbrand, Karen Bradford, Dan E. Rogers, Charlotte Gerson Strauss, and Shirley Cavin
    1996 "The Role of Follow-up and Retrospective Data Analysis in Alternative Cancer Management: The Gerson Experience." *Journal of Naturopathic Medicine* 6 (1): 49–56.
Hildenbrand, Gar, L. Christeene Hildenbrand, Karen Bradford, and Shirley Cavin
    1995 "Five-Year Survival Rates of Melanoma Patients Treated by Diet Therapy after the Manner of Gerson: A Retrospective Review." *Alternative Therapies* 1 (4): 29–37.

Moss, Ralph
  1995 *Questioning Chemotherapy.* New York: Equinox Press.
  1996 *The Cancer Industry.* 2d ed. New York: Equinox Press.
Nauts, Helen Coley
  1975 *Osteogenic Sarcoma: End Results Following Immunotherapy with Bacterial Vaccines, 165 Cases or Following Bacterial Infections, Inflammation, or Fever, 41 Cases.* Monograph no. 15. New York: Cancer Research Institute.
  1980 *The Beneficial Effects of Bacterial Infections on Host Resistance to Cancer. End Results in 449 Cases.* Monograph no. 8, 2d ed. New York: Cancer Research Institute.
Walker, Paulette
  1997 "Lawmakers Push NIH to Spend More on the Most Prevalent Diseases." *Chronicle of Higher Education*, April 18, A34.

| one | Sharon Batt |

Patient No More

Sharon Batt is the author of *Patient No More: The Politics of Breast Cancer* (Charlottetown, P.E.I.: Gynergy, 1994), an award-winning journalist, founder of Breast Cancer Action Montreal, and former editor of the consumer education magazine *Protect Yourself.* Breast Cancer Action Montreal is located at 5890 Monkland Ave., Suite 201, Montreal H4A 1G2.

Her Story

Sharon Batt was diagnosed with stage II breast cancer in 1988. "It was a big shock to me, partly because I had felt as though I had never been healthier in my life. I was on a cycling trip in France when I discovered a lump in my breast. I felt that I was living a healthy lifestyle. I have some cancer in my family, but the relatives who died of cancer have been diagnosed in their sixties or later. I was stunned to be diagnosed with breast cancer in my forties.

"At the time I was quite naive about cancer treatments, whether conventional or unconventional, because I had always been well. I hadn't thought much about cancer, and no one in my close circle had been diagnosed. At the time of my diagnosis, I was pretty much learning from scratch. I have worked all my life as a researcher, so my approach was to dig deeply to figure out what was going on and to look for answers.

"The doctors recommended a lumpectomy with axillary node dissection [removal of lymph nodes in the armpit area], radiation, and a very toxic chemotherapy cocktail. I received conflicting recommendations for the chemotherapy. The tumor board recommended CMF (cyclophosphamide, methotrexate, and fluorouracil), a fairly mild and standard combination for breast cancer. My oncologist asked me to go into a clinical trial to test three levels of CAF (cyclophosphamide, Adriamycin®, and fluorouracil), a more toxic regimen. They made no pretense that these therapies were going to cure me. They also didn't hide the fact that the chemotherapy might permanently damage my heart and the operation could leave my arm permanently disabled. They were throwing out all these potentially horrific scenarios that could result from the treatments."

She sought additional opinions and found that the specialists disagreed, although always within the range of which conventional therapies were appropriate (such as whether or not to have tamoxifen). "I found the atmosphere among oncology specialists to be very masculine; there was not a lot of warmth there."

Batt eventually found a woman general practitioner with whom she could communicate. Although Batt had questioned the wisdom of chemotherapy, the doctor suggested that there was a significant benefit for premenopausal women. "She had a friend who had just been diagnosed with breast cancer, and all her physician friends got together to help this woman decide about chemotherapy. They agreed that if it was them, that is what they would do. It was this conversation with my physician that tipped the balance for me, in terms of going ahead with chemotherapy, although I still had some grave doubts about it."

Batt tried to determine whether the toxic drug Adriamycin®, which her oncologist was recommending, would benefit her any more than a milder drug combination. She soon realized that patients were making decisions based on imperfect information. "The science just hadn't been done."

Batt also questioned having an axillary node dissection. She understood that its primary value was diagnostic, and she wondered if the diagnostic information was worth the risk of possibly having her arm paralyzed for the rest of her life. "I fought with the surgeon on that and he insisted we needed the operation 'to complete the staging.' I didn't understand the word *staging*. I went to another surgeon and he was a little less authoritarian, but he clearly recommended that I have my axillary nodes removed. I went back to *Our Bodies, Our Selves* and found nothing in the book questioning the operation. I was looking for support for rejecting the additional surgery and couldn't find it. I ended up going ahead with the dissection, which turned out okay, but I was not happy about taking such a big risk for a diagnostic procedure."

After surgery Batt entered a clinical trial for comparing three dosage levels of chemotherapy at four or six months; she also had six or seven weeks of radiation therapy. During this time Batt examined alternative therapies, particularly those in the dietary and psychosocial areas. Finding that she gained weight when she was on chemotherapy, she started to look into low-fat diets. "There was this general kind of advice to eat a low-fat diet. There wasn't the kind of information that there is now. I changed my diet quite a bit to eliminate cheese, whole milk, and dairy products in general. I also ate more vegetables and cut out meat almost entirely. I didn't go on a programmed anticancer diet. I just modified what I ate within that framework.

"I asked the oncologist to refer me to the hospital nutritionist, and he said, 'What for? Your diet is fine. What am I supposed to write here on the referral form? There is nothing wrong with your diet.'"

Batt did not get much support from her general practitioner on the dietary issue, either. "She did ask me if I wanted her to prescribe some marijuana to combat nausea from the chemotherapy. I never was really into marijuana; it just didn't interest me. She also talked to me about visualization and gave me some exercises. I tried them, but they didn't work for me."

Batt's skepticism came from extensive research of the various psychological interventions. Soon after her diagnosis, friends spoke to her about the purported cancer personality, and she was disturbed by the blame-the-victim undercurrent of that concept. "I felt somewhat defensive and angry that people were implying that I wasn't good enough as a person."

However, she attended one of Bernie Siegel's weekend workshops, which she liked, and she read the work of the Simontons. David Spiegel's study (1991) had also just come out, and Batt interviewed him, O. Carl Simonton, and other psychologists for a two-hour radio documentary. She found visualization difficult. "It takes a lot of concentration. I was really frightened at the time of diagnosis, so a lot of the images that I was conjuring up were terrifying. To use the Simontons' approach, I had to turn them around, but the images that I found in books were Walt Disney stuff. They didn't resonate for me. I was also skeptical as to whether visualization could make a difference in the physiology of cancer. I read Susan Sontag's book, *Illness as Metaphor,* a powerful polemic against the psychological theories of cancer that grew out of her own breast cancer experience. My starting point was the Simontons' book and Sontag's book, which were both compelling books presenting diametrically opposed views."

At a psychological level, Batt was working through her own intense fears that came from being diagnosed with stage II cancer. "I was thinking about a lot of worst-case scenarios. At times I felt alone. My friends didn't have experience with cancer and were even more ignorant about the disease than I was. I wanted to talk to other people who had cancer. I couldn't find a support group. I would strike up conversations with women in the oncology waiting room just to connect with other people who had cancer. I soon joined the National Coalition of Cancer Survivorship in the United States and went to two of their meetings. I eventually started a group myself, but that was quite a bit down the line. I had always had close friends, and their support became very important to me."

At the time Batt was having chemotherapy, Gaston Naessens was being tried in Sherbrooke, Quebec. She followed the case from a distance. "I felt that the medical community overreacted to people like him. Whether he was helping people or not, I didn't think it was likely that he was hurting people. The trial seemed to border on persecution and showed a closed-mindedness within the medical community. It was clear to me, having gone through the [conventional] treatments, that they weren't terribly advanced or based on a sophisticated understanding of how cancer progresses or develops. So I had sympathy for him as a researcher who was trying something different."

Although Batt did not try Naessens's 714-X, she did try supplements such as vitamin C. However, she was cautious about supplements as well. "I chose the ones that I did because they were fairly simple, easy to obtain, and not costly. Basically, they were extensions of the kinds of things that I did anyway. They were not particularly risky. I felt the same way about taking risks with alternatives as I did with conventional therapies. Risk was one of my criteria for both. Economics was another. Also, as I felt so healthy, it didn't make sense to try something that could have a noxious effect. So, logic was another criteria.

"I was very conscious about being frightened or used. If anyone was moving in on that vulnerability, I really backed off. I learned a lot about myself in making these decisions. Your own values come into focus when you have cancer. In the end, the 'right' decisions are the ones that make sense to you as an individual." When we spoke again with Batt in early 1998, she remained in good health.

Advice to Other Women

Batt began this topic by pointing to a central problem from the patient's perspective: the information that patients need is often not available. "You have to live with a certain amount of uncertainty. Even if you are using something that has been demonstrated as being effective, you don't know if it will help *you*."

She also emphasized that, for their own sake, patients need to assume responsibility for their decisions. "Whatever choices you make, you're the one who has to live with the outcome, and the outcome may be that you die of breast cancer. You will never know if a different path would have changed that, so if there's something you really want to try, it's important not to let other people discourage you. And if you're convinced a treatment is really *not* for you, don't be talked into it."

Although Batt does not advise individual women on choices, she has noticed that many women are "interested in finding a combination of mainstream and complementary therapies. I think that this ongoing war between the two sides is damaging to the patients. Patients have to realize that there is a lot of selfinterest on both sides. Then they have to find their own way."

Batt never found a support group, but she recognized that it could be helpful for some women. In general, she thought some sort of support, even if less formal than a support group, is vital. "I have always been politically involved. So, when I ended up with cancer, I gravitated to political action."

From a political perspective, Batt noticed early on that patients were disempowered in the decision-making and treatment process. "We were pawns in the power struggles that were going on, whether it was between surgeons and oncologists, or a surgeon who had one way of treating versus another who had another way of treating, or different alternative therapies. The patient was just a kind of football." As a result, Batt became involved in patient advocacy groups. Although she has participated on a national level, she decided to start a local group in order to work for change on an ongoing basis.

"Our Montreal group is very interested in prevention. We push the boundaries of the research agenda away from just treatment, the clinical approach, to looking at ways to prevent the disease. In 1991 four of us started to organize Breast Cancer Action Montreal, and the next year we held a public meeting where we had Ginny Soffa [see the interview, chapter 20 of this book] come up and talk. It was just overwhelming, the interest we had from women in the community coming out to the meeting. That is when we decided to really get serious.

"We define ourselves as an advocacy group rather than a support group. We have about 130 members with twenty to twenty-five active members. We have had a real impact in raising awareness and creating a community in Montreal. We've brought in terrific speakers like Susan Love and Devra Lee Davis. We are trying to promote the perspective of women in the community and, in the large sense, give people some power. The group in San Francisco is the group that has inspired me. A lot of women in our group are interested in writing and exploring cancer in a political sense.

"I think public involvement is necessary in the cancer field. I encourage women to get involved in advocacy and not to feel inadequate because they don't have scientific or medical credentials. The woman with cancer has a perspective that is legitimate and has not been heard. I'm really struck when I get together with women who have cancer, from all over the world, that basically our concerns are similar. A whole range of issues are common themes among women. They reflect the patient's holistic response to the disease, which means far more than controlling the tumor, preventing it, or trying to get treatments that are more effective and less damaging to your system. By *holistic* I mean recognizing that a life-threatening diagnosis affects you at a spiritual, social, and economic level. It has such a profound impact on your life. The medical community has to realize that medicine has a place, but it is only part of the picture from the patient's point of view."

Batt also recommended a number of books, including Susan Love's *Dr. Susan Love's Breast Book,* Kathy LaTour's *The Breast Cancer Companion,* and Susun Weed's *Breast Cancer? Breast Health!* She expressed concern that environmental carcinogens and pollution may be contributing to cancer rates, and she suggested that there should be more open discussion about the dangers of X rays. "With a lot of medical interventions, you are battering your immune system, and that scares me. There should be more discussion on the role of X rays and cancer. We, the patients, have to catalyze this debate, because health professionals do not want to talk about the overuse of X rays."

Opinions on Cancer Research and Publicly Supported Cancer Organizations

"It scares me that the corporate influence is so strong in cancer research. Researchers are losing control because there is not enough money at the university level. The genetic research that is getting all of the attention has the potential of being useful, but because of the economic incentives for developing tests for cancer susceptibility when we don't have a means of preventing the disease, priorities are out of whack. I think that we have to lobby and be involved in a very astute way to try to keep patients' needs on track. This is going to take an enormous amount of energy and awareness. It is tempting to get caught up in the idea that pouring more and more money into diagnostic and treatment research is going to help patients. That is not necessarily true. Tests and treatments can hurt patients. I'm optimistic that the involvement of patients can have a positive impact, but also feel that we are working against enormous forces.

"I was shocked when I looked into the history of the American Cancer Society in sources like Audrey Lorde's book *[The Cancer Journals]* and Rose Kushner's book *[Alternatives].* From the beginning the ACS promoted early detection and seeing your doctor. As a fund-raising lobby, they have succeeded brilliantly. I think they need to work more closely with patients or they are going to lose credibility. The pamphlets that were given to me as a patient in the oncology ward were so pitiful. They didn't provide me with information that I needed as a patient.

"As advocates, we have to work at the local level but be connected at the national and international levels, because it doesn't make sense for activists to fragment our energy. We now have many breast cancer groups here in Canada, as well as different groups serving people who are interested in alternatives, such as a new group here in Montreal focused on alternative therapies. The NCI [Canadian] has just completed a series of monographs on alternative therapies. There is mounting pressure for an office of alternative medicine to be set up at the federal level, similar to the one set up in the United States."

References

Boston Women's Health Collective
    1971 *Our Bodies, Our Selves*. Boston: New England Free Press.
Canadian Breast Cancer Research Initiative
    1996 *714-X: An Information Package*. Toronto: Canadian Breast Cancer Research Initiative.
    1996 *Essiac: An Information Package*. Toronto: Canadian Breast Cancer Research Initiative.
    1996 *Green Tea: An Information Package*. Toronto: Canadian Breast Cancer Research Initiative.
    1996 *Hydrazine Sulphate: An Information Package*. Toronto: Canadian Breast Cancer Research Initiative.
    1996 *Iscador: An Information Package*. Toronto: Canadian Breast Cancer Research Initiative.
    1996 *Vitamin A, C, and E Supplements: An Information Package*. Toronto: Canadian Breast Cancer Research Initiative.
Kushner, Rose
    1986 *Alternatives: New Developments in the War on Breast Cancer*. New York: Warner.
Latour, Kathy
    1994 *The Breast Cancer Companion*. New York: Avon.
Lorde, Audrey
    1997 *The Cancer Journals*. San Francisco: Aunt Lute.

Love, Susan
    1995 *Dr. Susan Love's Breast Book.* 2d ed. Reading, Mass.: Addison-Wesley.
Siegel, Bernie
    1986 *Love, Medicine, and Miracles.* New York: Harper and Row.
Simonton, O. Carl, Stephanie Matthews-Simonton, and James L. Creighton
    1978 *Getting Well Again: A Step-by-Step Guide to Overcoming Cancer for Patients
    and Their Families.* New York: Bantam Books.
Sontag, Susan
    1977 *Illness as Metaphor.* New York: Farrar, Straus, and Giroux.
Spiegel, David
    1991 "A Psychosocial Intervention and Survival Time of Patients with Metasta-
    tic Breast Cancer." *Advances* 7 (3): 10–19.
Weed, Susun S.
    1996 *Breast Cancer? Breast Health! The Wise Woman Way.* Woodstock, N.Y.:
    Ash Tree.

two

Gayle Black

The Growing Lymphedema Epidemic

Gayle Black earned a Ph.D. in clinical nutrition from the University of Southern California. She held the position of assistant administrator of Bennett Community Hospital in Fort Lauderdale, Florida; was elected the U.S. representative in health care to St. Thomas's Hospital, London; and for many years was an assistant professor and deputy chairperson in the Health Care Department at St. Francis College, Brooklyn, New York. She was a cancer specialist and directed the Breast Cancer Survival Center, 401 East 80th St., Suite 28E, New York, NY 10021.

Her Story

In 1987 nutritionist Gayle Black was diagnosed with interductal carcinoma of the breast. "I started out my diagnostic and therapeutic regime very conventionally. Then, when I was having my lumpectomy, they found a one-centimeter mass of invasive carcinoma. Actually, I had five separate cancers, three of which didn't show up on the mammogram." Black had interductal, invasive, lubula, in situ, and squamous cell carcinoma.

"I had a lumpectomy and an axillary node dissection with the removal of thirty-three nodes, which were all negative. Following the surgery, I had thirty-three days of radiation therapy and was told that it would all be fine and dandy, to go home and not to worry."

At the time Black was given no information that the removal of all thirty-three lymph nodes for her right arm would put her at risk for developing lymphedema. That disease is not a kind of cancer, but it is in some ways worse: it is a painful, chronic, progressive swelling of a body part (usually an arm in the case of breast cancer patients) caused by the abnormal accumulation of lymph fluid. As Black added, "The lymph system carries all the bacteria, toxins, and dead cells. If they don't have a way to get out of the body, bacteria develop in the arms and you get many infections. Because there is no ability to heal, when you get an infection it's *really* serious. Even antibiotics only help a tiny bit. The lymph system is so stagnant that little gets through to it. A small percentage of women die from the lymphedema because the infections are uncontrollable. I never knew it could happen. It's the silent killer that no one talks about."

The lack of information on the risks of axillary node dissection was complete: "Not only did they never give me advice; they never even told me that there was a possibility that this could happen in 25 percent of the women. It's the big secret. No one talks about it. What's so sad is that they don't give any education to the doctors on lymphedema when they learn oncology. They don't know the first thing about it. They don't know where to send you or what to do."

Four years and eleven months later, Black had a mammogram, and the results showed calcification exactly at the same place in her breast. "The doctors wanted me to have a mastectomy. I decided against it because with the earlier radiation treatments, reconstructive surgery would have been very, very difficult. I thought to have just this portion of my breast removed again and see what happened."

When the cancer did return, Black began to use alternative therapies. "At the time, I wasn't on chemotherapy or radiation and felt as though what I was doing wasn't enough. I started to take various therapies: Essiac tea, purple herb, high megadoses of vitamins, and a clean diet." Black had another lumpectomy and, within a year, another recurrence. "I was hoping for the best, but it didn't work. It returned again."

In 1994, when the recurrence occurred, Black had a mastectomy and immediate reconstruction. "When I was having my mastectomy and reconstruction, the doctors told me that I needed to have chemotherapy after surgery." Black decided against the chemotherapy treatments. Immediately after the surgery, she went on an autogenous vaccine therapy for six months. "It seemed to work the first three months, but it didn't seem to work for the remainder of the time. It was also during the last three months of my stay that I developed lymphedema. The right side of my arm began to swell up, and it became extremely painful."

No doctor had told her what not to do to avoid the lymphedema. Only later did Black find out that "you must never, never go into a sauna, steam room, Jacuzzi, or a hot whirlpool. After five years I was still doing fine. I was staying at a hotel that had a sauna, steam room, Jacuzzi, and a hot whirlpool. Every night after the end of the treatment I would go there, and by the end of the week I had almost what I have today. My arm swelled up to three times its normal size. It was burning and hot as the skin was stretching with the lymph that was trying to go through with the blood. From that point on it never got better; it only got worse.

"At that time I was told I had to use a compression bandage, which I did. I was told I had to wear it all the time, but I was not told I had to do anything at night, so I wore it during the day, not at night. My arm continued to get worse until I got back to New York and saw a doctor who has a company doing just lymphedema therapy. He said I had to wrap it at night, and my arm has to be bandaged twenty-three hours a day. The only time it's off is when I take a shower or bath. I started a full-time regime, but my hands got worse. As it progressed, I went (in 1996) from wearing a sleeve to a gauntlet, which covers the hand down to my fingertips. It's on all the time. If I take off the glove portion, my arm from my wrist to my fingers will swell, because the fluid can't go through. The glove holds it so my fingers don't swell any more than they are."

After her stay at the clinic in 1994, Black was fighting two diseases: cancer and lymphedema. "When I first came back, only the top part of my arm—from the elbow up—was swollen, and the part from my elbow down was fine. I had that for about eight months. So I was just watching it, and it wasn't terribly bad. Then it started to travel quickly down to my wrists." At that time there was little available in the way of lymphedema therapy, but Black eventually found a therapist who was trained in a method from Germany. "She said she was afraid to do any manual drainage. My cancer had invaded my brachial plexus [the nerves at the base of the neck and armpit], and that must be massaged front and back to get the lymph to drain. There was a chance the cancer could spread. She said as soon as I was off the chemo and in remission, she would do it, but I never was in remission long enough to do it. Some women who are in remission have the drainage, but that's every day, five days a week for one month, and it's very expensive and not reimbursable."

Because the vaccine therapy hadn't been successful, Black went to the Janker clinic in Germany for six weeks. There she received beta-interferon and gamma-interferon injections directly into her lesions. "They did debulk and reduce beautifully. I thought that it was the end and how great it was that I didn't have to go on chemotherapy."

While in Germany Black also received treatment for her lymphedema. "I was not on chemo then, so they were able to do the lymphedema drainage. It was wonderful, but of course twenty-four hours later it was back to where it was."

Black returned to the United States, and within seven weeks she noticed that the cancer had metastasized to the chest wall. "It was very obvious and apparent; all you had to do was look into the mirror and you could see it. It looked like a red rash and then it became more extensive. It reached up and around to my back. Where there were beta- and gamma-interferon injections, it was killed, but it wasn't systemic. I knew new ones were always coming up again."

In December 1995, Black went back to an oncologist and began a three-month regimen of tamoxifen. "After a month on the tamoxifen, we saw that it was working on approximately 20 percent of the metastases, but the metastases were more aggressive. They were getting ahead of us, and my doctor suggested chemotherapy.

"In February 1995, nine years after being diagnosed with breast cancer, I began my first chemotherapy treatment with CMF [cyclophosphamide, methotrexate, and fluorouracil]. I was very scared, very apprehensive, and nervous while I was going through the chemotherapy treatments." Black supplemented her chemotherapy treatments with various immune system stimulators to keep her body as strong as possible. "I was taking such things as thymus proteins and maitake mushrooms along with a great deal of other alternative substances.

"By August 1995, after completing six months on CMF, I thought it was like a miracle. Everything cleared up. I thought, 'The chemotherapy wasn't so bad; my hair didn't fall out.' I thought that I was free and clear, and it was all just wonderful. I continued to stay on all my alternative therapies."

Nine months later, in May 1996, Black noticed that she had started coughing regularly. She took the antibody test, AMAS, and for the first time, it went up 140 points. "It looked disastrous because it had never done that before; something was brewing. I went down to the Hoxsey clinic in Tijuana, Mexico, and went on the program for three months.

"By July 1996, I was coughing uncontrollably and my lymphedema was bad." Black had a CAT scan and it showed metastases to both lungs. "At the time, we knew that we had to work fast, because with the lungs involved, I was quite sick. On July 26, 1996, the oncologists put me on the chemotherapeutic agent navelbine." At the time of our first interview with her (early 1997), Black was supplementing her navelbine treatments with alternative therapies. "Just recently, I added another oncologist and am working on his alternative program. Also, I started a sixty-day regime of a highly concentrated soybean isoflavin drink." Black was taken off the tamoxifen because she noticed red pimples on her newly created breast and thought that it could be a hormonal response.

"I am at a place right now where I'm just waiting and praying. What is happening is that the chemotherapy is corroding my bone marrow. My bones are breaking very easily and as we speak, a bone in my chest is probably broken and pushing on my nerves." Black was taking morphine in the evening and awaiting a CAT scan.

"That's where we are; this is some story. I'm a combination of both: conventional and alternative therapies. My criteria for choosing among the conventional and alternative therapies included what I felt that I could emotionally and physically handle along with what I could fit into my life. I didn't want it if it made me feel like a freak or look like a weirdo. I didn't want to think of anything else except being normal.

"I kept thinking, 'I don't want to lose my hair; I don't want to lose my hair.'

"I'm not the type of person who could face going through chemotherapy feeling sick and losing my hair. The only reason that the oncologists got me to do the CMF and navelbine is because these two chemotherapies don't produce side effects. I felt that if I got sick, it was just going to weaken my immune system and I wouldn't be able to recuperate. I continue to feel that there is a very fine line where chemotherapy helps and where it does permanent damage."

Besides books, Black contacted the National Cancer Institute hot-line, 800-FOR-CANCER, to find information on clinical trials. "I would always check them to find out about new trials and any new therapies. It's amazing to me that medical doctors don't do this.

"I would have to go to my various doctors and say, 'Here, this looks like a clinical trial that I can handle, what do you think?' Then it would be fine with them.

"When I was originally diagnosed in 1987, the doctors didn't recommend chemotherapy if the lymph nodes in your armpits were negative. It was the standard practice until two years later. So not having chemotherapy at the time of my diagnosis was not my decision. When I did decide to have the chemotherapy, it was only after having my breast removed in 1994. At that time, I was the one to decide against having chemotherapy and for reconstructive surgery. That's when I decided to go like gangbusters with the alternative therapies."

Black looked at numerous alternative therapies and continually changed her treatments. "I found out about the various alternative therapies by obtaining the book *Third Opinion* [Fink 1997; orig. 1988]. Another book that I used for information was *Options* [Walters 1993]. In that book, I used the listing of contact places across the United States for alternative therapies. It just became a process of endless phone calls. As I called the contacts, they gave me the names of people who had gone through the program. I was forever on the phone with very expensive bills to show for it. I never found out about alternative therapies or their sources from a medical doctor. They never heard of them and only believed in chemo, chemo, chemo."

From the therapies that Black learned about, she chose those that she could do at home. "I read everything on alternatives. The ones with the best track record were the ones that I considered, but they also had to make sense and fit into my lifestyle.

"I looked at the Gerson therapy, and the reason I didn't choose it was because I had to live with the problem when I got back to the States. I knew that I couldn't chop, house, and store thirteen juices a day and still feel normal. It would be so emotionally disruptive that I knew that it wasn't for me. I had to feel as though I had a mainstay of normal living, to keep my emotional course.

"Prior to my diagnosis with breast cancer, I was what you would call 'eating very well,' never a junk food eater. I would eat chicken and eggs, lots of eggs. After my diagnosis I stopped eating the chicken and eggs, knowing that in the United States we use stilbestrol, a female hormone, on chickens. We also give them antibiotics so they won't be sick, and food and dye so they're nice and yellow. I didn't want to put that in my body because what I didn't need was any additional estrogen." Her estrogen receptors were already positive.

Black also switched to soy milk. "I started on a more grainy, vegetarian diet, but still with a good amount of protein. I didn't go macrobiotic, but more of a semivegetarian diet." She also switched from tap to distilled water. "I was trying to work all ends of the environment.

"I've also addressed my physical activity by doing what I consider a minimum amount of exercise. I had been exercising on the treadmill for half an hour, four miles an hour, three times a week. Recently, I had to stop exercising because I was having chemo and was just wiped. I think I will start again because my bones do better with exercise." Black could not do weight-bearing exercises or lift heavy weights because of the lymphedema in her right arm. "Right now, I am having a great deal of trouble with the lymphedema." Her arm was wrapped in a compression sleeve during the day and wrapped in bandages at night. It was totally compressed twenty-three hours a day.

From the time of her diagnosis, Black attended two support groups. "I went to a support group when I was first diagnosed. It seemed okay because it was a group for the newly diagnosed. Then, when it metastasized, I went to a group for metastatic cancer." It was while attending that group that Black had to leave. "It took me about ten sessions and I kept coming back crying every night.

"My husband said to me, 'Why are you going there?'

"And I said, 'Because I am supposed to be in a support group.'

"Attending the support group was actually harming me. What I was hearing was where people who were a little down the road from me were, with regard to their health. It just got me more nervous and crazy. Also, I felt like a lone turkey because I was the only one who was doing alternative therapies. I kept looking at them as the end-all and yet kept saying, 'I can't believe this because they aren't doing alternatives.' Finally I left and have been much better off for leaving the group."

After two years, however, the fears that Black was first facing when she attended the support groups had been realized, and being in that situation was not as bad as she had first expected. "I was now on a different level. I now needed the support group for its friendship with women who had traveled the same journey that I had. We were no longer fearful about what would be happening because it had already happened. I realized after going through this experience that our needs and desire for a support group change from year to year, and we have to be open to that change."

Black chose only doctors who would be open to alternative therapies. "I only allowed those doctors who would say 'Yes, you can do both conventional and alternative therapies' into my circle. If a doctor ever said 'This is garbage' or 'No,' then I was out of there; I was history. I ended up going to all parts of the world to find a doctor who would say 'Yes, you can do both.'

"I have had several oncologists since my last diagnosis but have stayed with this last one for the past three years. She believes in doing anything you can. Whether or not she believes in it emotionally, she knows that I am taking things that can't hurt me. I will stay with her because she knew that I was going on the Hoxsey therapy and actually encouraged it. She knows that they don't have the answer with straight chemotherapy and the eventual outcome with it."

At the time of the interview, Black had begun to consult an oncologist who also treats patients with Chinese herbs, and she was waiting for her first round of medications. "He's from a long line of doctors and chief of oncology at a major medical institution. He doesn't advertise it, but he is a practitioner of all the alternatives. I just heard about him last week and immediately made an appointment. My feeling is that if every oncologist could be this smart, if they could be this bright, to know about Chinese herbs and which ones to use, then I have a feeling that I'm in good hands. This is a forever search or journey, and you find people who will help you along the way. I was lucky that I came across him; it's a comfort to me."

At the time of our first interview, Black felt as though she had a little bit of cancer and had to work through it. "You wouldn't know it. I try to maintain a normal regimen, even though it takes a total of approximately one and a half hours to take all my products in the morning and evening."

In mid-1997 we talked with Black again. She was on Doxil®, which she described as "a sister clone of Adriamycin®, but it's delivered in liposomes, so it doesn't have the same horrible reaction. In other words, I don't lose my hair, and I can function on it and carry on my life other than being more tired. I've been on it for four months. In two months I'll get a CAT scan, and we'll find out if it's working. I think it's working because now that the cancer has metastasized to the lungs, any time it stops I start uncontrollable coughing.

"I had to stop the vitamin C intravenous drips because the fifty grams of vitamin C are delivered in a solution that is sodium-based, and the sodium was too much for my lungs to handle. My lungs would swell up. Now I'm on a fermented soybean drink that's equivalent to twenty-five pounds of soybeans. I'm on massive doses of Coenzyme Q-10 to protect my heart from the chemo, which does get weak from this particular type of chemo. There is a lot of research being done in Italy by a fellow named Lissoni. He feels that melatonin combined with tamoxifen is three times as effective for breast cancer. He has not done the work with Arimidex®, which I am now on. When tamoxifen fails, we now put women on Arimidex®. I was on tamoxifen for a year, but it wasn't working because the cancer metastasized to my lungs. Arimidex® is supposed to be better; it has fewer side effects. It's the new kid on the block. But the research has not been done on melatonin and Arimidex®, so I'm trying to decide about going on them."

When we talked with Black in mid-1997, it was during the middle of a heat wave that was affecting the northeastern states. "It's ninety degrees here in New York City. Although my body was able to handle it, my arm had another brain. My arm was so swollen that I had to have it in bandages all day long, totally immobile. I have to go out later today, and I am afraid to go out of the air-conditioned house, because I don't have to do too much and it will swell. When it swells and you're wearing a compression bandage, it's like torture. The bandage goes up to the armpit, so the shoulder is exposed. The lymph has to have a place to go, so all of a sudden the shoulder swells up like a balloon. It's tight because you have to have your compression bandage on, which is keeping it in. It's like somebody is trying to strangle you. If you take it off, your arm is going to swell. If you keep it on, you're getting faint from the strangulation.

"Aesthetically, I have to take a suit size bigger to cover the arm. I look thin but I have one fat arm. It just doesn't give me the freedom—I used to play tennis and golf. I can't play practically any sport because it's my right hand. I have no fun as far as any kind of exercise goes. I've become more of a couch potato, and I've had to accept it because it's not going to change.

"That's just a small taste of how debilitating the lymphedema is, and how it never gets out of your face. When I look in the mirror, I see one arm normal and one arm distorted. I try so hard to forget the cancer and to go on with my life, but this thing rears its ugly neck all day long. This is as painful as after surgery. The best we can do is control it, but we know that each year it does get worse."

Black did a series of exercises to help control the lymphedema. "Sometimes I am fiercely angry at the exercises because they take so much time. If you don't do it, your arm hurts. If you do it, your arm hurts. It gets to the point that when I use my computer on a bad day, I have trouble hitting the keys because my fingers are swollen. It plays on me, especially for little things like opening my blouse when my fingers are all swollen. I just can't. I've tried to teach myself to eat with my left hand. There are so many other limitations. I can't hold a hair dryer tight in my hand.

"I get infections because the lymph stops. I have to go on antibiotics, and I always wind up getting a vaginal infection because my immune system is low and I get a yeast infection. And the antibiotics are strong, plus they hold up my chemo cycle because I can't have chemo when I am on antibiotics.

"I pray every day that it won't get worse than it is. I know it's not going to get any better, but I just work so it won't get any worse." Unfortunately, her condition did get worse, and when we spoke with her husband in early 1998, he said that she was terminally ill.

Advice to Other Women

Gayle Black emphasized that in her experience probably the single most important decision about cancer is selecting the right doctor. She interviewed seven doctors before finding one who she thought was acceptable. "And *I* interviewed *them*. When they didn't pass my test, I didn't use them. You've got to feel that the doctor is a team person, a friend who is there for you. If you don't feel included, you lose control, and I think there is no greater fear to a person with breast cancer than losing control. You've got to find a person who's going to go along with you and accept the roads that you're planning to travel. If they won't, it's important to learn that from them right up front. If they're not your friend and not willing to work with you in a teamwork approach, you will need to search until you find someone who is. I've found that the people who do better—the patients who have longer success stories—are the ones who have a very fine friendship with their oncologist. The doctors really have to believe in their hearts that they are there to serve you, as opposed to you following the doctor's orders."

Black saw hundreds of women every year, and she found that there "is no question" that those women who have a teamwork relationship with their doctor, as well as a sense of friendship and support, do much better. "Many women don't understand that they have the right to find someone who is their friend. They are so governed by the medical myths that they think that whatever the doctor says is how it has to be. My journey has been easier because of the wonderful doctor I have."

Black advised women who are interested in alternative therapies to consider them, but she adds that women have to do much of their own work: "I would say that you have to be smart and savvy. You have to read all the alternative books, because no one is going to tell you a thing. It's your mission to do it.

"You've really got to be emotionally cancer savvy. Unless some major changes occur, you'll never be able to learn anything about alternative therapies from traditional doctors.

"It's a hard road and you have to be willing to persevere. Sometimes I have wondered if it's worth it. I had five separate cancers when they took my breast off. That's a lot to deal with, to make it to where I am today. I don't know any other woman who has had five separate cancers. I don't think that I could have possibly gone the traditional route, to have chemotherapy for all these years and still be here today. There is just so much chemotherapy that a body can take.

"I know that whatever I did along the road, I wouldn't change. I know that it was right for me, but I had to seek out everything else before I was able to know it. I had to spend time in the library and bookstores to really be able to handle cancer. I always believed in what I was doing. After all, I am a Ph.D.-trained nutritionist. It helped because I spent years and years learning about healing, including all these alternatives. In fact, I did my dissertation on alternative healing. I was researching it, never knowing that I would have to use it one day."

Black also had some advice to offer on axillary node dissection and lymphedema: "My advice is to tell your doctor that if you're going to go on chemo, you just want the first five or six nodes. By and large, if it's not in the first five or six nodes, it's usually not in the others. You have to be reassured that the doctors aren't going to take out all of your nodes, like they did in 1987 when I was having it done. I would have it in writing that my doctor would not take out more than one-third of my nodes, so that I would have some nodes to work with. What they never tell you is that mastectomy or lumpectomy will never bother you in your life, but the arm will. If there isn't something to filter out the lymph, you're guaranteed to have lymphedema forever.

"Now they can ask for this new gene detection. In the larger cities, they are just taking out the one node. If that gene is affected, you know it is metastasized. It only means taking out one node. They took out thirty-three for me. I had thirty-three—they took out everything! I have no nodes under my armpit. This is what they've done with most women. It's a diagnostic procedure to tell you whether or not you will need chemo, but the insanity of all this is that everybody who has breast cancer goes on chemo. So what is the point of mutilating a woman, who now has this possibility of going through life like me, with a real handicap, when in fact they're going to get chemo anyhow?

"The truth about it is that it didn't have to be. If you're told that you shouldn't be in the heat, never to put your arm in the sun, and never to go into saunas, steam rooms, Jacuzzis, or hot whirlpools, it doesn't have to happen. You have to keep it moisturized. You can't ever pick up a weight more than five pounds; you can't carry a pocketbook or anything. As soon as you put any pressure on it, it swells, and the more swelling the more likelihood of infection." Black has also changed her diet in ways that may reduce the swelling. For example, she eats fewer dairy foods and less salt, which may have a protective effect. She thinks all of these warnings and indications should be passed on to all women who are at risk of developing lymphedema. Instead, there is only silence.

"Doctors don't even know about it. When I told my oncologist, she looked at me in total shock and said, 'I didn't know that.' Of my friends, nobody's oncologist knows about it. When I go to the lymphedema services center, there are twenty or thirty women in the room and each of them has an arm like mine. They talk about how this could have *not* been done. They talk about how they had their nodes taken out. They were given chemo anyhow. They got the cancer back anyhow, and look at the arm. It's so sad to see how all the oncologists dismiss it."

Black suggested to women that they have to do their own research. "I can't let up. Doctors don't have the time to do it. Half the time I bring doctors new chemo protocols they've never heard of. Women have to decide they are going to get a degree in oncology. They have to never stop learning and never stop asking questions. Never just accept anything as the gospel, because there is always someone else who has a different direction." Black gave the example of how she pushed her oncologist to come up with a better chemotherapeutic option, and she eventually came up with Doxil®. "It's pushing to the ultimate limit, saying, 'I cannot accept it. You have to do better for me.' It's becoming master of your own ship and never letting go of those reins. Otherwise you fall into what we call typical protocol treatment."

Opinions on Cancer Research and Publicly Supported Cancer Organizations

Black found the publicly supported breast cancer organizations helpful for providing clinical trial information. In addition to contacting the NCI hot-line, Black contacted the American Cancer Society, the National Alliance of Breast Cancer Organizations (NABCO), and an organization in New York City called SHARE. "All these organizations were extremely helpful to me for finding information." She added, however, that the organizations did not tell her anything about alternative therapies. "They would only tell about traditional modalities and never anything alternative."

Regarding the NCI hot-line, 800-FOR-CANCER, Black commented, "It was the resource I used to find out about the locations and types of cancer clinical trials that were ongoing." Black also thinks that the PDQ (physician's desk query) for lymphedema at the NCI provides much good information. That address is <gopher://gopher.nih.gov...o/supportive/ lymphedema>, or it can be found via the National Institute of Health's Web site. "I use that when I get patients that have lymphedema to educate them about it. It's about the physiology.

"When I didn't know where to find anything, I contacted NABCO for directions to the various organizations. I went once or twice to hear speakers at meetings held by the SHARE organization, even though I stopped going to its support group." (SHARE now has a whole health group; see the interview with Ann Fonfa, chapter 8.)

Black gave an example of the type of helpful information that can be obtained from conventionally oriented organizations. "In 1995 I called the American Cancer Society to find some help for my husband because cancer is a family affair. We needed to get him into some kind of support group for husbands. My husband is a kind and wonderful man, and my cancer was just taking him down. He went to the support group and found it helpful."

Regarding lymphedema, when Black was first diagnosed with lymphedema in 1994, no one seemed to know anything about the disease or how to treat it. Black had to do her own research and found out about the National Center for Lymphedema in San Francisco. Now there are lymphedema service centers in many major cities, and more emerge every day. The National Lymphedema Network has a hot-line at 800-541-3259 and a home page.

References

Fink, John M.
    1997 *Third Opinion: An International Directory to Alternative Therapy Centers for the Treatment and Prevention of Cancer.* Garden City Park, N.Y.: Avery.
Walters, Richard
    1993 *Options: The Alternative Cancer Therapy Book.* Garden City Park, N.Y.: Avery.

three

Alice Cedillo

Giving Your Program 100 Percent

Alice Cedillo is a consultant to other cancer patients, real-estate broker, master gardener, and former flight attendant. She and her husband own a video production company that has produced the Burzynski patient organization's video, which is distributed worldwide.

Her Story

Alice Cedillo noticed a swollen lymph node in her neck and pointed it out to her gynecologist during various visits over a two-year period. At first the doctor thought it was a slight infection and did not seem worried. In August 1994 Cedillo switched doctors, and when she asked the new gynecologist to check her lymph node, which at the time had grown to the size of a walnut, the doctor was alarmed and immediately set up additional appointments for her. The doctors subsequently did blood work and ordered X rays and other tests in order to rule out other diseases. Cedillo commented, "To this day I really don't understand why it took them so long to find out that it was what it was." It was not until December 1994 that the doctors did a biopsy and made the diagnosis.

After the biopsy, Cedillo went to visit her mother. "I kept calling them to try to find out what they knew. They ended up leaving a message on my answering machine at home. The message was that it was non-Hodgkin's lymphoma and it was incurable, and if I had any questions to give them a call. This was Christmas of 1994. I still have the tape from when they left it. I cannot believe after all the calls I made from Austin to personally talk to them that the doctor left the message on my answering machine."

In January 1995 she saw an oncologist who explained that although the disease was incurable, he recommended chemotherapy. "I asked him, 'Well, how soon do I need to start it?'

"He said, 'Today.'

"I asked him, 'Is there anything else out there that I can do that is not poison to my system, or not quite so toxic?'

"He said, 'There is nothing else. People die from non-Hodgkin's lymphoma.'

"I asked him, 'Well, what kind of time are we talking about?'

"He said, 'Ten years doing chemotherapy, five years if you don't do the therapy.'

"I told him, 'I am going to have to think about it.'

"It was a lot of information. I think I was overwhelmed. To a great extent I was numb. My husband, Greg, was with me. He asked the doctor, 'Do you think we would be irresponsible if she waited on the chemotherapy?'

"He said, 'Yes, I think it would be very irresponsible if she waited.'

"Then I said, 'Well, I think I would be very irresponsible if I didn't check it out and started chemotherapy today.'

"He said, 'Well, do what you want, but there is nothing else.'"

Cedillo returned for a second appointment, when she asked even more questions. She wanted a second opinion, and the doctor offered her the opinion of another oncologist in the same office. When she said she wanted a more independent second opinion, they told her she would have to pay for it. She did a bone marrow biopsy in the doctor's office, which was disastrous in part because of her reaction to the anesthesia and also because the doctor apparently did not get a successful biospy. After a second biopsy at a cancer center, she learned that the cancer was stage IV, which meant that there was bone marrow involvement. At the cancer center she asked one of the doctors what his opinion was of antineoplaston treatment, and he dismissed Dr. Burzynski as the "pee doctor." (His antineoplastons were originally derived from urine.)

After doing substantial library research in a medical library, Cedillo developed a list of questions for her doctors, who were planning to put her on a chemotherapeutic drug cocktail known as CHOP (cyclophosphamide, doxorubicin, vincristine, and prednisone). Her questions showed the level of research she was doing. For example, she asked, "Is joint pain or muscle soreness associated with slight fibromyalgia?" She also asked for the names of patients who had been put on the same protocol, so that she could talk to them and find out their opinion. She did get the names of two patients, whom she contacted. One was very positive about the treatment, but she warned Cedillo of side effects such as pneumonia.

After some research, Cedillo decided to become a candidate for a trial of FND (Fludarabine). However, she thought about it some more. "I got home and began to think, 'no.' I had already started doing some herbs on my own, like echinacea, and Essiac tea. I had started reading all kinds of articles on my own." She also decided to visit an herbalist, who "put together a concoction of mistletoe and a few other ingredients. I did that and tried to clean up my diet as much as I could."

After a few months without doing chemotherapy, she went back to her doctor's office, where the doctor "said that I was a case of spontaneous remission. This was either from the herbs that I was doing or from what doctors say about lymphoma, the waxing and waning process. This was two months from the original December diagnosis when I went in to see him."

By March 1995 she had read several of the major guidebooks on alternative and complementary therapies, such as those by Walters (1993) and Pelton and Overholser (1994). She also called the Cancer Control Society in Los Angeles, which sent her information, and she talked with people locally, particularly at a local health food store in Dallas. Through the health food store she met another non-Hodgkin's lymphoma patient who was using conventional therapies and suffering tremendous side effects. That patient, who became her friend, was a medical librarian, and she helped Cedillo by doing library searches for her.

After talking to various people and learning more about alternatives, Cedillo decided to become a patient of Dr. Burzynski. When she became his patient, she found that most other doctors were unwilling to work with her. "I didn't get help from anywhere. I felt abandoned and very alone." She had difficulty finding doctors who would place the catheter in her chest (the tube for delivering the antineoplastons). Once she did manage to get a catheter placed, she had enormous problems with it. She had several trips to the emergency room, and at one point the catheter ruptured. "I had to go to the hospital for fluoroscopic surgery to remove the catheter because four inches of tubing had broken off and were now in my heart." Over time she found a doctor who seemed to do a better job of placing the catheter. She also learned about the different techniques, and found that a Groshong worked better than a Hickman technique.

Cedillo suffered a great deal of pain, including pain associated with either necrotic tissue or enlarged lymph nodes near her right kidney, and in October 1996 she went off the antineoplastons. She tried 714-X, an injectable substance made of camphor and nitrogen, for two twenty-one-day cycles in October and November. She took Haelen-851, a fermented soy beverage, for a fifteen-day period. In November she had a scan of the abdominal area, and the radiologist told her that the reduction was dramatic. "At that time, there was a 58 percent reduction. That was in November 1996. I had been off the antineoplastons since October 21." She returned to the antineoplaston treatment in January 1997. Although she is satisfied with her choice to use antineoplastons, she adds, "It is not to say that Dr. Burzynski has a total cure; it might just be a piece of the puzzle."

Cedillo's current program includes a radical change of diet. She visited the Optimum Health Institute, which taught her about a diet that she described as related to the wheatgrass therapy of Ann Wigmore. That diet emphasizes all raw food. "A typical day might be fruit juice or vegetable juice for breakfast, with citrus once or twice a week only. Lunch would be a green salad with sprouts. Dinner would be seed cheeses, guacamole, and crackers. I was at the institute for three weeks. It was a wonderful experience." She has limited tolerance for the wheatgrass juice, so she is on a modified version of the diet. She does eat some meat, cheese, and eggs—all organic. "Being Hispanic, I would want to eat tortillas with my eggs and maybe some bacon and potatoes. Well, that is considered all wrong on this diet. I think those are the kinds of things that helped me get into trouble. I feel better when I just eat fruit for breakfast or grain products. I drink goat milk because it is the closest thing to human milk."

Other key elements in her overall program for health include supplements, exercise, and meditation. She supplements her diet with a multivitamin, and she added, "I also started on a program with a kinesiologist-nutritionist that consists of oils and enzymes." She was once a runner and a bodybuilder; she ran three miles per day and nine miles on Sundays.

However, her joints are painful, so her exercise is limited to walking. She meditates at home, and she adds, "My faith is strong and I believe in God. My mother prays for me all the time. I certainly believe that my strength comes from my faith." Friends tell her that she looks healthy, and she attributes her feeling of health to the combination of factors that has been described here.

When we spoke with Cedillo in early 1998, she commented, "I'm still pumping the antineoplastons, continuing to do research, praying every day, and reading children's books."

Advice to Other Women

"When I talk to other people who call and are trying to find out what to do, one of the things that comes to mind is that I have had so many jobs in my life, and when I was doing them, I tried to give them 100 percent and then some. Why, then, shouldn't I do the same when it comes to saving my life? This is the most important job I have ever had. So why am I not going to do my very best? Why am I going to put my life in the hands of others and say, 'You take care of me'—somebody I really don't even know? It is scary. I have always been very independent, so why give this most important job to someone else?"

Cedillo believes that her "fighting spirit" has been an important ingredient in her battle against cancer. "I always think of Bernie Siegel, who found that cancer patients who were assertive and determined to beat cancer had a better chance of recovery, and that the uncooperative patient, and not the passive patient, does better." For her, being uncooperative meant questioning a conventional treatment option that basically provided her with a death sentence within ten years. "I don't think they have all the information. I think and believe that they have been through special training, and that doctors are as vulnerable as we are to the ravages of cancer. Their families are, too. I would like to believe that they care. At the same time, I think their knowledge is supplied by a very powerful medical and governmental body that has vested interests to make cancer prevention very unprofitable. The medical learning institutions are subsidized by foundations from the multibillion-dollar drug industry. This is why I think many doctors are so narrow-minded and are unwilling to go outside their comfort zones.

"I believe that doctors take a Hippocratic oath—which is, 'First, do no harm.' They know chemotherapy doesn't work on certain cancers, but they will still recommend the treatment, which will harm the patient. Common sense tells me this doesn't add up. I've talked with people who have undergone conventional treatment and can only imagine what they have gone through. Why, then, would I want to follow that path? It seems to me that it was harmful. Why not start out by doing something that isn't so toxic? I do realize that some people don't have a lot of time. In my case I felt that chemotherapy would be there for me at the end of the line, if after my search there was nothing else. But I have never believed that there was nothing else. Chemotherapy is still a choice for me, but it would be my last choice."

Cedillo added that if she were to opt for chemotherapy, she would work with a doctor in California who first tests the chemotherapeutic substances to see how they react to the individual's cancer cells. Surgery was not an option for her, but she said she would have considered it "if maybe I had a lymph node that was putting pressure on, say, a lung, and they could get to it."

She added that in her experience diet was also very important. "In my opinion diet is one of the main contributors or causes of cancer. No matter what you choose—Gerson, Kelley, or other programs—diet is the main focus. It means helping the body to heal itself."

Cedillo emphasizes the importance of choosing options that are tailored to each individual. "I would advise women to pick their own path. Don't allow anyone to lead you. Just pick your own path, whatever that may be. Probably none of it is ever going to be easy. But just know that if it is your own path; you are doing what is in your own heart. Listen to that."

In addition to being independent and finding the therapeutic options that make sense for the patient as an individual, Cedillo advises women "to do their homework." She adds, "If you are given a death sentence, just don't accept it. Do everything you can to arm yourself with vital information regarding your diagnosis. It may come from other people or from books or doctors. It is going to come if you look for it and are open to it."

Opinions on Cancer Research and
Publicly Supported Cancer Organizations

Cedillo had enormous problems with insurance, and she faced abandonment by conventional practitioners whom she informed about her choice to pursue alternative and complementary therapy. "I think this should really be called the catastrophe of cancer. I think the profit is in cancer and not in a cure. I think that medical research has failed to come to terms with the problems of cancer. They won't come to terms with it unless they take a different approach. Looking at this disease another seventeen or twenty years from now, we will be doing the same things: basically cut, poison, and burn. I think they really need to pay attention to and have an open mind to alternative therapies that are out there instead of doing what they are doing to innovative researchers like Dr. Burzynski. When someone comes up with a potentially innovative cancer treatment, instead of trying to suppress it, they need to look at it seriously. In his case, he should be given support. The American Cancer Society should spend some of its money for alternative therapies. I think that if you keep doing something over and over again and it doesn't work, you should try something else and it just might work. I do think that in this case this is what they should do.

"I really haven't tried to get information from the publicly supported organizations. I think they probably are helpful. I wonder what women would do if there wasn't a central place where they could go, even if all of the information is regarding conventional therapies. As far as the organizations, I believe they do serve a purpose. I have called the Lymphoma Research Foundation in California. That foundation only works on clinical trials, and the only way to get into a clinical trial is if you have done everything else. So, they really wouldn't give me any information. It really wasn't a viable source of information in my case.

"The Cancer Control Society, not being conventional, has been helpful. You can call, and they will send you whatever current information is available on alternatives.

"I think basically my role with Dr. B's organization, clinic, and patients is really not a big one. I do take calls from patients that call and want to speak to someone who is on the treatment. I try and encourage people, and check on other patients whom I have known for quite some time. As far as the actual (court) trial and the organization, everyone does numerous things, so there is not one specific role that anyone plays within the organization. You just do whatever you need to do and go wherever you may be needed. The important thing, besides being there and giving him support and informing patients what is going on, is talking to potential patients who are looking for help. I think that is the most important form of help.

"The way I see it, this is a job for God. He is my support group. I really don't go to support groups. I went once to Nancy's support group [her friend with lymphoma who is using conventional therapies], and everyone who was there had undergone conventional therapy. I hadn't done any treatment yet, and since I was thinking about alternatives, I felt like an outcast and like I didn't belong in that group. They were all very nice people, but their experiences with conventional treatment were really scary. I just said, 'This is not for me.'

"I know there are probably other support groups that are different, but basically I find that what I need comes from other people, whether it be friends or kids. I find kids to be good to hang around. I think they would be a wonderful support group. Last Friday we had the Ugly Bug Ball. You dress up as an Ugly Bug. Isn't that great? Kids are great. If you can get outside of yourself and whatever your problems are, then I think you'll be okay. That is how I feel. With kids nothing is a problem. The biggest problem or challenge to them is 'What are we doing today?' How are we going to have fun today? That is my therapy. So, go to the library and check out children's books."

References

Pelton, Ross, and Lee Overholser
    1994 *Alternatives in Cancer Therapy*. New York: Simon and Schuster.
Walters, Richard
    1993 *Options: The Alternative Cancer Therapy Book*. Garden City Park, N.Y.:
    Avery.

four

A Mother Battles the FDA for Medical Freedom

Kimberly Eckley is a Burzynski patient and support person.

Her Story

In 1994 Kimberly Eckley, a twenty-six-year-old mother of three from New Jersey, was diagnosed with breast cancer. Eckley immediately underwent a modified radical mastectomy for the removal of the seven-centimeter mass at the five o'clock region of her left breast. Because of her age and the type of cancer, Eckley's only therapeutic intervention was the surgical procedure.

"It was a situation where many doctors didn't know what to do with me. I was tossed around between medical practitioners at three different hospitals until one doctor finally made a decision that radiation and chemotherapy were not necessary."

Following the surgery, Eckley remained cancer-free for two years. However, a year after the surgery, her six-year-old daughter was diagnosed with a rhabdoid atypical teratoid tumor, a rare form of childhood brain cancer. Eckley's daughter was transported to Children's Hospital, where she underwent surgery and chemotherapy treatments.

"Literally, we were taken by the hand and told this was the only thing available to us, that we didn't have any other choices. The chemotherapy treatments were not curative but were to extend her life. It was all that was available to us, and since that was the only knowledge we had at the time, we started her on the chemotherapy two days after Christmas, 1995."

Eckley's daughter underwent six weeks of chemotherapy and an additional four and a half weeks of radiotherapy. "During that time she had ten different types of chemotherapy treatments, three of which were

41

directly administered into her spinal column. She was also receiving weekly spinal taps." Eckley's daughter lost more than 10 percent of her body weight and became devastatingly ill. "She had to be fed through a feeding tube because she couldn't tolerate solid foods."

While her daughter was a patient at Children's Hospital, Eckley heard about Dr. Stanislaw Burzynski's antineoplaston treatment program from another patient. "He sounded too good to be true. When people say things that sound too good to be true, they usually are. I accepted the information and just stored it in the back of my mind. A few months later, I met a patient's daughter who knew about Burzynski's patients, and I also had people anonymously put information about the Burzynski program in our mailbox. My husband said, 'We've got to call this guy and find out more information about his program.' We weren't hopeful about our daughter's progress, even though she was responding to the radiation and chemotherapy. The doctors didn't change their minds on her prognosis. They didn't give her any additional chances than from the day she began the radiotherapy and chemotherapy.

"As a concerned and loving parent, no one wants their child to die, so we investigated Dr. Burzynski's program. We called many different Burzynski patients, but mostly the families with small children facing brain cancer. They all had stories to tell, some very sad and others that made us ecstatically optimistic. One common theme throughout these stories was that, whether or not they lost their loved one, if they had the option, they would do it again. Hands down, they would have gone to Dr. Burzynski and refused conventional therapy. Unfortunately, from my understanding, many of the patients had already received conventional therapy, so by the time they started Dr. Burzynski's therapy, it was too late. Sometimes the antineoplaston treatments can't alter the effects of conventional therapies."

In March 1996 Eckley's daughter began her treatments with Dr. Burzynski's antineoplaston therapy. The residual tumor, which was the size of a golf ball when the primary tumor was removed, was the size of a baseball at the start of the treatment regimen. "We have been very fortunate. After three months with the antineoplaston treatments, the residual tumor was virtually gone. This was determined by MRI tests performed at our local hospital. The doctors here are completely flabbergasted by the fact that my daughter is doing so well. Currently, she is in her third month of being cancer-free, and I thank God for giving Dr. Burzynski the guiding hand for creating this therapy."

It was at this time, April 1996, that Eckley discovered a mass in her right axillary nodes. A mammogram also detected a lump in her right breast. "Due to my history, the doctors immediately performed a biopsy and the lump turned out to be malignant. As I stated earlier, when I was first diagnosed with breast cancer, I was tossed around the various hospitals and couldn't even remember the physicians' names. The issue was 'Do we treat her with radiation, radiation and chemotherapy, or maybe even tamoxifen?' After all that, the only therapeutic treatment they recommended was the surgery. Why? I still don't understand to this day.

"Now I have developed a totally different and very rare form of aggressive breast cancer. I am only twenty-nine years old, and my age makes me a fluke of nature. It is horrible, but true. To redevelop a totally different form of cancer is very far-fetched and isn't something that you commonly hear."

Eckley underwent a second modified bilateral mastectomy two weeks after the biopsy. "The results of the estrogen receptor status and nodal sampling were negative, but this time my physician and oncologist recommended chemotherapy." At the time of the interview (late 1996), Eckley had undergone four cycles of Adriamycin® and was scheduled to receive eight additional cycles of CMF (cyclophosphamide, methotrexate, and fluorouracil) for a total of eight Adriamyacin® and twelve CMF treatments. "I am almost done, thank God. Now they are deliberating over whether or not to recommend radiotherapy. I don't want to be on the chemotherapy or radiation."

In May 1996 Eckley submitted her first petition to the Food and Drug Administration after receiving the results of her pathology report. "Upon receiving my first petition, the FDA officials called me and asked me why I wanted to be on this medication." Eckley told them her daughter's story and her own reasons for requesting the treatment. "The reason I wanted the antineoplaston therapy was because there were no debilitating side effects. Initially, you may have some minor side effects: tiredness, nausea, and frequent urination from all the fluids that are being intravenously fed into you. Another side effect may be some problems with electrolytes, which are controllable, as opposed to the adverse side effects of chemotherapy.

"I laid it on very thick with the FDA; I just told them the truth. I told them I'm a twenty-nine-year-old mother of three-year-old twin boys besides my six-year-old daughter. My husband and I have only been married for five years, and I just don't have the time to be sick. And since my daughter is doing so well with Dr. Burzynski's treatments, why wouldn't they want to see her mother do just as well? Unfortunately, the FDA disagreed with me and refused my first petition for Burzynski's antineoplaston treatment."

She submitted a second petition five months later, and again the petition was declined. "The FDA officials called me back the second time, and when I asked them why they wouldn't allow me to participate in Burzynski's antineoplaston program, they said the reason was that I don't have a tumor. Well, I didn't have a tumor because it was surgically removed. The masses in my breast and lymph nodes were huge; the mass in my lymph nodes was almost seven centimeters. They're not something that a doctor, not even Dr. Burzynski, would want to remain in the breast area because of the chance of metastases. Also, the FDA officials felt that I would do just fine on conventional therapy. Chemotherapy seems to have positive results with breast cancers, but in many cases it still doesn't stop recurrence. Finally, they said if this was a recurrence instead of a totally different form of cancer, I would have been permitted to participate in Dr. Burzynski's treatment program, even though my first cancer was not as aggressive as the second cancer.

"Their reasoning didn't make any sense to me. I believe it's my body and it should be my decision for choosing among the various therapies. It's not someone else's life, and I want Dr. Burzynski's antineoplaston treatments. Who is the government to limit my medical choices? They haven't done anything for me or my daughter.

"Conventional therapy hadn't offered us any hope. What was available to us was not acceptable; we sought something different. Dr. Burzynski's treatment seemed to be the best thing for my daughter; the results showed it had such a strong affect on brain cancer.

"I chose Burzynski's antineoplaston therapy for myself because I got to know patients with breast, ovarian, lung, and prostate cancer over the course of a few months. Seeing them doing so well and able to maintain their quality of life prompted me to want to join the program. A better quality of life is definitely one of my criteria for choosing among the various therapies. Another criterion would be that the modality would have to boost my immune system, not suppress it. With conventional therapies, you don't have the ability to be selective. The therapies can't weed out the good and bad cells; that's why you lose your hair and your fingernails become brittle. They also do an incredible amount of damage to your internal organs, destroying your kidneys, heart, liver, and bladder. How can something that doesn't work half the time, or may only work for a short period of time, be any good for you? Conventional therapies don't make any sense to me, and why we keep going along this line of scientific inquiry and not in another direction is beyond me.

"Dr. Burzynski is looking for something that will be long-term, a cure for cancer patients. He is looking to redevelop the body's defenses and boost its immune system. How are you supposed to fight off an immunodeficiency disease when you don't have a functional immune system?"

At the time of the interview, Eckley was supplementing her conventional therapy with vitamins, herbs, and cleansing teas. "I take a lot of supplements and drink green tea along with other cleansing teas. My routine consists of having the chemotherapy and after a few days, when I think it may have been effective, then I do things to take the toxins out of my body."

She has also continually been making dietary changes. "With my initial breast cancer, my doctors told me to stay away from red meats and fatty foods. I was also told to cut back on caffeine and to be more discriminating with what I ate. So I have eliminated red meat from my diet and have cut back on my fat intake. Unfortunately, I have never been a skinny child, so I must confess that I fall off the wagon.

"I have looked into the information on macrobiotics and have incorporated some of it into my diet. For instance, I eat a lot of tofu and soy products. I have found that there is just no way that I can do the macrobiotic diet without some type of support. It is a big change and you have to be conscious of everything that goes into your mouth. Now, even when I had my first breast cancer, I would think, 'Oh, you don't have to be so strict on yourself.' Whereas now, I have to be more strict, and it really does make a difference. Some people can't do it; that is why it's not for everyone. Either some people have more willpower or they believe it will be more beneficial. Either way, it is a big commitment."

Eckley found out about vitamins and herbs through another patient in her oncologist's office. "This woman was wonderful and projected this glow all around her. One day we were in the treatment room and I said to her, 'You look fantastic. How long have you been on chemotherapy?' She said she had AML, a rare form of leukemia, and wasn't on chemotherapy. Previously, she had gone through chemotherapy treatments with little success. The woman became progressively worse and ended up having blood transfusions, so she decided to go holistic. In fact, her son is currently obtaining a degree in holistic medicine and herbology. He has worked up a comprehensive protocol of holistic medications for me to follow. I met a few people who are on holistic medications, and they agree that he has done his homework." Eckley started on his protocol, minus a few substances that she could not afford. "For instance, the colonics are a little too far-fetched for me to be an enjoyable experience. I rather do it myself, thank you very much. You think after having children that you wouldn't care about modesty, but it's not true. I also want to purchase a juicer and a bread machine because I would look for juices high in potassium, and it scared me what was actually in the commercial juices.

"I have also tried meditation and Tai Chi but find them difficult. Unfortunately, I have so many things that are creating uncontrollable stress for me that I can't seem to be able to clear my mind. Basically, I am what is holding my family together. At times, it can be difficult, and the stress is overwhelming, but I have no choice.

"My third petition has recently been sent in to the FDA; they basically just laughed at it. They said, 'No, we refused your petitions before and it's what we're going to tell you now.' Basically, they said I had to redevelop cancer in order to get Dr. Burzynski's medication."

Advice to Other Women

Eckley hopes that passage of the Access to Medical Treatments bill will allow doctors to inform cancer patients and their families about the availability of conventional and alternative therapeutics. "I feel that you have to figure out what is best for you, but I would recommend the alternative treatments. I don't think alternative medications are for everybody because it can be difficult and costly to follow the alternative therapy lifestyle. For instance, the supplements and health foods are expensive. I think they should be cheaper and more accessible."

Eckley emphasizes the fundamental difference of frameworks as the basis for her choice between the conventional and alternative treatments. "When my daughter was in Children's Hospital, she was having a hard time digesting solid foods. They said if she wanted a banana split for breakfast, give it to her. The more calories the better. They didn't care what she ate just as long as she was consuming calories, even if it was the worst thing for you. Well, calories aren't going to help you. Conventional therapies suppress your immune system and are destructive to your body. The alternative therapy approach is a healthier approach and, let's face it, the process is to become healthier, not sicker. It's like taking your car in for a total overhaul and paint job instead of giving up on that old Nova. It's a holistic approach, both mind and body.

"Again, I need to emphasize that it is an individual choice, whatever you feel is right for you. I feel that you should incorporate into your lifestyle whatever is helpful to your body. Who knows? It gets easier as you get into it, and you need to take some risks in life.

"Here I am, feeling like a hypocrite by receiving conventional therapy, but right now I really don't have the option for anything else."

Opinions on Cancer Research and Publicly Supported Cancer Organizations

"I have quite a few organizations in my life right now, mostly those that are directed toward my daughter's well-being and others that are helping our family through this crisis. With regard to publicly supported cancer organizations, I am disappointed with the American Cancer Society (ACS). It has not followed through with helping our family. We have called them numerous times after my daughter was diagnosed with cancer, and they haven't done a thing for me, ever. They also told me they would get me a wig. Well, sorry, but I don't want a wig. I find it ironic that we have been included on the ACS mailing list and are constantly solicited for donations."

Eckley views her experiences with the ACS as indicative of the large, nonprofit cancer organizations. "I believe when you donate moneys to these organizations, in many ways your money goes toward the wrong research. Most of the time, you are paying for some executive to have a beautiful home and expensive cars. It's unfathomable that the cancer industry is a billion-dollar enterprise.

"In general, I don't believe our medical system has its heart in the right place. All that they care about is the almighty dollar, not the patients and their families. These cancer organizations go hand-in-hand with the mainstream physicians in this nation. For instance, the Breast Cancer Foundation wants me to do things, to raise money, but again I haven't been offered help as a woman with breast cancer."

Eckley doesn't believe the publicly supported cancer organizations address women's health issues. "I think the organizations' focus is on raising money, and we don't really know how this money is being spent. My family and I don't have much use for these publicly supported organizations."

Periodically, Eckley has been involved with the Reach for Recovery Program. "After my mastectomy, I had a visit by a woman from the program. Her visit was extremely uplifting, and the experience has made me want to do the same thing for other women. The program requirement for being a volunteer is a year of being cancer-free. At the time, we were living in Pennsylvania, and my husband's job transfer forced us to relocate to New Jersey. Shortly after we moved, my daughter and I were diagnosed with cancer, so I no longer qualified." Eckley is waiting another year in the hopes of beginning the training program. "When I had my second mastectomy, I was disappointed that no one from the program called or visited me in any way, shape, or form. I guess they felt I had been through it once and this time would be a piece of cake. I'm just guessing this was their reason, but believe me, having cancer the second time around isn't a piece of cake."

Eckley and her family are continually receiving support from the Burzynski group. "As I said, what we went through on a personal and professional level with Dr. Burzynski, caring for loved ones and making sure their needs are met, it has just drawn us all closer. It's not only fighting for ourselves and loved ones, but we also have to fight to keep the government from imprisoning Dr. Burzynski. The struggles have created this incredible bond between his patients and their families. Hopefully, by being included on the Burzynski patients' hot-line, I can help as many individuals as possible."

In one week's time after starting on the patients' hot-line, Eckley was contacted by eight people. "It is very beneficial because we are getting the necessary information out to the public about the ludicrous persecution of Dr. Burzynski. And when the American people become aware of what is happening to Dr. Burzynski's patients, they are going to say, 'Okay, enough is enough. How dare you? This man has something that is helping these patients.' I am hoping for a rebellion, and it's working."

five _____ | Alice Hopper Epstein

Using Visualization and Fantasy for Healing

Alice Epstein, Ph.D., is a sociologist and the author of the book *Mind, Fantasy, and Healing: One Woman's Journey from Conflict and Illness to Wholeness and Health* (New York: Delacorte, 1989). The book is no longer available from Delacorte, but it can be ordered from Balderwood Books, 37 Bay Road, Amherst, MA 02202, for fifteen dollars including postage.

Her Story

In February 1985 Alice Epstein was diagnosed with hypernephroma of her left kidney. Within two weeks, the primary tumor and her left kidney were surgically removed. "At the time of my diagnosis, they already knew that there was a metastasis in my left lung. The issue was what should be my next step. Since the metastasis wasn't big enough, they just wanted to wait." After a month, the malignancy in the left lung grew, and Epstein's oncologist discovered an additional metastasis in her right lung.

By April 1985 Epstein was diagnosed with stage IV metastatic renal cancer. "At that point, the oncologist who had reviewed my X rays after the surgery suggested that there was no point to chemotherapy. He felt it wouldn't be effective with this particular type of cancer. His only recommendation was an interferon clinical trial program at Boston's Dana Farber Medical Clinic."

During the interview with the oncologist, Epstein broached the topic of the Simonton method, and he dismissed it as ridiculous. "He became very defensive and said that he had made his recommendation, it was beyond a doubt my best chance, and I should take it. Later, when I knew there were the two interferon programs, I called him and asked for his advice, and he almost hung up the phone on me. He gave me no infor-mation and said, 'I gave you a recommendation and my recommenda-tion is Boston.' He was very, very defensive, and obviously I never went back to him. He expected me to be dead in three months, so what was I fussing about?"

During the next month Epstein made a trip to the Dana Farber Clinic for examinations and evaluation. "It wasn't an automatic entrance into the program, but after they examined me, they immediately accepted me as a patient." The next step was for Epstein to decide when she would begin treatments. "It was at the end of their program, so I didn't have a lot of time to make my decision. I didn't commit one way or another, and the doctors were a little disturbed with me. They couldn't comprehend why I was taking so long to make a decision. To them this treatment program was my best chance."

It was during this period that she also learned about the interferon pro-gram at Yale University Medical School. "I went down to New Haven and was examined by the clinical staff. Finally I made the decision to begin treatments at Yale's interferon program. In May 1985 I was to begin the program by having a baseline X ray and blood work. When the oncolo-gists examined the X ray, they discovered that the metastasis in my right side was disappearing and the other one was considerably smaller. It wasn't what they would consider a significant change, but to us it was very signi-ficant. At that point my husband and I decided against my starting that particular interferon program. Patient enrollment in the program was winding down, and the oncologists told us they would wait for two weeks while I went home and thought through my decision.

"We didn't get a second opinion from an oncologist that perhaps at another time we would have obtained. However, there didn't seem to be any question about the diagnosis. We looked at the X rays and spoke with the physicians who examined them, and they were very open with us. We approached our physicians in an open way but we didn't get a second opinion. It seemed clear to me that at that point the interferon program was the only possibility."

At the same time, Epstein was in an intensive psychotherapy program that she began shortly after her diagnosis. She began very intensive psy-chotherapy with her husband, a trained psychologist, and also a form of therapy known as psychosynthesis, with a therapist. She and her husband thought that the psychological interventions may have affected the reductions in the metastases that they found in May 1985. "After two weeks I went back for an X ray and it was obvious there was a dramatic reduction. Again, my physician said it wasn't a significant change because the malignancy was not more than half reduced. Also, he said that it would be a great time for me to start the interferon program. I said, 'No,' and that I would continue the psychotherapy and give up my place in the interferon program. We left there with him saying, 'This is your decision and you could always come back. There are other experimental programs. If you come back in six months, there may be other new things that we don't even know about, and keep in touch.'"

The other alternative therapies she considered included the Livingston-Wheeler program in California, a self-inoculation program, macrobiotic diet, and Simonton visualizations. She decided against the Livingston-Wheeler program because of the distance and because she had unanswered questions about the therapy. "It wasn't something I would have done instead of the interferon program. My husband and I also considered a self-inoculation program in Albany, but that was futile because I didn't have the tissues from my cancer."

She also looked at some other psychological interventions. "Bernie Siegel was just beginning at the time with tapes, but he had not written his books. I had a contact in Boston who had taped his Boston lectures. We wrote and called the Siegel group, which was informally organized at the time, and I went to one of his lectures in western Massachusetts (in the Berkshires) and attended one of the evening sessions. He was not as impressive in the flesh as he had been on the tape. I just had the sense that it wasn't for me. He is a guru and I just didn't feel that it would help me as much as what I was already doing. With my personal approach we were making tremendous progress, so I did not pursue the Siegel approach any further."

Instead, she chose to work more with psychotherapy, visualization, and meditation. "In that year of therapy I really worked out a lot through visualizations, and I currently don't feel the need for visualizations at this time. Now, I should distinguish Simonton visualizations from the other type of visualizations I was doing. I was doing Simonton visualizations several times a day, visualizing the cancer getting smaller and smaller. I believe this was very important for me to do.

"I would also lapse into fantasy, working with my subpersonalities as I had been taught in psychosynthesis. In psychosynthesis, you break your personality into subpersonalities and deal with whatever conflicts there are among them. My therapist and I just really clicked, and my husband and I would discuss what I went through in therapy. It was a fantastic combination. In two months, the cancer decreased discernibly. I don't do that anymore and only use it if something is really bothering me and I don't understand it."

Epstein added that part of her program included meditation, which she learned to do before she was diagnosed with cancer. When she was battling the cancer, she meditated four times per day, and at the time of the interview she continued to meditate once or twice per day. In addition to meditation, she and her husband take long walks in the woods or, in the winter, they go cross-country skiing. They are fortunate to live on land that is connected to a state park. Her exercise regimen also includes tennis and morning calisthenics. Furthermore, she made some dietary changes: "I went to a physician who specializes in diet, and he recommended some high-potency vitamins. He also recommended the usual diet that people are on now, but the main recommendation was the vitamins. They are called Pioneer vitamins; they are all natural and made locally. You take six a day, and they have all the things that people say are essential." They also went on a low-fat diet.

Unlike some of the other interviewees, who relied more on serendipity and intuition, scientific knowledge and research played a significant role in the decisions that Epstein made. "Certainly the two cancer interferon programs were at respectable hospitals connected to medical schools. The one was recommended by my oncologist, and he had a direct connection with them, and so both programs were what we considered high-level recommendations. As for the other alternatives, as with the Siegel group, I tried either to write or talk to people, or to experience what they were talking about before making my decision. My husband did research, and he certainly researched my condition and what the documented probability of my recovery was. He discovered very early on the connection between the psychological aspects, the cancer-prone personality, and cancer. When we decided that I was not going to participate in the interferon program, I was concerned that I fit the description nicely [of the cancer-prone personality], so I decided to stick with the therapy. There were good alternatives, but they could mess things up.

"My husband is a Ph.D. psychologist, and he certainly is capable of reading scientific journals and his own psychological journals for helping to make decisions. We read the Livingston-Wheeler book, and both my husband and I were not convinced just by reading it. Both my husband and I have a Ph.D., and we are used to evaluating scientific information. The criteria were experiential and research of information. In regard to the conventional therapies, I was not convinced that I would benefit by taking chemotherapy. We were told twice that chemotherapy was not a good recommendation, and from research we found that it was not good for stage IV kidney cancer. We knew the statistical results of the interferon program were very low. We knew what the possibilities were and knew the New Haven interferon program did not have as good a response rate as the other program, but we chose it for convenience and because it was a self-administrating program. It was a very hard decision to make and we also used gut feeling in the end." Ultimately she decided not to begin the New Haven program, either.

"I continued with the therapy and monthly X rays, and each time the radiologist noted no change because he was looking for something very dramatic. But if you look for something over six months, there were obviously changes. The one lesion that was left kept getting smaller and smaller. By 1986 I finally got a reading that said there was nothing significant on the chest X ray. And every X ray since then has been the same thing. It has been eleven years and they still have found nothing."

When asked if she was seeing a physician during this period, Epstein replied: "Yes, I was now back with my family physician, who was a great believer in alternative medicine. He told me originally, before the oncologist spoke to me, that chemotherapy is really no good for what I had and that perhaps I should do nothing. I would go every month, perhaps every two months, and I felt fine going for the X rays. The X rays kept getting further and further apart, going from six months to a year. I don't have X rays now. The physician who is taking care of me said to just consider the kidney area cured. They can't find anything on the lung, so they consider that cured as well." As of early 1998, she remainder in good health.

Advice to Other Women

Epstein's story appeared on the Fox television network in a program called "The Heart of Healing." As a result of the television show and her book, she has received many telephone calls from cancer patients and people who were interested in psychosynthesis. Consequently, as for many of the other women we spoke with, she has been put in the role of advice-giving.

"I think the main thing that I tell the many people who call me is to be open. They need to consider a lot of things, to be open to many alternatives, but to choose what is right for them. In the end each one of us has to choose the path or the type of therapy that is best for us. There are so many things that are available to people.

"I would certainly say that everyone should go to a support group. At a certain level, support groups work. They don't cure people, but they do prolong their life. So I would always recommend them." Epstein was referring to the work of psychologists whose studies have documented longer survival among cancer patients who were in support groups or receiving psychotherapy. She personally did not use a support group when she had cancer; she was not even sure that they existed at the time she was diagnosed. Instead, she relied on family and friends for support.

Epstein added that she considered the various psychological interventions and therapy to be more important than the support group, at least in her own recovery. Along with therapy she added that spirituality was important as well. "For some people prayer is the thing. For some, religion or therapy is the thing. And a lot of people like to do visualizations. I went to someone who did visualizations and had her check it out before I used it, because some are better than others. I would say, 'Leave no stone unturned and pick whatever therapies are best for you.'"

Opinions on Cancer Research and Publicly Supported Cancer Organizations

"I don't have a lot of information on publicly supported organizations, but I certainly would not recommend any organization to anybody, because I don't know anything about them. I think that with all organizations that are soliciting money, the money is going toward the organization and not to whatever task they set for themselves. I am rather suspicious of national organizations. For instance, I'm sure the American Cancer Society is a fine organization, but I'm just not as impressed with national organizations as I am with local organizations. The national organizations would not be a recommendation or choice of mine because, first, I don't have a lot of experience with them and, second, I am suspicious of their effectiveness. With local organizations, you know that they are not collecting money for maintaining their bureaucracy. I recommend looking into local hospice organizations and support groups affiliated with local hospitals."

References

Livingston-Wheeler, Virginia
    1984 *The Conquest of Cancer*. New York: F. Watts.
Simonton, O. Carl, Stephanie Matthews-Simonton, and James L. Creighton
    1978 *Getting Well Again: A Step-by-Step Guide to Overcoming Cancer for Patients and Their Families*. New York: Bantam Books.

six

Diet, Faith, and the Manner Protocol

Pat Fogderud is copastor with her husband David of the Overflowing Life Cup Total Life Center and Harbor for the Homeless in Beloit, Wisconsin.

Her Story

In July 1987 Pat Fogderud, who today works as a minister for homeless people, noticed some irregular bleeding. At the time she was busy taking care of her mother, who was recovering from open-heart surgery. "After taking care of my mother, I went in for a gynecological checkup. Two pap smears were taken and both were negative, but my doctor noticed some bleeding when he bumped my uterus. He took six biopsy samples, and five out of the six samples indicated stage II cervical cancer. The cancer was invasive and had grown through the uterine wall. More tests were conducted, and the results showed that the cancer had metastasized to my left lung. My doctor told my husband, Dave, that I had a 40 to 60 percent chance of living five years, with or without treatment.

"First of all, I believe in the power of prayer and have learned not to do things that are not approved by the Lord. I've been a Christian for thirty-five years, and over those years He's taken good care of me. I have learned to listen to His voice. The day after my diagnosis, I was reading the Bible for comfort and was getting ready to go in for more tests. He directed me to open Psalm 118:17, which says, 'I shall not die, but live, and declare the works of the Lord.' The verse told me that perhaps the Lord had a purpose in all this. That's what I always look for: purpose. In 1973 my oldest son was killed in a car accident. There was such a purpose that came out of that, and I have seen it fulfilled in the past twenty-some years.

"In 1974 my husband and I started a coffee-house ministry for teens and youths. The first night we were open, my husband and I realized there were people who literally didn't have a place to go. Because of our availability, the coffee house evolved into a homeless shelter. In the first two and a half years of our marriage, we brought home fifty-four people. I had three children before my oldest son was killed, and my husband had two children. It really wasn't good to have people staying in our home; there was too much risk and stress. We moved away from the ministry, about ten miles, and rented a house for emergency housing. It went under because of lack of funding, but a task force was formed to see what we could do about the people who were homeless. Putting these people in a motel was just a one-night Band-Aid."

Fogderud was asked to be on that task force, and the resulting shelter, Harbor for the Homeless, was established in 1984. "In 1985 we started a church in our facility. It was for the homeless who didn't feel comfortable in the organized church and didn't have nice clothes to wear. By 1995 we had helped over three thousand people. Unfortunately, the city took over our property by right of eminent domain and sold it. We have since relocated our ministry and have ended up in three separate facilities. We had to close the shelter in February 1997 because we had incurred thirty thousand dollars in debt due to insufficient funding.

"I look for purpose in things but couldn't understand why I had been chosen for the task of facing cancer. Somehow, I just knew that it wasn't God's will for me to check out at this time. It was just a strong conviction that I had in that inner man. With every day that went by, I had a stronger conviction. Every time I would get more opposition, I would just get stronger in the route I was going."

Fogderud's doctor recommended radiation therapy at the University Hospital in Madison, Wisconsin. "He told my husband that if it was his wife, he would take her to Madison for radiation therapy since their facility wasn't equipped to treat cancer that had advanced to this stage. The treatment would consist of six weeks of daily radiation along with three days of radioactive isotopes inserted in my uterus, and I would remain flat on my back for those three days. He suggested that after the radiation, I might have to have a radical hysterectomy since I had a tumor the size of a four-month pregnancy.

"Flags went up for my husband and me. Dave asked the doctor if it was true that radiation killed the good as well as the bad cells. The doctor said, 'Yes, it is true.'

"He then asked, 'Is it true that it damages your body's ability to heal itself?'

"Again, the doctor said, 'Yes. It's true.'

"It is so funny, so strange, because neither my husband nor I knew anything about cancer before this happened. We never expected it to happen to us. When this happened, it was like he had a word of wisdom or knowledge that it does damage to good cells as well as bad. We didn't know that of our own knowledge. It was something the Lord put in his spirit to know what to ask. We looked back on it later and said, 'Hey, that was something that God was trying to tell us.'

"My husband took over the management of my illness because I was emotionally distraught and just couldn't do it myself. Even though I had a strong faith in knowing it was going to be all right, I just didn't know what to do next. He just took over and did it. I think it's important to note that because we are married and are one, my husband and I were in agreement with things. I had a friend whose husband was not in agreement with her taking alternative therapies, and he insisted she have chemotherapy. He's now a widower.

"It wasn't the normal thing for me to question the doctor's suggested treatment plan, because I had always been taught that doctors are next to God. I didn't know why, but everything within me rose up against the very thought that I should have radiation. The radiation treatments just didn't make sense to us, and we began to search for alternative treatments. Dave had been in the data processing field for thirty years prior to my diagnosis. He was real tenacious, like a dog with a bone, trying to find out information on different treatments. We called doctors in this area, but it was to no avail. They all gave us the same referral—the radiation therapy at the University Hospital in Madison. We found that we were mostly on our own because neither of us believed that I should go with traditional therapy.

"Earlier in the year, at a time when we really needed some encouragement, we had been given a trip to New Orleans to attend the 1987 Congress on the Holy Spirit. The doctor said to cancel the trip because I wouldn't feel like going. I said, 'Forget you! Somebody gives me a free trip; the Lord must know I need it, so I'm going!' Before we left for New Orleans, we were discussing our dilemma of not knowing what to do or where to go for the best treatment. One evening Dave's mom called from North Dakota to ask if we had heard of Dr. Harold Manner. She remembered hearing him speak at a Gideon Convention in North Dakota about six or eight years before. At the gathering, he spoke about his forty years of work on perfecting a nontoxic cancer therapy."

Fogderud and her husband began calling around the country, trying to find more information on Manner. "We accessed information in libraries, and my husband spent a lot of time on the phone with anyone who was a referral. We thought we could get more information on Manner from the American Cancer Society, but they told us his therapy was unproven and he was a quack."

Finally, Fogderud and her husband called Loyola University, where Dr. Manner had taught. "He had been dismissed from his position at Loyola because of the laetrile controversy back in the 1960s. However, they did give us an 800 number to call; it was for Manner's public relations director, Nadine Rogers. She sent us a packet of information on Manner's Metabolic Therapy."

Fogderud and her husband further researched Manner's Metabolic Therapy and the admission procedures for his clinic. "Manner's therapy consisted of high doses of laetrile, vitamin C, and DMSO [dimethyl sulfoxide]; nutrition detoxification; and what we called 'coffee breaks' (really coffee enemas used to stimulate the liver to detoxify itself). After going through the information, the therapy just made sense to us, and we really thought that God had answered our prayers.

"From the beginning there was a church that we had attended until we started our own church. They put me on their prayer list, and we called the elders and they anointed me with oil. Everywhere I turned it seemed that I was hearing an encouraging word, or book, or someone's testimony. Church members brought me stories of other people who had used alternative therapies. One woman, Dodie Osteen, who was a pastor's wife in Texas, had been given six weeks to live. She is still living today because she went the natural route and defied the odds by refusing to believe in her prognosis.

"The doctor who diagnosed me was very reluctant when I chose Manner's therapy. He made it clear he was not in favor of what I was doing. He was very nice about it and genuinely concerned about it, telling me that it wasn't a wise choice, that it wasn't a proven therapy and about all of its pitfalls. So I just patronized him and said, 'This will be my choice. It's my body, and I should have something to say about what is done to it. I don't think that I have anything to lose by trying this therapy. If it doesn't work, I'll be back to see you.'

"He was very hesitant to hand over my records unless he knew and approved of my treatment. Since he didn't approve of the metabolic therapy, I had a hard time getting my records. In fact, I was at Manner's clinic in Mexico for a week before he sent them. The doctor at the clinic had to request them, or shall we say, demand them.

"On July 31, 1987, we returned home from New Orleans and went directly to Tijuana, Mexico, where I checked into the Manner Clinic. The day that I left to go to the clinic, I was having second thoughts because my mom was against it. She was concerned for me and my odds. Her sister called and told me about a friend with stage IV cancer who had gone to Manner's clinic and is still living today. The story was a confirmation to me. I thought, 'Hey, this is the right thing to do. Get going.'

"When I checked into the clinic, I hadn't eaten, so they fixed me this wonderful, nutritious meal of things that at first I couldn't recognize. The next day I started on a detoxification program that consisted of nothing but fruit juices. Every hour, on the hour, I had juice, nothing else. I knew I was detoxifying my body because I had the worst headache. After a day or two, I went on their diet, which is organic, mostly raw fruits and vegetables. I was also put on a daily regime of high-dose enzymes and other supplements, which consisted of sixty-five pills and trace minerals.

"When I started on the nutritional program, I saw their psychologist and we talked a lot about stress and biofeedback and the importance of the body working together in all three areas: the mind, body, and spirit. That was a very important part, I feel, of my progress. I think stress suppresses the immune system a lot. I had a lot of grief—deaths in my family—and had to deal with that. I think that is another large part of it.

"The theory of the metabolic therapy is that if you have a tumor, you just don't attack the tumor site the way they do here in the United States.

You try to find out what else might be occurring in the metabolism to cause that tumor to grow. They explained to us that when you have cancer cells, the body tries to isolate them from the rest of your cells. A hard shell forms around the cancer and becomes a tumor. In their program, the enzymes break down that hard shell and the laetrile goes in and gobbles up the cancer cells, but it doesn't hurt the good cells.

"Basically, my daily routine consisted of the Manner Clinic diet, enzymes, massages, and exercise. Every afternoon at 4:00 we would have our 'coffee break,' or coffee enemas. I also had whirlpools to stimulate the therapy. At the same time, we had free time for shopping and visits to the cultural center. It was like a wonderful vacation, really.

"After ten days on the Manner Therapy, tests were conducted on me at the clinic. My chest X rays showed that the spot on my lung was completely gone. A few days later I had more tests done, and a surgeon from San Diego came down to the clinic to examine me. He said that the stage II cervical cancer had gone to stage 0, that the cancer wasn't invasive and I could have surgery.

"The staff psychologists at the Manner Clinic met with me one day and said, 'Well, we have to visualize your cancer.' I am a strong believer in the faith walk and not into New Age biofeedback, visualization, or psychology. Sometimes I think we need to see ourselves well, to see ourselves whole. I said to the psychologist, 'Well, it is going to be hard to visualize "my" cancer because I am not going to own it. It is not my cancer; God didn't give it to me. It's not mine, and I am not going to claim it.'

"He said, 'Well, you're going to have to come up with something or this is going to be a long therapy session.'

"I thought, 'Oh, well, okay, what can we do?'

"He said, 'Well, how do you see it?'

"And I said, 'Well, I see it as a big zero.' This was the day before I had gone from a stage II to a stage 0, and I just said off the top of my head, 'I see it as a big zero.'

"He said, 'Okay, well, a zero is shaped like a watermelon. Let's have a watermelon party and we'll have the watermelon seeds gobble up the white corpuscles.'

"I don't think like that and so I said, 'Yeah, whatever,' and went along with it.

"But he kept saying things like, 'As a man thinketh, so is he.' He would put the emphasis on how you think. It was from the Bible and he would even say that it was a Bible Scripture, but that is not the complete Bible Scripture. It actually says, 'Whatsoever a man thinks in his heart, so is he.' And your heart is wicked unless you have it cleansed and redeemed by the Lord Jesus Christ. I just couldn't go along with the psychologist, so I asked my doctor, 'Who decided whether I see this psychologist or not?'

"He said, 'You decide. If you don't want to see him, you don't have to see him.' Several patients started to opt out of his program, and he decided to take a sabbatical and went up in the mountains to meditate.

"I stayed at the clinic for three weeks, until August 18, then returned home. I didn't have insurance or the money to have the surgery in Mexico, so I came back to the States to have the surgery at the University Hospital.

"The doctors at the University Hospital refused to do the surgery without radiation treatments. My husband asked, 'Why won't you do it?'

"The doctor said, 'Because you could sue me for malpractice.'

"We offered to sign a waiver, and she said, 'No, if you want to kill your wife, just go right ahead.' So we took my records and returned to Mexico for the surgery."

On Labor Day 1987, Fogderud had a hysterectomy/oophorectomy (removal of the uterus and one ovary) at the Del Rio Mexican Hospital. "I was in the hospital for two and a half days, then flew home after a short recuperation period at the Manner Clinic. I was back at my desk the next week and have felt absolutely perfect ever since.

"After returning to the States, I had a hard time finding a doctor who would treat me because I was still taking laetrile. There was one doctor in Beloit that my husband knew from a church he formerly attended. He was a nice Christian man who could read Spanish. (All my records were in Spanish.) He was not taking any new patients, but for some reason he decided to take me as his patient. It started out okay, but there was a point where he became hostile to my treatment choices. He was very thorough. He gave me ultrasound and every other kind of test you could imagine to prove that the doctors at the Manner Clinic had missed something. Then one day he said it wasn't the kind of cancer that needed radiation. I started to have second thoughts about the whole thing. I thought, 'Why were they going to put me through radiation treatments if it wasn't that kind of cancer?'

"Eventually, it got to the point that I felt such hostility from this doctor when I would go in for a checkup. He was so determined to prove that I had done something terrible that my blood pressure would go up and I had to leave. It was about that time that I found out about a doctor in Illinois."

Fogderud continues to monitor her progress with a doctor in Illinois not far from her home in Beloit. "I still have him as my doctor because he believes in the use of alternative therapies and is supportive of my choices. From September 1987 until now I have been cancer-free. I stick to the Manner diet as close as I possibly can. I stay away from things that they suggest, like red meat. I eat chicken and fish, and most of the enzymes are in whole foods, not processed or canned. I shop the perimeter of the grocery store now instead of up and down the aisles. I am also juicing, mostly carrot juice but also apples, pineapple, and a lot of mixtures.

"A friend of mine introduced me to barley green after I got back from the Manner Clinic. Barley green is a whole food, probably the most perfect food you can get. It is made from young barley plants before they are matured. As a nutritional supplement and an immune booster, it is one of the things that I am faithful to take. For exercise I am a mall walker. My schedule is pretty hectic, so I walk whenever I can.

"I didn't utilize any support groups. I usually feel like a fish out of water when it comes to things like support groups. I have such a strong faith and knew that it was a gift at the time, that God planted it in my heart.

"In trying to find out about therapies, I read just about everything that I could get my hands on. I have had to learn how to order my life. After I was diagnosed, I read a book by Gordon McDonald called *Ordering Your Private World,* which helped me learn to pace myself. I was so immersed in family, ministry, and sometimes working a secular job to survive that I would go home late at night and eat, skip meals, grab a donut on the run, and drink a lot of coffee. I would eat late at night, which is not a good thing because the food just lies there and ferments. It is true: we are what we eat. So I had to alter my thinking and learn to deal with stress. That was difficult for me to eliminate because of the ministry putting so many demands on me, and the people-helping business is the hardest job that there is. I had to learn to say no. I decide when I am going to do it, if God is asking me to do this or if someone else is just trying to drain me.

"I can't explain why. I guess you would call it a witness of your inner spirit or inner man that said I should go with the Manner Clinic. It was an intuitive feeling to go with the Manner Therapy and not try the other alternative therapies. It is really strange. I don't know why I chose the Manner Therapy versus other alternative therapies. I think it has to do with when we got his tape in his free packet of information; he gave his own personal testimony of how he had become a Christian. Before he became a Christian, he was an atheist and would talk against God. After becoming a Christian, he felt such an urgency to go back and tell others that he had been wrong and that God is real. He said that he thought God had given him this therapy. It was so much in tune with our beliefs and value system, and I think that is the reason I chose his program. I have since visited most of the places where other alternative therapies are being practiced. They are very similar."

As of early 1998, Fogderud had recently gone through surgery on her sciatic nerve. From her physical examinations, it was determined that her immune system was in "tip-top" shape.

Advice to Other Women

Fogderud advises, "Don't take conventional or traditional therapies; you will have a better chance of living. I really believe that in my heart. Two of my mother's sisters had the same type of cancer as mine; one had chemotherapy and one had radiation. They're both gone, and I don't know how much clearer it has to be. I watched the therapies take them away, just take them right down. They just couldn't recover, and then they told me, 'Well, my doctor didn't tell me that radiation would burn my bowels and I would have diarrhea for the rest of my life.' It's sad; they were my ancestors. I just lost my own mother in July from lung cancer. Yes, her smoking was a contributing factor. My grandmother also died from the same type of cervical cancer as mine.

"I would advise women to just try and educate yourself. If a person reads, you can learn an awful lot. I have always been a reader, so I just increased what I have read for my health's sake. While I was at the Manner Clinic, besides the Manner cocktail, which was the intravenous feeding of the laetrile and DMSO, they had teachers come in and teach us about nutrition. It was awesome. So I have learned a lot from the nutritionists down there. And I have people who I can call if I have a question.

"Before I was diagnosed, when I was taking care of my mom, I was reading everything I could get my hands on about faith and about healing. I didn't know why. It was just the Lord going ahead of me and preparing me, and it was my spiritual vitamins. So when it hit, it was no big deal. I was just going to believe in God for which way to go. We are going through the same thing with my four-year-old grandson. My grandson, Josiah, has brain cancer and was at the Burzynski clinic for antineoplaston therapy." Although her grandson was alive at the time of the interview, many complications had kept them from continuing with the antineoplaston therapy. In early 1998, after thirty-six hours of brain surgery and four months in intensive care, Fogderud's grandson was rehabilitating well. Josiah celebrated his fifth birthday and was looking forward to going to school.

Fogderud advises against women trying to treat themselves. "A lot of people think all they have to do is go to the health food store and get tea, make some juice, and whatever else they find at the store. You need to have someone who knows how to get your system back into the proper balance. It is a lifestyle change, if anything. I try to put people in touch with one of the doctors I had at the Manner Clinic—I am now working with a Dr. Narvaez in Juarez, Mexico—and let them decide what type of therapy they need. They will use anything that will help, and one person may need this and another that.

"I have been asked to speak at a few places, like support groups, and I take every opportunity to tell them my story because it's always different from what they have heard. But the medical profession usually doesn't ask me to speak to support groups. However, I have people calling me from all over. In fact, I just got off the phone with a woman from North Carolina who was diagnosed with stage II cervical cancer. She got my name from the National Cancer Institute's Directory Listing. I have talked to hundreds of people that way. I am quite high profile in my area because of the ministry, and perhaps that is one reason I was chosen for this mission.

I get a lot of calls from people whose relatives or friends tell them about me. I talk to people almost every day. There is quite a network for people with cancer. It touches everyone's lives and there is no such thing as a cure for cancer. You can manage it and control it, but everyone has cancer cells. The more we live in this polluted world, the more we are going to see. I look in the paper every night, and if a person doesn't die of old age, they usually die of cancer or an automobile accident."

Opinions on Cancer Research and Publicly Supported Cancer Organizations

Fogderud is critical of publicly supported cancer organizations that do not support alternative cancer therapies. "The American Cancer Society was downright hostile to us when we mentioned Dr. Manner's name. Their statement to me was enough to make anyone critical. We couldn't get any information from them about Dr. Harold Manner. They just came out and said he was a quack with an unproven therapy and that they were not going to give me information on it. I tend to believe that the NCI has a little more going for them. It's more open and supportive of alternative therapies.

"With regard to public organizations focused specifically on breast cancer, I was working on a time factor and didn't solicit any of these organizations. If my husband heard about some group, we contacted them for information purposes.

"As you can tell, I am not real crazy about the American Cancer Society because they have been collecting money and saying that they are spending it on research for twenty years. At $20 billion a year for twenty years, we are no closer, as far as they are concerned, to a cure than we ever were."

References

McDonald, Gordon

   1996 *Restoring Joy: Three Complete Works in One Volume.* New York: Inspirational Press.

   1997 *Ordering Your Private World.* Nashville, Tenn.: T. Nelson.

seven

On Becoming a Cancer Activist

Ann Fonfa is cochair of the Alternative/Whole Health committee of SHARE, an organization that offers support and
education programs for women with breast or ovarian cancer.
She has also been active in the National Breast Cancer Coalition. Through her work in these organizations, Fonfa has
helped publicize the options available to women who wish to
pursue alternative or complementary approaches to cancer.
She has also written a fifty-six-page compendium, "A Consumer's View of Alternative Medicine," which she handed out
at the 1997 NBCC advocacy conference. She also spoke about
the topic at the World Conference on Breast Cancer. The
phone number for SHARE is 212-719-0364, and its address is
1501 Broadway, Suite 1720, New York, NY 10036.

Her Story

When Ann Fonfa was diagnosed with breast cancer, she did not have
much personal knowledge of cancer: "I knew only one woman with breast
cancer—she died maybe fifteen years ago—so I didn't know much about
it. The only thing that happened that I recall is that she let me feel her
breasts when she was in an advanced state and they felt like petrified
wood. That is the only memory I had around breast cancer. No one in my
family that I know of ever had breast cancer. My uncle, my father's
brother, died of a malignant brain tumor, and my mother's brother had
colon cancer, and he is still alive. That was my only close personal experience of cancer. About five years ago I made a decision to start donating
money to breast cancer organizations. My friend and I had been talking

about Susan, who had died of it, and it was the tenth anniversary of her death. We decided to make a donation, but I never thought for one second that it would become personal.

"I discovered a lump in December 1992. It had been only two months since my female internist/gynecologist had examined me. I was doing monthly breast self-exams, so I knew that the lump had not been there in October or November. I didn't think it was cancer, since I had no family history and never felt at risk, but I showed it to a friend who was my acupuncturist. She said I should have it looked at, so I had a mammogram. The lump itself did not show up on the film, but the doctors at the Strang Clinic were very concerned and told me to see a [breast] surgeon right away. A friend was with me at this time, and she and I proceeded to see the recommended doctor. Everything happened very quickly. One day later, a Thursday, the surgeon examined me. He told me I was a perfect candidate for lumpectomy and not to mention mastectomy! The only thing I knew about breast cancer was that you kept your breast or you didn't, so of course I agreed to a lumpectomy. He told me he had an opening in his surgery for the following Monday. I understood that to mean I was in dire need of this life-or-death surgery, and I agreed to go right ahead. I had everything done all at once without a biopsy. Even though I thought of myself as an educated consumer, I never thought to ask for a second opinion or find out exactly what the surgery involved."

The procedure that Fonfa underwent involved axillary node dissection or removal of the lymph nodes under the armpit. As for many women, this procedure led to lymphedema, an accumulation of excess lymph fluid and a permanent swelling of the tissues. "I never had radiation or chemo, so I developed the lymphedema solely from the surgery." Her own experience with lymphedema led to her organizing events at SHARE for women about lymphedema; that work is described in the next section.

"I have had many recurrences, all of them local and at the original site, at this moment I think I have two more microscopic tumors there. The original recurrence was two years after surgery; it was a complete shock. I thought I was cured as I was diagnosed stage I with a 1.5-centimeter tumor and no node involvement. I was a vegetarian and took vitamins, supplements, organic food, and exercised daily. There is no across-the-board protection against cancer. The risk factors for breast cancer mostly involve estrogen production and of course one's genetic structure. I had no children and had taken birth control pills beginning at age eighteen for eleven years.

"From the beginning of my experience I used vitamins and minerals. I did not go for chemotherapy or radiation. Having seen my uncle go through it with no gain of quality of life or extension of it, I had felt those treatments to be too extreme and damaging to the patient. I had stage I disease and felt I could deal with it in other ways. Strangely, when you have breast cancer, you do not necessarily feel ill, and it is a real shock to be told you have cancer. I truly thought I was cured by the surgery. I understood radiation to be used as a local preventive. I was told that about 16 percent of women with radiation had recurrences and about 40 percent of those who did not take it. I thought I could risk it; as it turned out I did have recurrence. But I still think radiation is overkill. With cancer, the main thing is that if it spreads, it is really bad, and radiation does not really prevent the spread of cancer. I believe it is important for the host (myself) to stay as healthy as possible. Radiation and chemotherapy are very destructive to the body, even using herbs and other protective agents, and for me it just didn't seem the way to go. From my readings I learned that about 30 percent of the women who took chemotherapy for their breast cancer could be said to benefit. In fact from 1989 to 1994, available statistics show a 5 percent increase in survival (the only valued area to measure success as far as I see). This survival increase is said to be the result of chemotherapeutic advances. I say what the hell is (only) 5 percent?"

After her cancer recurred, Fonfa began to follow a dietary and metabolic program developed by William Kelley, D.D.S. She chose this option after reading extensively; consulting on options with the cancer educator Ralph Moss, Ph.D.; and considering what made sense to her, given her own tastes. She followed a version of the Kelley program based on long-distance telephone consultations with a doctor who developed her individual protocol from data that included blood tests and an extensive questionnaire. "It's supposed to be very specific for each individual; however, I felt from the beginning that it was not personalized enough. Here I was a vegetarian with a strong awareness of health issues, yet I got test results back that indicated anomalies. Example: I was drinking between sixty-five and one hundred ounces of chlorine-free water daily, yet the test showed I needed more water in my diet. When I questioned the doctor as to what this could really mean, I got no useful feedback. This kind of thing occurred with several aspects of the results. So even though this was supposedly based on my particular blood test and my nervous system that was being evaluated, I had doubts and confusion from day one.

"I followed the program very strictly. It even involved waking at 3:00 A.M. to take enzymes, which I did. I incorporated twenty minutes of exercise at that time, too. I was also making lots of organic vegetable juice daily, and I did feel great.

"I continued to have recurrences at the local site, resisting a mastectomy until September 1995. After that things were fine until May 1996. I developed Paget's disease of the nipple, usually indicative of invasive cancer. My original diagnosis of invasive lobular carcinoma had included the information that the disease often went to the second breast. I had been told many times to go ahead and have a prophylactic mastectomy. So here I was with a real symptom. I decided rather than have a series of lumpectomies (as I had on the left side), to go for the mastectomy immediately. Surprise! No tumor was found and it was diagnosed as stage 0, noninvasive. For this breast I did not consent to axillary node dissection, as I had become persuaded that there were much better (safer, less invasive) ways to stage the disease.

"I decided to go the Gerson clinic (located in Tijuana at the Centro Hospitalario Internacional Pacifico, S.A.) in July 1996 because of the continued problems. I was probably the healthiest person who had ever gone to the hospital there. They were saying to me that I really didn't have to do that much because I was basically fine and could go with whatever aspects of the program I was comfortable with. I was there for only two of the required three weeks and felt I understood the program. I saw dramatic things happen at Gerson. My feeling is that people who come there having eaten unhealthy diets with lots of meat, junk food, soda, etc. will benefit the most since they create such a big change in their body chemistry. For me not too much seemed to change because I had been following a plan much like the program. I saw people literally get up from wheelchairs while I was there. This did not happen to me, although once again I began to have that glow I now identify with juicing.

"The worst part was that within a few months I realized I had developed chest wall lumps at the original (left) site. They were microscopic, which is very unusual. Each time that I was diagnosed with these recurrences over the years, I was told that the cancer itself was very slow-growing and unaggressive. I had been told by several oncologists in 1995 not to have chemotherapy because the slow growth rate would not allow the cells to respond appropriately (chemo acts on fast-growing cells of the body—the fastest of which is usually cancer). Because I had refused the various conventional cancer treatments except for surgery, I did not fit into any of the patterns established. Cancer diagnosis and treatment is not really personalized—you simply fit into a category and are part of a statistical pattern. Well, in my case I had stepped out of that pattern, so no doctor can be too sure how I am doing at any given time. Incidentally, I have never had my cancer show up in blood work or on mammograms."

Fonfa returned to the Gerson hospital for a second treatment, where she experienced ultraviolet blood irradiation and Coley's toxins, a bacterial vaccine. "Coley's toxins is quite an amazing treatment. It's usually administered as an IV in the intensive care unit. Reactions can be incredibly strong—muscle contractions, violent chills, and high fever. The recovery can take three to five days. It is very difficult, but several people had overnight measurable tumor reductions. One woman with breast cancer was told she probably no longer needed a mastectomy since she had such a strong response. When I found out she was to be spared this, I found it so poignant that I cried."

Fonfa continues to follow the Gerson program at home. "The Gerson doctors who continue to follow my case use monthly blood tests." In addition to the strict diet, "I have also developed my own program of additional supplements based on my readings. I see that most of the people who recommend supplements suggest the same ones. It is the dosages recommended that usually vary. One woman will tell me that her nutritionist said to take thirty milligrams of X and another will say she was told to take fifty milligrams. So I began to feel that it wasn't so critical how much (within obvious limitations) you took as the substance itself that was important. I read a ton of publications, and I often find out what is being recommended in Europe or Japan or China. I boost my dosages by experimenting with my own responses. I always know when I take too much or the wrong thing since my body responds by feeling wrong. As soon as I don't feel well, I cut back. Obviously I try one thing at a time.

Dosage increase should always be done slowly. My supplements program evolved from a combination of those substances most recommended, but at my own dosage levels. I take Coenzyme Q10 at six hundred milligrams daily, green tea capsules, evening primrose oil and EPA/DHA gel caps, N-acetyl cysteine, grape seed extract (pycnogenol), flaxseed oil and flaxseeds, melatonin, garlic tablets, enzyme-rich (organic) vegetable and fruit powder capsules, and a lot of acidophilus. I have had over eight years of yeast/candida problems (which, by the way, went away for the last four to five months but just returned). I see it as a sign of a suppressed immune system and am rethinking my current program." She did not use antiangiogenesis products such as cartilage because she doesn't really feel they are appropriate for her. She also does not use soy products because they are not part of the Gerson program, so she has not yet paid attention to the developing controversy over soy.

When we spoke with Fonfa again in early 1998, she commented, "Since March 1, 1997, I have been using high-dose vitamin A and E to reduce the fifteenth chest wall tumor I developed in December of 1996. It has been very successful—my first success in reducing a tumor without surgery."

Advice to Other Women

Although Fonfa is college-educated, she commented, "I didn't learn any of this in college. Everything I learned came from trying to find information for myself and for the group. I found information from books, reports of studies, news articles, and just learning how to research the topic. I was politically aware and I knew that I could use my knowledge to make changes."

At first she did not understand how she had not received enough information to give true informed consent for all the risks and options when she had her first lumpectomy with axillary node dissection. "My anger over the way the whole thing was handled, as I realized much later, brought me a long way toward activism. I grew up in the Vietnam War era and was very active working against the war, for the civil rights movement, and later for the women's movement, so it was not very difficult to define myself as a cancer activist.

"I joined SHARE, which is a New York City–based grassroots survivors network for women who have had breast or ovarian cancer. They run support groups, educational meetings, hot-lines in English and Spanish, and wellness programs. About four years ago (1993), coincidentally just as I became involved, SHARE started an advocacy committee and generally expanded services from one location to about fourteen citywide. I was able to put together a program on lymphedema and also became the founder and cochair of our study group on alternative/whole health issues. At the time I developed lymphedema, I went back to my surgeon and showed him my swollen breast and swollen arm/hand. He simply said, 'Yes, you have a swollen arm.' He never told me it was lymphedema, never explained about getting treatment. When I later found out about this chronic illness, I realized how little information there was available. I wrote him a letter telling him what I had found out and then helped sponsor an educational meeting at SHARE. That meant that I contacted doctors, massage therapists, and others who actually dealt with lymphedema in the New York area and asked them to speak at a forum. We at SHARE had never held a meeting on the topic and actually had no idea how many women had lymphedema, as statistics ranged from 5 to 50 percent! We held this meeting in a good-sized room featuring five speakers and hoped for twenty women. Seventy-two showed up. We were thrilled and horrified. One speaker after another told the women this was a lifelong chronic condition. It could improve but would never go away. The women in the audience were gasping; it was a very powerful and painful evening for us. We already had breast cancer and now we had another illness that wouldn't go away.

"Once we gathered this information, I wrote a summary of the meeting, which was published in our quarterly newsletter, and a permanent packet of material on lymphedema was made available to the women. On our hot-line, I handle the calls on lymphedema. Many women are amazed to develop it several years later. One woman told me she had continued to play tennis after her diagnosis and treatment and only developed a swelling after fourteen years. I still hear that physicians do not properly diagnose it or advise on treatment."

There is another area where Fonfa thinks more consumer information needs to be available to women: she believes they need better options on pathology reports and noninvasive testing measures. "I am an educated consumer, and I have figured out how to send my tissue samples to various labs for special testing [i.e., angiogenesis], or how to cajole pathology departments to help me out. Not everyone is as pushy as I am. I have been gathering information on alternatives to axillary node dissection. Many surgeons are willing to say that it will be a thing of the past within five years. One paper suggested that four tests would be as good as the surgical option. When I further researched this, not one hospital in New York City did all four: tumor size, grading, overexpression of the oncogene C-Erb-2, and laminin receptors (the missing test). It is very frustrating, and I have discussed this with my various health providers. I've been told that since that test is considered experimental; it isn't done. This is somewhat like the problem of persuading doctors to switch to lumpectomies if justified instead of continuing to perform mastectomies on all patients. How long will it take until women are spared this (soon-to-be) unnecessary surgery?"

We also asked her what she thought of the experimental test known as AMAS, which measures a blood antibody thought to be an indicator of tumor activity. "You cannot get this test done in New York state. The blood has to be sent to Boston, and New York doesn't allow that. We have a state department of laboratories and testing, and it has not granted permission for the AMAS test. This seems to be a function of fees and registration, although there is an inspection of facilities involved also. However, I organized a group of women and arranged to take the blood test in New Jersey. The first result I had showed tumor activity. The blood was taken three weeks after a lumpectomy, and the results were expected as tumor cells are in the blood stream at that time. I waited several months and then had a test three months in a row. All of these showed no tumor activity. I was told the test is usually accurate to 99 percent after at least two are taken in a row. It was suggested that my current pathology report showing a malignant tumor was inaccurate. In fact I had the second of my several recurrences, so for me AMAS was not helpful. Maybe I am an anomaly, but I am the only person to have closely followed with this test and it did not work for me, although I should point out that *no* blood test of any kind has ever shown cancer to this date."

What is her advice on choosing a program? "I always felt that nutritional programs would work for me, so I based the original design of my choices around doing programs that I knew I could comply with. People have to do programs they are comfortable with; otherwise, they are going to fall off the wagon quickly. If you hate the program, you'll drop it. I felt that the metabolic program was meaningful to me and something that I could follow."

Other advice includes: "I think they should check out bookstores and start looking at overviews of options because there is a lot of information available now. I think Oriental medicine should be examined. And I really think people should get involved in organizations, because that is the only way we can get any real strength or power to fight pharmaceutical companies and insurance companies to get the medicine and insurance coverage we need to live."

Opinions On Cancer Research and Publicly Supported Cancer Organizations

Fonfa is the cochair of the Alternative/Whole Health study group of SHARE, an important committee because it provides a key source of information on alternative and complementary therapies within the universe of breast cancer organizations. "SHARE is a fabulous place. Aside from its main concern, emotional support, it is a learning based area. When you have surgery, for example, and you have specific follow-up questions, it is great to be able to ask a woman who has gone through it for advice. Who knows better exactly how it felt, what stages occurred, and other basics? Many doctors are just too busy and, frankly, may not even pay attention to the 'minor' details of healing, but SHARE people do. We have groups for newly diagnosed women where they grow used to handling the disease together. Or you can talk to women who have been there, can tell you about it and help to normalize your feelings and reduce the fears. I kept telling my mother that I had just met a hundred women I really liked. It is such a community. There are overwhelmingly good feelings and people you can respect. They are doing things and going forward.

"At SHARE, it's a volunteer, a grassroots network. So if you get a good idea, you usually end up implementing it. That's what happened to me. I said, 'Wouldn't it be great to find out what alternatives to chemotherapy exist?' And the group said to me, what a great idea—why don't you form a committee and explore it? SHARE gave me a room and an announcement in the newsletter. At the first meeting about twelve women showed up, and we took it from there. Women were interested in meditation and visualization, and we agreed to look into that. There were women interested in very specific hands-on treatments, and we agreed to explore that. Everyone took a research area and we began putting together a resource book. That was how SHARE's library of information was begun. We began to sponsor speakers to the larger group. Our first was Ruth Sackman, who runs FACT (Foundation for the Advancement of Cancer Therapy). About seventy people came to the meeting. It was tremendous. Then we had Ralph Moss, Ph.D., and others. SHARE sponsors many meetings with conventional doctors and research facilities, too. I created monthly summaries of our meetings and began mailing them to women in breast cancer organizations in other states.

"For several years I've been involved with the National Breast Cancer Coalition. It was created to increase awareness and raise research dollars. It has been very successful to date. Funding went from $40 million to about $500 million, although we have to lobby strongly each year to keep the momentum going. Each year that I attended the advocacy training conference, I went around asking, 'Wouldn't it be great to find out about alternative medicine?' Well, last year a group of women suggested that we begin a petition. We passed it around at the 1996 meeting, and about a third of the women present signed it—it asked for Dr. Wayne Jonas, the head of the Office of Alternative Medicine, to be one of the keynote speakers for 1997. And that is just what is happening. It is a really big step forward. We hope to interest him in our cause as well as find out what is happening with his office. Next year I hope we can have workshops on alternative medical issues. I'd like to start confronting insurance companies on coverage issues too.

"I am planning to bring a lot of information on alternatives to hand out to activists from around the country. There is obviously a great deal of interest. Many people with cancer are beginning to realize that it simply cannot be true that only chemotherapy and radiation work. As an activist, I want to use those feelings to help prevent FDA and the conventional medical establishment from stopping alternative cancer treatments."

Fonfa is hopeful that the pressure of women breast cancer activists will lead to randomized, controlled trials of nontoxic cancer therapies. "We will offer ourselves as candidates for trials, but we want recognition of the fact that most often there is a synergy among treatments. We should examine a body of supplements rather than one thing at a time. Almost all trials use stage IV cancer patients. This is understandable, but most often the criteria include having gone through chemotherapy. I would like to see an arm added to all trials for people who have not had chemotherapy. Let's see how people respond to treatments when their immune systems are less damaged. How about comparisons between matched groups of conventionally treated patients to groups of patients using nontoxic methods? In other words, new ways of conducting trials should be examined. It is something to strive for."

eight

Maintaining Hope after the Doctors Give Up

Anne Frahm is the author of *A Cancer Battle Plan: Six Strategies for Beating Cancer from a Recovered "Hopeless Case"* (New York: Putnam, 1997). She and her husband founded HealthQuarters Ministries, an educational and resource center at 41 Sinton Rd., Colorado Springs, Colorado 80907, 719-593-8694.

Her Story

In May 1989 Anne Frahm was diagnosed with stage IV breast cancer. "I was told that I probably only had a few months to live. At that point, it was so far spread that I had tumors covering my head, shoulders, ribs, and sternum. In fact, my sternum was broken and several of my vertebrae had no bone matter. A copy of a report from the time states that every single one of my vertebrae had tumors growing through them."

Prior to her diagnosis, Frahm had found a lump through a breast self-examination. "I have a family history of cancer; my grandmother died of breast cancer." Frahm had always been extremely careful with her self-examinations. "Immediately after discovering the lump, I went in the next morning and had a mammogram followed by ultrasound. Unfortunately, they said that it wasn't cancerous and that there was nothing to worry about.

"My doctor had been treating me all this time but thought it was one thing or another: pulled muscle, kidney infections, or some other malady." Finally, when Frahm was correctly diagnosed, she had been bedridden with incredible pain for several months. "He didn't have any idea what was causing my pain. I was only thirty-five years old, and it didn't cross his mind that it could possibly be cancer. It never occurred to me that it could be cancer.

"At the time of my diagnosis, my doctor made it quite clear what to expect. Radiation, chemotherapy, and surgery would work for a little while. He stated that the cancer would build up a resistance to the chemotherapy. But if I was going to beat this thing, I had to go beyond what he had to offer me.

"I had a mastectomy and was informed that the tumor was the entire size of my breast. The surgery was followed by several weeks of radiation and months of ten-day intervals of intensive chemotherapy. About nine months into the treatment protocol, what my doctor had predicted came true. I began to lose ground very fast: five months worth of progress in a couple of weeks. The cancer was growing back so fast that I had never completely gone into remission.

"I was able to walk and move around even though there was a lot of cancer left. Several different kinds of chemotherapies were tried, but nothing was effective against the cancer. Hormonal therapy was also tried, but was also ineffective. As a last-ditch effort, I underwent a bone marrow transplant."

In the summer of 1990, Frahm went to the University of Nebraska Medical Center for an autologous bone marrow transplant. "I ended up spending fifty-two days in isolation. Initially, my body was saturated with chemotherapy for a week. Then we basically waited, for three reasons: first, to see if I would survive the chemotherapy treatments; second, to see if the bone marrow would graft back; and third, to see if they got all the cancer cells in one fell swoop. It was a hard experience. There was a month of my life that I don't remember because I was so heavily drugged to counteract the chemotherapy effects. My skin turned a chocolate brown color and was burnt from the inside out. With fair-skinned people, their skin actually peels off; mine just turned a leathery brown."

Frahm was constantly receiving blood transfusions over the course of a few months. "I received one hundred blood transfusions just to stay alive. I was coughing and vomiting the whole time. The more serious side effects were that my kidneys shut down. As a consequence, I began filling up with fluids and had also contracted pneumonia. There was one night when they told my husband not to expect me to live through the night, because my one lung was completely filled and the other one was half-full with liquid. At 2:00 A.M. that night, I was rushed into emergency lung surgery and was sent back to my room. There was nothing else that they could do for me.

"This all occurred as a result of the bone marrow transplant, and it was a miracle that I survived at all, but eventually I recovered from the pneumonia. When it was time for testing, toward the end of the fifty-two days, they told me that they thought there was still a considerable amount of cancer cells growing in my marrow. After taking two days to get back with me, my doctor came into my room crying. She said, 'We're very sorry but it just didn't work for you.'" Frahm was sent home with many cancer cells still in her bone marrow and no white blood cell count. "While at home, I was still receiving four blood transfusions a week just to stay alive. I was basically told to 'eat, drink, and be merry'; there was nothing more that could be done for me.

"In terms of other options with conventional therapy, they really had exhausted every possibility on me. They tried all the best guns and nothing worked. Besides that, I really couldn't have anything else. My body just couldn't take anymore. The conventional therapies gave me temporary relief, but they certainly didn't destroy the cancer that was going to claim my life."

Frahm's oncologist in Colorado Springs confirmed her prognosis. "He said that there was nothing that could be done for me. I knew that without hope you already begin to die.

"My family and friends were very supportive throughout my experience. My husband, David, was my biggest supporter. He made me feel as though we were going through it together. When I was first diagnosed with cancer, he said, 'Well, then, I have it, too. We're going to fight this together.'" Frahm had a few good friends who were also supportive. "I remember when I couldn't move, my best friend, Pam, came over and gave me a manicure and a pedicure. She listened and cried with me—she was just a great friend. I just kept hoping that an answer would come. I'm a survivor, a fighter, and I just wouldn't succumb. Finally, the answer did come in the form of a book."

Someone sent Frahm a book on the link between nutrition and cancer. "It was Maureen Kennedy Salaman's book, *Nutrition: The Cancer Answer*. Maureen and I don't agree on everything concerning nutrition, but she understands that the key is the immune system. Her book is what started me into doing my own research. I love to do research and would go to my doctor's medical library and bookstores for resources. At that point, it came as a revelation, but I finally realized that we all have cancer cells in our bodies. It is our immune system that is constantly keeping the cells in check. If I built up my immune system and it was working properly, I might have a chance.

"I didn't know anyone personally who had used nutrition as a therapy." Frahm found out about individuals using nutritional therapies in the books that she read. She was also given the name of a nutritionist practicing in Colorado. "The nutritionist taught me quite a bit about dietary and supplemental needs as well as helped me to outline an immune-building program.

"The day before I was to begin this intensive program, I went in for a checkup with my oncologist, just one of my regular visits every five weeks. After he was done with his examination, I told him about my nutritional program. I will never forget his reaction. He looked at me, then his chart, and said, 'Your cancer has nothing to do with nutrition.' I took his comment with a grain of salt because I had gotten to know him and had seen him eating candy bars and drinking pop for lunch. I thought, 'Maybe he doesn't know everything there is to know about nutrition. What do I have to lose?'

"My oncologist's objection to my exploring nutritional treatments didn't come as a surprise to me. I had learned over the years that many medical doctors don't receive extensive training in nutrition. Basically, everything that I learned was self-taught. Whenever we're sick, we want to see an expert in the field that we are pursuing. I didn't expect my oncologist to be an expert in nutrition; it's not his area of expertise."

Frahm perceived herself as a general in charge of her own cancer battle. "My own experience is that I needed an oncologist, nutritionist, metabolic physician, and a chiropractor on my war cabinet." Her oncologist was one advisor who was good at chemotherapy. "I referred to him when I thought it would help, and when it didn't I went elsewhere. The metabolic physician was most concerned with my immune system. When I first went to him, I had no immune system. I was already on a program when I consulted with him; all he suggested was intravenous vitamin C."

Over the years, Frahm consistently went to a chiropractor for consultations. "I have also had massage therapy; it has been a great help. It has been shown to boost the immune system by increasing lymphatic flow and lymphocyte production."

After her research, Frahm felt very strongly that nutrition was the foundation. "There are certain foods that will feed the cancer. If we put bad fuel into our cars, we are eventually going to break down. The same is true of our bodies. Having eaten the typical American diet, I had fed my body bad fuel. No matter what other therapies I pursued, I had to stop eating foods that fed the cancer.

"During those five weeks, I concentrated on the dietary aspects and used a lot of detoxification agents. I juiced, fasted, used coffee enemas, and ate 80 percent raw foods."

Frahm added several other alternative therapies to her program. "I also used some vitamins, supplements, herbs, and teas. After studying Linus Pauling's work, I added intravenous vitamin C to my battle plan. Over the past six years, I have tried many different therapies for which my immune system has responded very quickly."

Five weeks later, Frahm went back to her oncologist for another checkup. "I will never forget his reaction to my test results. He had just gotten the results from my latest CEA [carcinoembryonic antigen] rating, and it showed no trace of cancer. He couldn't believe it—thinking the results were wrong. Another set of tests were ordered, and those also came back negative." Frahm had another bone marrow biopsy, and that also came back negative, that is, with no trace of cancer. "My oncologist said, 'You've come to play stump the doctor, haven't you?' He also wanted me to have a bone scan, but that would have involved injecting a radioactive substance into my body. I had just worked so hard to cleanse my body that I really didn't want to expose it to any further toxic substances.

"I had researched visualization when I was first diagnosed with cancer and concluded it wasn't important to me. What was important was my attitude and state of mind throughout the day. I dealt with a lot of emotional issues that couldn't be swept under the carpet. They were issues that had to be dealt with on a daily basis, sometimes minute to minute.

"When putting together these various alternative or complementary therapies, I trusted my own logical sense. When referencing the citations in my doctor's medical books, it didn't make sense to me that in the results section it stated diet was a factor, but the authors would conclude nothing could be concluded from the data. I think many of us are aware that what we eat has an effect on our health. To me it's just a simple thing to understand. I don't think that it is a real complicated thing; anyone can understand this."

Frahm's intuition also played a major role in her decision-making process. "I looked up quite a bit of information but also trusted and relied upon my intuition. As a Christian, I believe that Salaman's book ended up in my mailbox for a reason. It was the direction that God wanted me to head into. His guidance was part of my decision-making.

"Working on my spiritual self throughout my experience was a constant for me. At times, it was my only comfort. Sometimes, others' comfort was shallow in comparison. When I read the Bible, I would get strength. Reading about David and Goliath, I felt like David: I was up against a giant, cancer. I felt helpless and small, but it was the stories of impossible situations in the Bible that kept me hoping. I thought, 'This is possible. God is good at impossible situations.' The stories kept me going; otherwise, I would be dead right now. If the doctor said I was going to die, I was going to die. I would have given up. And that's not so bad; heaven is a good place to go. But I think a lot of us give up too early."

After being diagnosed cancer-free, Frahm went on a maintenance program. "I was pretty strict on myself: no meat, dairy, or processed foods. Along with the diet, I used antioxidants, vitamins, minerals, herbs, and occasional cleansing. Obviously, I was able to get rid of the cancer very quickly, but I also had a lot of damage from the radiation and chemotherapy." She views herself as continually improving from her experience with conventional cancer treatments. "I wasn't supposed to have normal blood counts after the treatments, but they are back to normal. Also, I was always supposed to have damage to my female organs, to become sterile, but I think regaining that function is still a possibility. My thyroid was burned up by the chemotherapy but has been restored to complete thyroid function.

"I also incorporated exercise into my wellness program. Usually five days a week, I would go for a three-mile walk that was helping my lymphatic system. By moving well, my lymphatic system was stimulated, and it is also a good aerobic exercise. When my nutritionist saw my blood work, she almost fainted because she thought I would keel over and die right there from all the heart damage. I had a huge amount of heart damage from all the chemotherapy and now have a good heart and great circulatory system. It has been rebuilt from the ground up."

In August 1996, Frahm had a recurrence. "I went in for my regular CEA count and it was elevated. It was a small spot on my ovary, but I handled it through natural healing methods. I just went on the program that I know how to do."

She went on a fast along with other therapies, but her CEA count remained elevated. Frahm consulted with several nutritionists and physicians about her condition. "It was interesting. I found out I had a cavitation from an old molar that had been pulled out years and years ago. It left a pocket of infection that was just cooking away for twenty years. The bacteria placed such a stress on my immune system that cancer just started checking in again.

"The infected area in my jaw was identified by a technician who uses a Computron, a computerized diagnostic system. It's widely used in Europe, and I was able to see some areas that were compromising my immune system. The one that seemed to be the most prevalent was the one in my jawbone." Frahm had the infected pocket taken care of by a dentist.

Frahm was checked three or four times after her recurrence and was deemed in remission again. "I eventually got to the point where my oncologist only wanted to see me once a year." She continued to have checkups with her alternative doctor. "Currently, I also go to a general practitioner who is supportive of my choices toward nutrition. It is rare to find practitioners like them, but it does happen.

"One of the things that surprised me after first being diagnosed cancer-free was that my phone began to ring. It just rang and rang from strangers around the country who wanted to know what I did to regain my health. I was spending hours every day on the telephone detailing my experiences with people. Finally, my husband and I tried to write it down so we could send it to people. Eventually we wrote a book, *A Cancer Battle Plan: Six Strategies for Beating Cancer from a Recovered 'Hopeless Case.'* The book has sold over a quarter of a million copies. In fact, it was just bought out by the second largest publisher in the world, Putnam Publishing. They plan on selling another half million copies in the next two years.

"By the time the book came out, I was cancer-free for two years. My husband and I realized that we were heading into new territory, and it was becoming a full-time job for me."

In 1992 Frahm and her husband started the HealthQuarters Ministries, an educational and resource center in Colorado Springs, Colorado. It became a full-time job for both of them, and they had a staff of fifteen people. "We do phone counseling and run a lodge for people to work on their health for eleven-day programs. We teach them about making those lifestyle changes that can help prevent them from getting cancer or, if they do have cancer, maybe help rebuild their immune system. We teach them so they know what to do when they go home."

Sadly, when we called Frahm again in early 1998, we learned that the cancer had returned and that she had died on February 5, 1998. Her husband attributed her decline of health to excess iron in the blood from the transfusions received in previous years and to ongoing infections in the dental cavitations, both of which had weakened her immune system.

Advice to Other Women

"The number one thing that I would tell women is that there is hope. There is no type of cancer out there that someone hasn't overcome, so don't ever feel that you are helpless or hopeless because there are things that you can do to help yourself.

"Secondly, I would say educate yourself. Read the books out there from people like me who have beat the odds. That is the type of information that you need to know. Obviously, find out what your doctor has to offer and find out exactly what he expects to achieve by the therapy that he is promoting. Many times we are told that there is a 40 percent chance of a cure, but that is usually based on a five-year outcome. I don't think people realize this. We need to know exactly what is meant by the term *survival*. Ask a lot of questions when you consult with your doctors. I used to go in there with at least a list of ten to twelve questions to ask my doctor.

"I would also advise women to pray about it. What is right for you is not necessarily what is right for the next person. I saw someone who really thought that chemotherapy would kill him, and that is exactly what happened. You've got to do what you believe. I encourage people to make up their own minds. Don't have a relative or friend pressure you into something that you don't believe. We're not carbon copies of each other; everyone is different. Do what you believe in, whether it is conventional or alternative therapies. After you have educated yourself, go with your own guidance.

"Carefully select your professional help. In our book, chapter 8—which is titled 'Coming Alongside in the Battle'—offers a checklist for helping individuals locate resources. Our HealthQuarters Ministries really is a health resource center. We publish a listing, called the Health Resource List, of nutritionists and doctors from across the United States who are knowledgeable on various methods to get well. The listing is several thousand names long."

Frahm also advised women to network with other people, and she suggested going to the local health food store as one starting point. "When people call me I offer the three points that I mentioned (maintain hope, educate yourself, and pray). You need to have hope because if you lose hope, it has been scientifically shown that your immune system will drop about 50 percent. I would also encourage them to find out about nutrition, how what you are eating today is having an effect on the cancer cells. You are not helpless; there are things that you can do. I think knowing this encourages people. The first thing my doctor said to me after he said that I had cancer was that he didn't want me to think that I had anything to do with getting cancer; it was just strictly genetic. If I had accepted that no-fault cancer scenario, I would be equally as helpless to do anything about it."

Opinions on Cancer Research and Publicly Supported Cancer Organizations

"Since Nixon declared war on cancer, billions of dollars have been spent on cancer and cancer research. Still, we haven't seen much reward from it.

It was recently stated that the war on cancer was being lost." Frahm noted that cancer rates are increasing and may soon reach one in two Americans. "I would say that maybe we are barking up the wrong tree. Maybe we need to start looking in a different direction. What I notice when I research the books in the medical libraries of my doctors is that we don't know what is causing cancer. If you don't know what causes cancer, how do you know the right way to treat it? That makes no sense to me. Maybe we need to start at the basics again."

Frahm did not think we were heading in the right direction. "I have met a number of M.D.'s and D.O.'s who are looking into this whole area of natural remedies for building the immune system. They are excited in what they are doing and are seeing results. I attended a symposium with approximately four hundred doctors on cancer and nutrition, and these doctors were excited. They knew that they were onto something, that it actually works. I think that is the wave of the future."

When she was looking for various groups focusing on bone marrow transplant recipients, Frahm accessed the computer to get information. "Overall, there wasn't any particular organization that helped me in any way. My doctor had a great exercise program, but that was out of his own office.

"I would have to say that the cancer organizations were of no help to me whatsoever." For example, Frahm described one national organization that sponsored a support group she attended. "To tell you the truth, it was really disappointing. What they did for these people with cancer, including myself, was to have a lawyer show us how to make out a will. That was one meeting, and there were five meetings. Another meeting was focused on nutrition. I didn't know a lot about nutrition then but was horrified by what she was telling us we should eat. It was a dietitian from the hospital who gave us recipes for Jell-O and buttermilk. It was full of fat and sugar. All she focused on was the calories, and it didn't matter how you got them. I felt as though she was putting nails in my coffin. I left early because I became physically sick; I just couldn't believe it."

Frahm predicted that alternative and complementary therapies will become more accepted because people will demand them. "I heard someone say that doctors are going to come around to educating themselves in alternative methods because their patients will demand it of them."

References

Salaman, Maureen Kennedy

    1984 *Nutrition, the Cancer Answer*. Menlo Park, Calif.: Stratford.

    1996 *Nutrition: The Cancer Answer II*. Menlo Park, Calif.: Stratford.

nine

Saying No to a Mastectomy— Twenty-Five Years Ago

Myrna Gene is a long-term Contreras patient, a Master Herbalist, a sales representative for Sunrider products, and a consultant to cancer patients. Her forthcoming book is titled *Count It All Joy.* She requested that her interview be published entirely in her own words, and we have honored that request.

Her Story

"In October 1971, during a routine examination, my general practitioner found a lump in my right breast. After doing a needle biopsy, he was extremely concerned, saying, 'You've got to have the biopsy.' I refused.

"The early part of 1972 my husband, myself, and another couple were vacationing in Mexico, and my husband contracted an intestinal parasite. On the trip home I was feeling unusually exhausted, and this didn't improve after I got home and rested, so I thought I might have contracted the parasite. By the end of March I went to the doctor's for a culture test to verify if I had it. When I returned to the doctor's office about ten days later for the results, which were negative, I asked him to check the breast lump. He exclaimed, saying, 'The lump has doubled since the first examination' and that I definitely needed to do something. I told him he could set up the biopsy, but I'd call him if I would do it.

"The biopsy was scheduled for Friday, April 25th, at which time I did go to the hospital to have the biopsy. I went as an outpatient because I felt sure of the findings. I told my husband, 'If they find anything, I am not going to have surgery.' He wasn't happy, at that time, about my decision, but it was really out of his hands. Now he's very glad I made the decision that I did.

"Following the biopsy, I was told to call the following Monday for the results. It was two and a half weeks before I got through to the doctor. In the meantime, about a week after the biopsy, I had a dream that conveyed everything that the doctor was going to say to me. In the dream when the doctor told me, I was to call all of my family together, and a church elder and his wife, and we were to take communion together and be blessed. It was to be a time together, before I saw the doctor. I believe this is one reason I didn't have the fear that is so associated with hearing the diagnosis.

"My family and pastor backed me 100 percent with my decisions. They may have been frightened; I don't know. One day my oldest daughter called and said, 'Mom, we were talking and you should know you don't have to be afraid of crying in front of the family.'

"I said, 'Honey, I'm not dying for anybody, and I'm not going to be burned up or cut up.' The next day I went to my doctor's office and was informed I should have the mastectomy because the kind of cancer found was an unusual kind, not normally found in the breast, and it was a very fast-moving kind. I blanked it out in my mind. I didn't want to hear the kind it was because I was not going to own it. It seems a portion of the biopsy was sent to UCLA and to Loma Linda Medical Center. The doctor had already scheduled me for the mastectomy the following week. My reply was, 'I am *not* going to have the surgery,' then I asked the doctor, 'What would you do if it were you?'

"His answer: 'I have to make a recording of the diagnosis first.' He did this, turned around in his chair, and said, 'If it were my wife or daughter, I would do the same thing you're doing. This is a very fast kind. Next week we will remove the breast; three months later we may have to remove something from the stomach; three more months maybe a leg or something; and I don't want to cut you all up.' I firmly believe he would never have told me this if I had not already made up my mind. I've thanked the Lord over and over for this man, that he didn't pressure me. If doctors and families just trust the decision of the patient, there would be much less pressure on everyone involved.

"One of the reasons I refused to have the breast removed was because, to me, that wasn't an answer. You can remove all the lumps that appear, and you still haven't taken care of the problem. The problem is internal—

it's spiritual as well as physical. There are many, many books out now revealing it's a lot of things—stress, emotions, poor diet—just a lot of things. Removing the breast is just a piecemeal thing; it's just the beginning of being cut, then burned. I just wasn't going to do that. My mother was a nurse, so I knew those results.

"When I refused the mastectomy, nothing else was suggested, so I was on my own. After the diagnosis, I just started praying and searching for information on what I could do. At that time, twenty-five years ago, you had to keep your mouth shut about what alternative treatments were out there. I didn't have anyone to talk to; I just had to do it myself. Today, there is a lot of information on nutrition, diet, and all kinds of things. I read books on all of these topics including what was behind it spiritually. One book I read was *One Answer to Cancer,* by William Kelley, which led me to the dietary changes necessary. You can't build live cells with dead food, and that is what meat and meat products are.

"The book suggested to get Dr. Walker's book *The Vegetarian Guide to Diet and Salad,* so I started there, changing to a vegetarian raw food diet and juicing daily. I also did the coffee enemas that he suggested. (Dr. Gerson was the one who discovered the value of these.)

"A friend wrote to Dr. Kelley for me, and he suggested, because of the diagnosis and the type of cancer I had, that I might need to contact Dr. Ernesto Contreras. I wrote to Dr. Contreras and received instructions for a blood test called A-MID and a urine test. I did as he suggested and the results were returned. Approximately a month later I received an airmail letter from Dr. Contreras again with the results. We prayed about it and decided I needed to go to the clinic and have the tests taken again. If it hadn't been for the support of my family and the body of believers I am involved with, it probably would have been difficult for me.

"Twenty-five years ago, you pretty much only heard about orthodox treatments. You had to really want to live and really fight for your life by yourself, because everything was hush, hush. In November 1972 I went to the clinic to have the tests retaken. One thing that really impressed me was the fact that when my husband and I arrived, we were waiting for me to be taken to the laboratory, when we saw a man being carried in by his family. He was not able to walk; he had bone cancer. My husband and I left after the tests and went to Ensenada for the five days (we were to wait for the results of the tests). When we returned to the clinic, this man was walking around. This really left an impression on me.

"The test results were not good, and Dr. Mellado said, 'Myrna, you have got to do something.' As my doctor who had done the biopsy in the States had said, it was very fast-moving. I made the appointment to begin the treatment the twelfth of December, which was two weeks later. You see, I still had a daughter in school. I needed to get things in order and prepare for three weeks away.

"I stayed at a hotel near the clinic. It had just cancer patients from our clinic. Incidentally, there were two doctors being treated, and one doctor had his mother there, also for treatment. In my hotel there were patients from China, Canada, Nebraska, Kansas, and California, so they weren't all just going from California.

"I love the doctors at the clinic. Their philosophy is 'Don't do anything to the patient you wouldn't do to yourself.' They believe in teaching you how to live—not how to die.

"The therapy I had is different from the currently improved therapy. Once a day, before breakfast, all of us would walk to the clinic and have our laetrile and Wobe Mugos implant. Then once a week we would have an appointment with our doctors to monitor our progress. If there was any adverse reaction or additional therapy needed, they would find that out at that time and begin the therapy. Basically, they started me out on the strict diet. After your testing was negative, they began you on the modified diet, which did include meat in small amounts. However, I have stayed on the strict vegetarian diet (I did all raw for approximately one year), feeling that if the vegetarian diet helped to get me well, it would help to keep me well. Through self-education I learned more about nutrition. After all, I was fighting to stay alive and I couldn't just depend on others. I had to learn for myself why I was needing to eat certain things.

"After my initial three weeks' stay, I made monthly trips to the clinic. This went on for approximately three months more. The checkups got progressively further apart, and now I just have the checkup once a year.

"I stayed on laetrile and enzyme treatments for approximately five years. I also went to a doctor in Los Angeles who helped me understand the vitamins and minerals needed, and he did additional counseling on nutrition. At the time the FDA was harassing him about the work he was doing with cancer patients: the result was they raided his office to put him out of business. He was put on trial and he was sent to prison for several years. To me he is a hero. Governor Brown commuted his sentence. We have many doctors in this country who have given much of their lives because they are committed to their oath.

"Because of my own studies, I did additional things, besides the normal from the Contreras clinic. I contacted Ann Wigmore and started growing the wheatgrass and juicing it. I wasn't overjoyed at the taste, but I was set to do anything that would get me through this. I incorporated many things, but I would never let go of the program that Dr. Contreras had put me on.

"A year later, when my tests for the cancer were negative, I went back to my U.S. doctor. He walked in the door and said, 'Myrna, you look better than I've ever seen you,' to which I replied, 'I'm on laetrile.' He was looking at my chart. He didn't say a word, and when he was done with the chart, he turned around and said, 'Well, good luck to you,' and walked out the door. I know the doctors are hampered in many ways from really wanting to encourage us to do things such as this, but I thanked the Lord for his giving me this doctor for the original diagnosis.

"I'd like to tell about an experience I also had. I was sent to a clinic in San Diego for what's called a darkfield test. I went to the clinic, had the test, and when the doctor started to talk to me, he began pressuring me into doing their treatment. I persisted in refusing the treatment they were offering, and he went on about how my diet and the laetrile treatment I was doing wouldn't help me, etc., and how one day I was going to have to depend on the doctors because I wasn't smart enough to know what to do for myself. Since I kept resisting, he was getting more angry and my husband was looking more frightened, so I said, 'I suppose you're not going to give me my results.' He threw the paper across the desk at me and said, 'You're doing remarkably well, but your kidney is still in trouble.'

"I said, 'Yes, but I'm doing remarkably well,' so with that I took the paper and quickly left. When we got to the car, I told my husband I wanted him to take me back to the Contreras clinic so I could walk around. I knew my spirit could tell me if it was right or wrong. After walking around the clinic, I thought, 'This is where I belong and I'm not going any other place.' I refused to accept the fear that doctor was trying to instill—I took charge of my own body.

"I don't believe you can say you are cured. I feel you are controlled. I would fluctuate back and forth between negative and positive for a while, before I stayed at the negative. I remember my parents went down with us one of the trips and my test was positive. I just cried. I was doing all that I knew how to do, and my mother said, 'Dear, it took you forty-five years to get this way; it's not going to be cured in a month.'

"During the early part of my experience, I took such heavy amounts of vitamins and minerals that I had a hard time looking at a pill. I subsequently began to study about the herbs, having learned about them through different books. I began to study nutrition, iridology, and herbs with Dr. Bernard Jensen and Dr. John Christopher. I got my Master Herbalist degree from the School of Natural Healing in Park City, Utah, in June 1980. I also studied nutrition with Dr. Robert Preston at the American College of Healthology. I knew I had to educate myself because nobody else was going to do this for me. As you can see, it was an ongoing process.

"I'm not an animal rights person. I just believe I don't need to eat them. I eat good vegetables, fruits, grains, beans, nuts, seeds. I take a lot of a Chinese whole food product called Sunrider. The philosophy is 'regeneration,' and that's just what I've been trying to do for all these years: 'regenerate.' I know when I eat these foods my immune system will stay strong, and that's what I need. One thing I have learned through this whole situation, the most important thing is to keep that immune system strong. It's your fighter.

"I maintain the diet and the periodic visits to the Contreras clinic. I haven't gone to a doctor here in the States since the year after the biopsy. If I need something, I go to my doctor at the clinic or to the BEST (Bioenergetic Synchronization Technique) therapist here (but not a regular M.D.). This type of therapy is far better than the regular chiropractor, I feel, because they get the body back in line: spirit, soul, and body.

"I now help people set up their nutritional programs and teach them about the use of the herbs and the Chinese whole foods of Sunrider. I just suggest the different things that I learned that may help them. My life is definitely that of a teacher. There is a saying, 'Feed a man a fish and you feed him for a day. Teach a man to fish and you feed him for a lifetime.'

"From my own experience and what I saw of other individuals' experiences, I was determined to make my own decisions. I was able to see how quickly I made a turnaround, not just with the test results, but with my energy level and the ability to resume various activities. It showed me I was definitely making a very positive difference.

"My intuition, or spirit—whatever you wish to call it—played a major part in my decision-making process. And that is what I was leaning on probably more than anything else. I really am grateful that all my family and friends let me make my own decisions and didn't try to influence me. I don't very often have dreams that I remember, but when I do they are specific dreams. The one I had certainly prepared me for this experience in my life.

"Science had no role in my decision-making process. The only answers I got were from the reading and studying I did, starting with Dr. Kelley's book. I chose the alternative therapies that I did because I wasn't aware of any other alternative therapies at the time. If Dr. Kelley hadn't written us about Dr. Contreras, I wouldn't have known about his treatment program, either. I wouldn't have learned about all the other things had I not searched on my own. I was searching, searching all the time.

"From the books I also learned much about the Gerson therapy; however, I used only the enemas because I felt the rest of their program was too stressful for me. I was still a mother and trying to care for my husband and one daughter, and still do all my household chores and my program at the same time.

"My feelings are that the conventional therapies aren't health-building and they most assuredly are not an answer, because most of the time the doctors aren't trained on diet and nutrition, which is a major part of the change needed. You can't put poison into the bloodstream and have it do good for you. Chemotherapy is a poison.

"Today if I had to do it again, I would rush back down there and do the same thing. But a lot of people who I have talked to through the years started on one thing, then jumped to other things. I never stopped using the Contreras program, but would just incorporate new things found to see if I felt they did good for me. I was convinced of this therapy because his was the only clinic, at that time, that was having consistent results. I've got twenty-five years to prove that Dr. Contreras has an answer.

"Another point to remember is if you wait too long or have a lot of the chemicals or radiation, you can't blame the natural treatments for not working. Many people do all the orthodox treatments, then go down, and when they don't live the families accuse it of being quackery. I look at the orthodox as being the quackery. It costs thousands and thousands of dollars, usually from your insurance. By the time the insurance runs out, you find out it's too late to do anything else. The success rate of all the treatments hasn't improved more than 5 percent over the years.

"When your body is badly damaged by chemicals, it is hard for anything to bring it back. My father died in 1983 of prostate cancer—he was on the same program that I was. Didn't it work? Of course it did. He was ninety-one and the cancer had gone to the bone, but he had no pain. It was his time to go and he went peacefully with his family around him, but he had no pain. That is not heard of with bone cancer. Of course it worked! *Big* time.

"You have to want to get well, and you have to not blame others for what you're going through. You were responsible for it yourself. Stress, bitterness, poor diet . . . many things had a part in it. The second thing is you can't destroy the immune system with the chemicals.

"I know with some breast cancers, like open sore breast cancer, generally they have to have the breast removed. It's open and gone too far. So there are times when a person needs the surgery. Dr. Francisco Contreras is a top surgeon who studied in Vienna for five years. This is Dr. Contreras's youngest son. He has the love and beautiful spirit that his dad has. After a surgery, if one is vital for your survival, you must go on the good diet, less stress, and seek to find what there is in your emotions and spirit that has contributed to this.

"I don't suggest anything unless I've searched it out, but then I tell anyone this is what I have learned and it might help. If you choose to do it, fine. If you don't choose to do it, that is fine, too. You see, it's their body. I know I can share with them the things that I have learned, but I never try to take away their decision, their responsibility for their own selves. If you balance the three things in your life, your body is going to respond. The majority of the doctors are looking at science; they are not looking at the complete body."

As of early 1998, Myrna Gene and her partner were working on a plan to open a facility called "A Peaceful Place," where they will have classes on food preparation, colonics, massages, and "counseling for spirit, soul, and body." Guests will be able to stay for one or two weeks.

Advice to Other Women

"All I do is tell people about my experience. I can't legally tell someone what choices to make. I just don't think it's my responsibility anyway. I share with them what I did and what I know, but it's their decision. No one should make the decision for them — doctor, family, or friends. Love them and give them all the support you can, but let them make their own decision.

"The main thing I would say to anyone that has just been faced with this big "C" word is, Don't blame anyone else for what is happening to you. Realize you have to take responsibility for your life. A doctor isn't going to hurt for you and he isn't going to die for you. You need to search for all the information you can get. My girlfriend in Washington, D.C., had her librarian print out from the Internet everything she could find on her kind of cancer, and guess what? The place that had the best success rate with her cancer was Dr. Contreras's clinic.

"Just because I chose the alternative therapy, not everybody needs to do the same. I think you have to be convinced of what you are doing. If someone talks you into something, someone else will come along and talk you out of it. If someone would choose the other therapy, no one should try to convince them they are wrong. It's their life or their death.

"Don't blame anyone else for your condition. You need to accept the fact that your lifestyle has created it. Because you are spirit, soul, and body, you have to work with all three, and that is what they help you with at this clinic.

"I feel as though I was, in a measure, spiritual before the diagnosis, but it certainly teaches you. It's a learning and growth experience. I've learned you don't do something just for yourself but also for those you will be able to help down the road. It certainly got me digging into the Scriptures and into other spiritual things as well as nutrition.

"If you can find one, I think you would be fortunate to supplement any other therapies with the BEST treatments at the same time. I would also suggest colonics, at least for a while. I did the coffee enemas and then bought a colonic machine.

"Everyone needs to exercise, but one thing a cancer patient needs to know is that you don't exercise to the point of exhaustion. Your body is needing to use its energy to heal, and if you become exhausted, it has to use its energy to recuperate from that exhaustion before it can use it to help heal. Swimming, bicycling, and walking are good exercises. Be mindful of how you address each aspect of your life. Gardening was my exercise. I loved it and was outside working with nature.

"If you have someone in the family or a friend who is facing this, you need to support them in any way you can, including emotionally, physically, and financially. I'm on the Cancer Control Society listing and have had many people call me saying they want to go the natural way, but their families are totally against it. So many people feel they're going to lose their wife, husband, mother, sister, or brother, and they panic because the media has so controlled the thinking that this way will never cure the people. People are afraid of it. My suggestion is pray about what your loved one wants to do—when you know it's what they want, then encourage them and encourage others to help them in any way you can, most of all *love* them. It's a time in their life when they need that more than any other time. And for heaven's sake *don't* sympathize with them. They sure don't need that. That is draining.

"Look at the quality of life involved with each method. I didn't lose my hair; I didn't vomit every day. In fact I began gaining energy, feeling happier, and was really as busy as I had ever been. With the orthodox method you not only, most of the time, lose the hair and vomit, but you feel like dying, not living. I just didn't want to live that way.

"I would say to anyone, Listen to your body. It can tell you what you need. I would wager that a woman who has cancer somewhere in her body has had something of a benchmark. She could look back and say, 'I felt this or that; there is something not quite right.' Pay attention; check your breasts frequently.

"When my pastor taught us to listen to our bodies, I started to do it, and I could tell what organ was needing help. For most of the women who call, I stress the need to read the book *Feelings Buried Alive,* by Karol Truman. I stress they need to pray and search their spirits and do a lot of

Scripture reading. There were two Scriptures that helped me so much. One was about the woman with the issue of blood (Mark 5:25–34); she spent all her money on physicians and they did her no good. It was when she touched the Lord that she was healed. The other was a Scripture in Hebrews that talks about how Christ died to conquer death for those whose fear of death caused them to submit to slavery all their life (Heb. 2:14–15). I feel there is nothing more slavish than the medical profession and feeling captivated to where you have no other answer than to do what they say.

"We are trained to think we aren't smart enough and that we need to go to a doctor for the slightest headache. Insurance companies get rich . . . based on the fear of getting sick and needing to go to the doctors.

"I have people come into my office and say they are on this or that medication. I say, 'Did you go to the library and look up in the PDR *[Physician's Desk Reference]* what the side effects are?' They need to search the answers for themselves. It's a matter of educating yourself about all major areas of your life, particularly your health. Don't just take the doctor's word. A lot of them don't want to play God, but people have put them in that place.

"I'm sure that turning to raw foods may be the answer for some people, but it isn't the answer for all people. When you are getting started, you need to look into the wheatgrass and raw organic vegetables. Another alternative therapy is Essiac tea out of Canada. My husband had prostate cancer. Our BEST therapist told me to put him on a program and give him the Essiac tea, which I did. They found the cancer in July 1991, and by April 1992 they couldn't find any cancer. They keep checking but it just isn't there."

Opinions on Cancer Research and Publicly Supported Cancer Organizations

"There are several good therapies used in various countries around the world, but they aren't recognized in this country. If the money factor were removed, you would find the openness to use them, but most wouldn't make much money for the medical establishment. It is rumored the American Cancer Society makes a percentage off the 5-FU [fluorouracil] treatment. How right is it that they make money off any treatment? It has also been proven that in all the years these organizations have held fund drives, there hasn't been a 5 percent increase in their success. Any time an organization makes money off cancer, I question whether or not they are really fighting cancer. We need to donate to those that are seeking and using the natural methods.

"Through my studies I've learned only about one-third of the medical doctors in the United States belong to the American Medical Association, but they are controlled by it. They are a union that has such a strong hand in the regulations along with the Food and Drug Administration and the availability of the therapies used in the United States. I think it's very sad that we have to go to another country for treatment, when it's known that there are effective therapies that do exist.

"Years ago I met a Los Angeles police lieutenant who said, 'You know. I'm so angry that I have to sneak things into this country just so my wife can live.' I felt the same way. I understand it's now legal to bring the laetrile into the United States, but if you declare it, there is a 10 percent duty on it. So if they can't control its coming in, they'll make money off of it. Does this make you see the money issue involved in treatments? If they can't stop it, they'll make money off of it.

"There are many more things I could share with you, both funny and sad, but I share those in my book *Count It All Joy*, which will be coming out soon. This has been a joyful experience, for me, that I love to share. In every pain we go through, there can be blessings also."

References

Kelley, William Donald
  1969 *One Answer to Cancer: An Ecological Approach to the Successful Treatment of Malignancy*. Grapevine, Tex.: Kelley Research Foundation.
Truman, Karol Kuhn
  1991 *Feelings Buried Alive Never Die . . .* Las Vegas, Nev.: Olympus Distributing.
Walker, Norman
  1971 *The Vegetarian Guide to Diet and Salad*. Phoenix: Norwalk Press.

Overcoming Cancer with Diet

Louise Greenfield is the author of the book *Cancer Overcome by Diet: An Alternative to Surgery* (Livonia, Mich.: Published by the author, 1987). This book is currently available in health food stores. Greenfield holds an M.A. in English from Ohio State University. Now retired, for twenty years she was a poet, short story writer, freelance journalist, and novelist.

Her Story

In November 1977, Louise Greenfield, a forty-nine-year-old office worker, was so overwhelmed with fatigue and physical ailments that she went to her family doctor for an examination. While examining her breasts, Greenfield's doctor found two small lumps and immediately recommended a mammogram. The results indicated that the lumps were malignant. Greenfield's doctor informed her of the urgency of removing the lumps and recommended an oncologist.

"My experience with the oncologist was not very good. Here I was, sitting with a man who is knowledgeable and experienced, and he's recommending conventional therapies.

"I thought, 'I don't think so,' then, 'Where is this assertiveness coming from all of a sudden?' I grew up in a generation of women who were socialized to stay home and be passive, not to question authority or be reactive. Here I was, in the face of this very learned man, saying 'No.' It was scary. Besides refusing the operation, I didn't have radiation, chemotherapy, or any other form of conventional therapy. I felt that radiation and chemotherapy were not my choice of therapies. It's general knowledge that they are invasive and poisonous therapies."

Greenfield felt very fortunate that her husband supported her decisions. "If he hadn't, I probably would have remained in my ordinary submissive mode. I might have succumbed to the oncologist's recommendations, but I didn't."

When the surgeon recommended a mastectomy, Greenfield postponed her decision, eventually refusing the surgery. "Actually, the mastectomy was never really an option for me. My breast was such an important part of my body; I didn't want to part with it unless I was sure."

At the time of her diagnosis, Greenfield was working, along with 130 other people, in an office space located in a warehouse front in Michigan. "Of the 130 workers, 10 of them were diagnosed with some form of cancer. The majority of them chose to use conventional therapies, and within a span of several years 7 out of the 10 individuals who chose conventional therapies died. I knew these were not very good odds. It was very sad to be working on that floor and seeing people coming down with these various types of cancer. The majority of them came down with colon cancer. Then, three friends or acquaintances I knew were diagnosed with cancer.

"Much later, someone remarked to me about the high rate of cancer in large companies. At that point, I thought that from my own experiences with large corporations, when you work in that type of environment, basically the personality of the person at the top filters down and is borrowed by all the supervisors and managers." Greenfield thought that at her company people didn't feel respected or valued and resented their employers. "I was aware of the negativity and tried not to have this attitude, but after a while I just absorbed it. In an atmosphere of pressure and where people are devalued, it could be a hotbed for a lot of things." She suggested that this workplace culture could have been a contributing factor to the cancer incidence among her colleagues.

"At the time of my diagnosis, there weren't many alternative therapies available. The only other thing I heard about was macrobiotics, but in November 1977 there were very few practitioners. A few years later I began to hear more about macrobiotics, but I didn't think it would be something suitable for me. It was too formalistic and I didn't like that type of regimentation. It suits some people, but it didn't suit my personality.

"The reason I turned toward using a nutritional approach for my treatment was that I read Dr. Goldstein's book [1977]. By drastically changing his diet, Goldstein was able to overcome a very serious case of ulcerative colitis. He water-fasted for six weeks then gradually switched to a pureed vegetable diet."

Greenfield considered Goldstein's book very inspirational. It read like an adventure story. "I thought, 'If he could do it for this, even though cancer is different, maybe there is some possibility that it may work for me.'

"With my husband's support and suggestions, I visited with Goldstein. After talking with him, I realized he was a brilliant chemist and physiologist. He had such a thorough knowledge of the human body that I felt that I could rely on his recommendations. Goldstein believed chlorophyll, obtained through dark green vegetables, was important for your health. He also felt that beta carotene, a precursor of vitamin A, was very important."

From 1978 through 1985, Greenfield followed Goldstein's dietary regimen of raw fruits and vegetables. The diet consisted of raw juices, raw blended salad, raw milk cheese, and raw unsalted nuts. "Dr. Goldstein told me that I had a low-grade allergy to wheat, and for a long time I was eating rice cakes. I stayed exclusively on Goldstein's diet and did not use any other dietary therapy."

Greenfield found it hard to remain on the raw-food diet while traveling. "At first, I used to get sick on the trips and then resumed the diet and got plenty of rest. You may say that I backslid on trips. No matter how hard you try, it's hard to get your diet the way you want it.

"I also tried a therapy by a local man, but the Food and Drug Administration stopped him from giving it to people." She used the remedy, CanCell, for about a year. She added, "It contains catechol, a naturally occurring substance that has anticancer properties. The local man was experimenting with CanCell on mice and consulting with Sloan Kettering. I thought they were just jerking him around by having him examine tumor regression and requesting more and more tests. Finally, he also realized that they were just trying to delay him from getting the drug to the market. Their delay tactics worked pretty well because by the time they were through, he was very old and just couldn't fight anymore."

Greenfield used both rational and emotional criteria for evaluating conventional and alternative therapies. "One criterion was my emotional reaction to the therapies. I also studied the scientific literature because I did not want to fly off into the wild blue by myself. I would go to the library and study the various books and periodicals. Science played an important role in my decisions. I would go off, study, and compile folders of all the things doctors and universities had said. In fact, I had a six-inch stack at one time. Afterward, I would let it percolate and went with my gut feeling.

"I am sure science had a lot to do with it because science is such a respected thing these days. But I do have to say that for me, when it came down to it, the fact that my husband supported me was important. Other than that, it was a gut feeling. The Goldstein diet was something that would work and it was something that I could handle. As time went by, Dr. Goldstein wouldn't tell me anything, but would just say, 'Go study. Find out for yourself.'

"For instance, I heard about a woman who was taking an herbal treatment. I'm sure it was working for her, but it was extremely cumbersome. Mine was cumbersome enough, scrubbing the vegetables and cleaning out the juicer, but this poor lady was doing something every half hour. She was able to handle it because she had a daughter helping her. I know I wouldn't have been able to handle that routine.

"At the time of my diagnosis, I had to go to the other side of town to get cheese because there were only a few health food stores and only one that carried food products. What distresses me is that General Nutrition only sells supplements. You can't buy one good loaf of bread, turkey sausage, or chicken hot dog. They're just going along with what most people want, which is 'silver bullets,' that is, one easy thing that works fast.

"Currently, I am back to a somewhat ordinary diet. I drink a glass of carrot juice once a day and try hard to eat pure food. As I go to the market, it's getting harder and harder to get food without additives.

"I also use vitamins and supplements. The brand of vitamin that I use, Thompson, is an older and smaller company. It hasn't been given over to the large production companies." Greenfield is leery of the larger supplement companies because of the issue of quality control.

Greenfield also practices stress management by meditating once a day for twenty minutes. "I think stress management is very important for maintaining your health. Occasionally, I will attend an anger or stress seminar to refresh my technique. It helps me handle stress because things do go wrong in life. My two sons, Stuart and Keith, are grown, but as they say,

'Once a mother always a mother.' If I think one of them is going to be having hard times, I suffer along with them and allow myself to get stressed.

"I haven't gone to an oncologist in quite a while. As long as I don't have any lumps or bumps, and I'm feeling good and functioning well in my daily life, then I don't need to go. Another reason is because the tests that they would give me would put poisons into my body. Sometimes I feel like an oddball because I'm questioned about this all the time."

Greenfield has been healthy for twenty years. "I always thought that in one or two years I would be gone, but I have had all this extra time. Here I am, twenty years later."

In June 1997 she wrote, "I'm in good health. I take no medications. My heart and blood pressure are fine. I do my own housework, run my own errands, and grow vegetables and flowers. I've retired from fiction writing but do the occasional essay. People often tell me I look very healthy. My hair and fingernails look great, my eyes are bright, and my outlook is generally optimistic." Greenfield passed her twenty-year anniversary as a cancer survivor in November 1997.

Advice to Other Women

Greenfield advises women to take the time to educate themselves. "I would advise women to read, study, and collect clippings, then sit down and put them all together. You have to find your own way.

"I would say to look into alternative therapies; the more natural the therapy the better. Our body has its own built-in killer cells, or T-lymphocyte cells, and if you correct your body's metabolism, it will kick out the cancer.

"As a writer, I would collect books for research on the weekends." One book that Greenfield found helpful was *Remarkable Recovery: What Extraordinary Healings Tell Us about Getting Well and Staying Well,* by Hirshberg and Barasch. "In the book, individuals were trying to compile evidence for the scientific basis of studies on alternative therapies that medical doctors are always trying to denigrate.

"This reminds me of the alternative practitioner Dr. Harold Manner. He was head of the biology department at Loyola University and testing laetrile on mice with tumors. He found the tumors would go away if the mice were treated in a certain way with the laetrile. Manner traveled the country trying to popularize laetrile as a cancer treatment. He believed that large quantities of emulsified vitamins would break down the fiber shell that the cancer cells use for protection, then laetrile could be used."

In 1988, Greenfield heard Manner speak at Livonia, Michigan. Often Manner went on lecture tours to solicit money from the public. He avoided government funding because he didn't want his results dictated or swept under the carpet. Greenfield heard him say,

> Everyone in the U.S. gets cancer, at least once a week, but our body kicks it out because the immune system is functioning the way it should. Unfortunately, our environment is so polluted, our foods are so adulterated, and our lives are so stressful and fragmented, that with all those forces our immune system is breaking down. If it gets weak enough, cancer begins to kick into action. Of course, this can also apply to other metabolic diseases.

Greenfield also advises women to take the time and think through the various therapeutic options. "Don't let the medical doctors push you into making a choice by scaring you. I have heard more than one story about a woman who has been rushed into making a choice for either radiation or chemotherapy. She wasn't ready to make a decision, but the doctors scared her into it. They said she only had one or two weeks for beginning treatments. I say, 'Don't let them scare you into it.'

"I have a fair number of individuals calling me over my book." Greenfield usually keeps a file on them and consults with them when she finds information that may be helpful. "I don't try to influence them but just tell them my story, explain it, and answer their questions. It takes a lot of self-discipline, but they have to make their own decision. It just makes me feel good to know that I've been helpful to people."

Opinions on Cancer Research and Publicly Supported Cancer Organizations

Greenfield believes that the current history of AIDS research is similar to that of cancer research. "In the early 1920s Krebs, who came up with one of the original cellular theories of cancer, eventually came up with laetrile. America had a mentality that they wanted a silver bullet, and everyone thought that it was wonderful. We wanted to have one thing that we could take to cure everything. Then we could go back to our ordinary lives the way we had lived them.

"After congressional hearings, Congress was going to come out and endorse it. However, behind the scenes a congressman told Krebs that he wanted to give the exclusive rights of laetrile to his brother, a medical doctor. Krebs wanted the public to have access. Therefore, Congress came out and said that the laetrile was not worthwhile.

"There are millions, even billions, of dollars going into cancer research, and I think it is very unfortunate. I think the basic assumptions are all wrong. Cancer is being attacked as if it was a big, bad bully, as if it was something outside of you. It's actually something that is going on inside of you. Something needs to be done inside of you. It needs to be done gently, either by going on a raw diet like I did or by going macrobiotic. But, of course, there is no money in that approach.

"With regard to the publicly supported cancer organizations, I didn't use them for support. I had my husband and doctor for my support." Greenfield disapproves of the organizations that are focused on conventional therapies. "It's just unfortunate that these organizations follow the medical line so exclusively."

References

Goldstein, Jack
    1977 *Triumph over Cancer—By Fasting and Natural Diet.* New York: Arco.
Hirshberg, Caryle, and Marc Ian Barasch
    1995 *Remarkable Recovery: What Extraordinary Healings Tell Us about Getting Well and Staying Well.* New York: Riverhead Books.

eleven

What Your Doctor May Not Tell You

Cathy Hitchcock, M.S.W., is the coauthor with Steve Austin, N.D., of *Breast Cancer: What You Should Know (But May Not Be Told) about Prevention, Diagnosis, and Treatment* (Rocklin, Calif.: Prima Publishing, 1994). She is also a psychotherapist in private practice in Portland, Oregon. Hitchcock has now been disease-free for over eight years.

Her Story

In February 1989 Cathy Hitchcock, a forty-three-year-old social worker from Oregon, discovered a breast lump. "According to a good friend of mine, I had mentioned the lump a month prior to my diagnosis. I had totally put it out of my mind." Hitchcock actually discovered the lump twice before acting on it. "I think it is a psychological testament to how much we don't want to believe what our bodies are telling us when it's bad news." She discussed the lump with her naturopathic physician in Portland, who ordered a mammogram on the urging of her husband, Steve Austin, who is also a naturopathic doctor. The results were inconclusive, probably because of the density of her breast tissue.

"I became alarmed at this point; somehow I knew there was something wrong. I asked the radiologist if there was anything else he could do for me. At this point, I was fairly ignorant about the medical diagnostic possibilities." Pressed, the radiologist said he could do an ultrasound. The ultrasound involved an odd coincidence. "The technician happened to be a client of mine in psychotherapy. I didn't know this prior to showing up for the ultrasound. Here was my patient, and then I became her patient."

The radiologist examined the ultrasound and found it unremarkable. As he left the room saying there was nothing to worry about, the technician noticed a tiny dark spot on the screen. She called him back into the room. The radiologist proceeded to recommend a biopsy. "I didn't have an allopathic physician at the time. My health care concerns were taken to licensed alternative medicine doctors. Obviously, I needed a surgeon because I needed to have a biopsy." After a few hectic days that involved considering the restrictions imposed by the insurance system, and her husband screening various surgeons for her, Hitchcock decided on a surgeon. "He examined me and said, 'I can usually tell by the feel, and this doesn't feel like cancer to me, so I don't think you have anything to worry about.'"

While Hitchcock was at her first appointment in this surgeon's office, he proceeded to perform a biopsy. "From my husband's point of view, this was our first mistake. Because he did not take some extra tissue around it, I would be required to have a second surgery if I had cancer." The doctor removed the lump, looked at it, and said that he was still quite sure that the lump was not cancerous, based on his visual inspection. "He threw into the trash receptacle the portion of the lump that would have gone to the lab for the determination of the estrogen-receptor status, thinking I didn't need it. Ultimately, there was a way to reconstruct it, but it was an interesting example of medical arrogance."

Hitchcock and her husband went out celebrating, thinking that she was cancer-free. "A few days later, the surgeon called and Steve picked up the phone. I heard, 'Oh, no,' and I knew what it was."

The surgeon presented Hitchcock with two options, which were to have either a mastectomy or a lumpectomy combined with radiation. "By that point, Steve had read a lot of breast cancer research, and it was clear that radiation therapy didn't extend life. It only increased the chances of not having a local recurrence. The surgeon didn't present the information in this manner; he said either I had to have the lumpectomy with radiation or the mastectomy. Steve and I raised this issue with the surgeon, and he eventually backed down. He said that it is true that radiation doesn't extend life according to current research, but he believed that would change in time." The surgeon presented his philosophy as fact until they confronted him. "He was nice enough about it, but it wasn't his place to make that decision."

During the period after the biopsy and before the second surgery, Hitchcock and Austin extensively researched the breast cancer literature. In addition to radiation, one of the main issues Hitchcock had to face was whether or not to have an axillary node dissection, which is considered standard with most lumpectomies. "The package deal was you get a lumpectomy, nodal dissection, and radiation, but I chose to simply have the lumpectomy. It was quite scary to go against the rules, and my doctor was not pleased with my decision. But I appreciate the fact that he was willing to go along with me." Hitchcock chose not to have the nodal dissection because its main use is to determine staging. "That is not the only thing it's used for, but from the way I understood it that's its primary function. The idea was that if I was diagnosed with stage II breast cancer, then from the conventional point of view, chemotherapy would be mandatory."

It was shortly after Hitchcock's diagnosis that chemotherapeutic treatments began to be used for stage I breast cancer patients. "I decided that if axillary node dissection was basically being used for diagnosis, and I had already decided against chemotherapy, even if I was diagnosed with stage II breast cancer, 'Why have the extra surgery?'"

Hitchcock had known a number of women who had had permanent impairment from the nodal surgery. A tennis pro could not keep playing tennis, and someone else was still having extreme pain and soreness raising her arm five years after the surgery. "I figured that if having the nodal dissection was necessary only for their curiosity, I had received such bad news so quickly, after doctors had said that I was probably fine, that I didn't want to know if I had stage II breast cancer. Unlike many women, I certainly wasn't going to change my treatment decisions."

The other issue that Hitchcock found problematic was the speed at which the surgeon required her decision from among his recommendations. "I felt extremely pressured to make an immediate decision. It was helpful that my husband was present at the appointment. In retrospect, I think that if I hadn't had the information my husband gleaned for me, I would have followed the surgeon's advice. One of the experiences that really kicked in for me psychologically, and that happens for many women, is that we may be these nice, intelligent, adult women who think for ourselves and make our own decisions, but when placed in a life-or-death situation, it is very scary to go against the medical establishment. The experience may be easier for some women than for others. I have seen a wide range of women in my clinical practice who have been diagnosed with breast cancer, and it's interesting to see that some of these women have had considerably more courage than myself. I think the only reason I was courageous was that my husband was able to obtain the research information. It brought me back into a position of strength so I was able to make decisions from my adult self. I was able to say, 'No, I don't want an axillary node dissection for X, Y, or Z reasons,' or, 'No, I don't want radiation because the research is saying X, and you are saying Y.' I was able to stay strong, but if the information had not been available, I suspect I would have been a blubbering idiot. This, more than anything else, is why I wrote the book on breast cancer with my husband. I wanted other women to have the same access to the research that I had because of Steve's ability to not only understand the technical jargon in the research, but to put it into layperson's language."

It was at this same point that Hitchcock pursued a second opinion from a medical doctor. "He was not a surgeon, but he was recommended by a number of friends because of his friendliness toward alternative medicine. We discussed the pros and cons of radiation and chemotherapy and what I wanted to do. He thought my reasons for not having the axillary node dissection made sense, and his validation of my decision-making process was enough for me to carry through with not having the surgical procedure."

Hitchcock also consulted a naturopathic doctor three hours away. He became her out-of-town doctor, guiding her nonallopathic cancer treatment with input also from her husband. Her treatment team at this point consisted of two allopathic and three naturopathic doctors. Her primary naturopath wanted to review her pathology report before commenting further on radiation therapy. "He was concerned about my not having radiation, in terms of the future need for another surgery." The naturopath examined all the markers on Hitchcock's pathology report and felt he could support her choice to forgo radiation.

Hitchcock stopped visiting the first surgeon for follow-up after a year. "During my follow-up visits after the lumpectomy, he would go on and on about breast cancer not being like any other cancer and how recurrence could happen anytime. I was aware of this fact, but I felt he was giving this lecture for liability purposes and from his own unconscious fear that I was not optimizing my therapeutic regimen.

"When I consulted a second surgeon, my husband and I were fairly impressed. She listened intently, writing down all my alternative therapies, and said she would be glad to follow me. However, after I had sent a note to my first surgeon indicating that I was switching to the second surgeon, she called and said, 'Well, I have changed my mind. I feel as though you are not being treated in a proper manner because you have not chosen conventional treatments. I am not comfortable following your case.' It was an awful experience, but it made me question why I would want to be followed by a surgeon. The whole psychological piece that came out of the experience with the surgeons was quite useful for me. Ultimately, I realized I had lined up the surgeons and was just waiting for the recurrence to happen."

By this time, Hitchcock had her allopathic physician, two naturopathic doctors, a psychotherapist, and her husband on her health care team. After the lumpectomy, she continued to consult with her allopathic physician while simultaneously working with her naturopathic physicians. She was using many alternative modalities, including vitamins, herbs, and a "clean" diet. "My history is that I have been involved with alternative medicine for over twenty years to create and optimize conditions for self-healing. And with my husband being a naturopathic physician, it has remained a natural choice for me. The unnatural choice for me would be the invasive, suppressive treatments: radiation and chemotherapy.

"However, I didn't want to throw out the conventional therapies blindly. I chose surgery. My philosophy is that there is a place for everything. I think your choices with conventional and natural therapies don't have to be a battle; it can be a marriage. It has sometimes become a politically charged issue because the medical establishment has too often used its power to discredit alternative medicine unfairly. However, I see a change happening in recent years."

Hitchcock added a second psychotherapist who was a creative imagery facilitator. "In addition to my naturopathic choices, including abstaining from alcohol, using herbs, vitamins, hydrotherapy, the Hoxsey formula, homeopathy, and getting plenty of exercise, I also added psychological interventions that included nine months of individual psychotherapy for dealing with a life-threatening disease." Hitchcock was also part of a guided imagery group for nine months at a local hospital. "I found the guided imagery group to be extremely powerful; it was a visceral experience that brought me back into my body and relieved my stress." She attended several time-limited support groups for people with cancer or other serious illnesses. "I finally ran out of options as the groups ended. I didn't want to be a part of the hospital support groups because they were focused on conventional treatments, which I wasn't doing." Hitchcock later began meeting with another psychotherapist/survivor, forming a minisupport group of two that continues to this day.

Hitchcock had two criteria for choosing among the various alternative treatments. "Either the therapy looked promising from the research evidence or it just made sense to me." Her choices and treatments have gone through some changes over time, but in terms of the alternative treatments, she is still doing most of them. "I will admit to being lax about a few things, but I am basically in a prevention mode, trying to remain cancer-free." Hitchcock has included hatha yoga and meditation in her wellness program. "After four years, I found that I had memorized the creative imagery tapes and was no longer receiving the same benefit from them. I switched to a more formal meditation practice." At the time of the interview, she was not in psychotherapy or attending support groups, but she continued to meet with her minisupport group.

Hitchcock has a yearly mammogram and checkup. She does an annual checkup with her naturopathic doctor in town as well. "I chose not to be followed by an oncologist because their main job is to do radiation and chemotherapy. I am not having MRI scans with my follow-up examinations. My mammograms remain clear."

Hitchcock continued her clinical practice throughout her experience with breast cancer. "Working was helpful for me because it allowed me to take my mind off my own problems and throw myself into the struggles my patients were facing. Especially when newly diagnosed, my work with clients helped me take a break from my own problems. Not missing a day of work made me feel hopeful instead of burdened." When we spoke with her in early 1998, she had just completed a mammogram and remained in good health.

Advice to Other Women

Hitchcock finds that giving advice to cancer patients really depends upon their types of cancer. "If it's a fast-growing cancer, your decisions need to be made quickly. Many breast cancers are slow-growing, and we jump too quickly toward action because we are afraid. We want to get the decision behind us when in fact taking a little more time, even for just a week to sort out the various issues, might be helpful. Again, it really depends upon the characteristics of the cancer.

"My personal opinion is that every woman with breast cancer should have surgery. To me, even if the body can heal itself, it is logical if you remove the unhealthy mass, you give the body more of a fighting chance.

"There are compelling reasons to consider radiation: age and the characteristics of the cancer determine the risk of a local recurrence. These need to be considered before deciding on radiation. This is an individual decision. What I would like is for every woman to have access to the research literature so they can use this information, along with their own common sense and self-knowledge, for making educated choices.

"If someone came up to me off the street and said they were going to be diagnosed with breast cancer in a month and asked, 'What should I do?' I would recommend a trip to a good bookstore to review the books. The unfortunate reality is that there are very few people who read cancer books who haven't already been diagnosed with breast cancer." Hitchcock stresses that in the case of the book written with her husband, Steve Austin, it would be helpful for women to read it prior to facing a diagnosis. "It would help them to have some real choices about their options, even at the diagnostic stage."

Hitchcock also points out that it is possible to make timely decisions. "One thing I appreciated about my surgeon was that when he knew I was waffling on the issue of radiation, he said, 'You don't have to make that decision right away. You can wait until after the surgical procedure.' I had time to gather information and talk with other people.

"It may be helpful for people to make their decisions about conventional therapies first. Then they can move to decisions about natural treatments. You don't have to do it all at once."

For finding out more information on alternative medicine, Hitchcock suggests consulting with a licensed naturopathic doctor. Another resource would be the bookstore. Regarding the more traditional cancer organizations, Hitchcock has some questions about the available resources. "I just don't know; it really depends on the type of information. For instance, the American Cancer Society is a good resource for individuals facing questions about conventional therapies. Also, 'The Race for the Cure' is an inspiring running event for women and a wonderful networking resource." Another resource for information and networking, but on a grassroots level, is a support group. "What was interesting for me in the guided imagery group was that everyone would be talking alternatives until the facilitator would enter the room and begin the session. In fact, the 'alternative speak' scared him so much that he brought in an oncologist to squelch our discussions, but people are talking alternatives, and that's what they want. Again, depending upon the type of local group, there may be more openness to alternatives than in the larger organizations."

Conventions, such as Portland's Issues after Breast Cancer, are another resource for information and a forum for seeking out others. "Conventions of that type speak to the political change that is happening nationwide. The Portland convention was sponsored by the Susan B. Komen Foundation, the ACS, Kaiser, and several local hospitals. This is an example of mainstream breast cancer organizations and hospitals providing information on conventional and alternative options for breast cancer. Steve and I were speakers last year."

Hitchcock also advises women to seek out individual and/or group therapy. "I think groups are very powerful and for the most part it is advantageous to be in a group. However, not everybody is comfortable with a group. For instance, I initially chose to be in individual therapy and later went into a group. At the beginning, it was too much for me to think of a group, but I was willing to do individual therapy. To me, the research on psychotherapy is just too strong to ignore. The statistics on group therapy show that it doubles your life expectancy. How can you turn away from that type of evidence when it is noninvasive and relatively cheap in comparison to other treatments?

"Another thing, which may be more nebulous, is that people talk about cancer as being a wake-up call. It has definitely been a wake-up call for me. I think it has reminded me and continues to remind me that when I am not happy, I need to address it."

Opinions on Cancer Research and Publicly Supported Cancer Organizations

"My feeling concerning the current direction of breast cancer research is pessimistic. It was disheartening that the budget for the National Institutes of Health's Office of Alternative Medicine (OAM) was just a pittance. The OAM's budget also went primarily to allopathic physicians. In other words, they gave the alternative medical doctors the money as opposed to naturopaths, acupuncturists, and other licensed practitioners in the alternative field.

"I didn't access the major breast cancer organizations because their support was largely to deal with the conventional treatment I didn't receive. That doesn't mean I don't think they are a useful resource; it just wasn't the right choice for me at the time. I know there are many sincere individuals working in these organizations."

Hitchcock's concerns are focused on what is happening at the top of these organizations. "The political ideologies, more than anything else, have kept me away. Historically, the money raised in these organizations has gone to support more research on surgery, radiation, and chemotherapy, or 'slash, burn, and poison.' Some of the individuals affiliated with these organizations are also associated with these treatments.

"Finally, if I was to convey one message to other women, it would be to have faith in your own ability to think rationally enough to come up with a decision that is right for you. The bottom line is that everything is an individual choice. Use the information and your own common sense in making decisions. I think that is what is taken away when we get scared and lose faith in our ability to sort through issues. The reality is that there are no perfect answers out there; ultimately, we have to make our own decisions."

References

Austin, Steve, and Cathy Hitchcock
    1994 *Breast Cancer: What You Should Know (But May Not Be Told) about Prevention, Diagnosis, and Treatment.* Rocklin, Calif.: Prima.
Love, Susan
    1991 *Dr. Susan Love's Breast Book.* Reading, Mass.: Addison-Wesley.

twelve

Confronting "National Breast Policy"

Susan Holloran is an international development planner and evaluator specializing in Asia, where she lived for ten years. Currently, she is completing a book about her experience of moving from conventional to alternative therapies for early-stage breast cancer. The working title of her book is *Journey for Life*. This interview is recorded verbatim, with some editing.

Her Story

"I was diagnosed with breast cancer in 1994 while living in Bangkok, Thailand. Just a month before my diagnosis I had a clear mammogram—nothing suspicious, or so I thought. I returned to my doctor two weeks later because of a persistent small lump in my left breast. Both he and I thought it was another one of my cysts, and he wanted to see if it would subside after my menstrual cycle. Several weeks went by and I again went to see him. He tried to aspirate it, but it was a solid lump, not a cyst. He said that I should have it removed but seemed in no hurry. I, however, wanted it out right away. I had a lumpectomy biopsy and was stunned when I learned it was malignant. I immediately flew back to Washington, D.C., which is my home when I am living in the United States, carrying my tumor tissue in a paraffin block along with the slides from my surgery. There I went to see a surgeon and an oncologist and I got second opinions. All the doctors agreed with the proposed treatment— that I could have a mastectomy or a lumpectomy and radiation. I could choose. I was astounded that I was going to be the person to make that choice. As I came to understand later, I was just entering the world of what I soon began to refer to as 'national breast policy,' where there would be many choices to be made.

"Essentially my diagnosis was early-stage breast cancer: infiltrating ductal carcinoma; the tumor size was 1.1 by 0.8 centimeters, a fairly small tumor. At the time I didn't know all the factors that contribute to the so-called staging process; I only knew that 'early' sounded better than 'advanced.' Nor did I know whether the cancer had spread to my lymph nodes. In fact, I didn't even know that lymph nodes were part of 'national breast policy' in terms of the staging of breast cancer. I began to gather information. To my knowledge I didn't have any history of breast cancer in my family.

"In any case I was stunned by the diagnosis of breast cancer and doubly stunned to know that I would have to make significant decisions about my treatment, the first of which was the choice between mastectomy and lumpectomy. As things proceeded, the doctors told me they wanted to reopen the site of my lumpectomy biopsy—apparently the margins were not clear and they wanted to go in again and get clear margins. At the same time, the surgeon told me, she would do a procedure called the axillary dissection, which would remove the lymph nodes under my arm to see if the cancer had spread. I remember it was at this time that bells started to go off in my head, and I was saying to myself, 'Wait a minute.'

"I started asking around about the axillary dissection, which sounded absolutely primitive to me. I said as much to my surgeon: 'You mean to say that you have to carve out all of the lymph nodes under my arm just to see if there's cancer there? And then what will you know?' I asked. My oncologist had told me that he considered the surgery to be relatively trivial. They would take out a lump of lymph nodes about the size of a 'dollar pancake,' as he referred to it. As I look back, I think it was at this point that I began to suspect that the world of breast cancer treatment might be much less refined—less sophisticated—than I had believed.

"In the meantime I was trying to find out more information on radiation therapy, which had been recommended as a follow-up treatment to my lumpectomy. I thought that certainly since radiation had been around for a long time, there would be a lot of information on its long-term adverse effects, and I set out to find what those might be. I talked to everyone—patients, pathologists, medical oncologists, surgeons, and radiation oncologists. The pathologists' views were different from the others—they were less confident that radiation was the right course. These physicians are out of the doctor-patient interaction loop where high visibility creates super-star doctors, but they are certainly closest to where the real action is—the cells. I was told essentially that the technology for radiation therapy had continued to improve over the last ten or twenty years and that research showing the damaging long-term effects of radiation was based on old technology. The secondary cancers occur sometimes near the organs of the breast which get into the radiation field—the lung, for example. Every time I brought up these dangers, they were explained away by the various improvements in the technology. The bottom line was that I could find no studies on the long-term adverse effects of radiation as it was currently administered.

"I talked again with my oncologist and told him I was very apprehensive about radiation. The more we talked, the more apprehensive I became. He explained that radiation was a treatment for the breast only; it did not treat any of the systemic aspects of the disease. We also discussed the research which indicated that breast cancer is not a disease of the breast. It is a systemic disease, and it is assumed that the cancer cells have already started to travel in the body at the time of the removal of the primary tumor. This assumption is based upon research done by the renowned Dr. Bernard Fisher (Fisher et al. 1985; Fisher et al. 1995), among others. So I now understood that breast cancer is not a breast disease; breast cancer is a systemic disease. I understood also that radiation would only treat the breast. I thought, 'This doesn't quite make sense, because this is not a disease of the breast so it can't possibly cure the disease.' I still had the idea of cure in my head at this point.

"It was about this time that I began to be aware of the language hang-ups that seem to cause so much misunderstanding about breast cancer. 'Cure' for most of us means that we don't die of breast cancer. But that's not what it means to most medical doctors. When they speak of survival, we think they mean our natural life expectancy, but often they are referring to the next five years. When they speak of avoiding recurrence, we infer that avoiding recurrence means improving survival, but that is not necessarily so either. The language needs to be clarified, and there are some signs that this is happening. There was an article on a new method of expressing survival in the *British Medical Journal* in June 1997 on just this point (Vaidya and Mittra 1997).

"My oncologist explained that treating the breast reduces the risk of recurrence—quite substantially so—but that reduced recurrence did not correlate with survival. I tried very hard to listen to what he was saying, because it was so counterintuitive and I had so much difficulty processing what I thought he was saying. I could have a recurrence, but it really wouldn't make a difference in terms of my long-term survival? I would have the same chances of survival regardless of whether or not I had radiation, or whether or not I had a recurrence. I was amazed. Actually, this was only statistically true, which means it could not predict my case at all. This use of statistics, upon which national breast policy is based, is another significant source of misunderstanding between doctors and patients.

"He continued to tell me about the short-term effects of radiation: the breast gets red; it becomes more firm; it would age differently; possibly I would have damage to the ribs, which might break at the force of a strong cough. All of this sounded ghastly to me, but he seemed to think it was relatively trivial. I noticed that he seemed to think a lot of things were trivial that I considered quite unacceptable. Of course I realized, too, that dealing every day with scared, sick, and dying patients gave him a perspective quite different from my own, or from that of any of his individual patients for that matter.

"At the same time that I was thinking of not having radiation, I was thinking that I needed to do *something*. We're told basically by conventional medicine that after our treatment is over, we should go home and get on with our lives. I think many patients do that, and it is a great temptation. But for me, I understood that something in my life had allowed me to get cancer; that is, whatever propensity I might have had for it and whatever was going on in my immune system, something about the way I was living or something that I was doing had allowed this cancer to come forward. By definition if I wanted to prevent a recurrence, I had to change something to swing the odds more in my favor.

"In the end I refused to have radiation treatment, and I adopted a whole-health plan for myself. Part of that health plan was an alternative therapy called Iscador, which is a mistletoe-based pharmaceutical therapy that my mother had told me about. It is used in anthroposophical medicine, based on the work of Rudolph Steiner, and its center is the Lukas Clinic in Arlesheim, Switzerland. Mistletoe therapy is used quite extensively in Europe, and I found a doctor in Baltimore who was an M.D. but was also a holistic and anthroposophic physician who was familiar with it. We talked about using it to try and deal with whatever residual cancer was left in my body, which I was sure there was. Iscador is alleged to have both cytotoxic as well as immune-enhancing effects. This sounded like it might be helpful and wouldn't cause the kind of permanent damage that I would have with radiation.

"My choice of mistletoe therapy could, I suppose, be interpreted as alternative, although I wasn't thinking in those terms at the time. I think the issue of defining the terms *alternative* and *complementary* is important because they are being used interchangeably in the literature and in general conversation. The term *alternative* seems to have negative connotations, and most medical professionals shy away from it. Interestingly, the Office of Alternative Medicine, which was created within the National Institutes of Health to capture the alternative medicine wave, may be changing its name to include 'complementary' in its designation. It's true that the term *alternative* implies a rejection of what conventional medicine has to offer if a patient chooses not to do something that is recommended by her doctors and does something else instead. But this really has nothing to do with the actual therapy itself—only with its use. In my opinion, complementary and alternative therapies are the *same* therapies. People prefer to use the term *complementary* because they think you should try the available mainstream options before turning to alternatives. Those who refuse a mainstream treatment and choose a different therapy are actually using this treatment as an alternative. Another person might go through all the mainstream options and use the same therapy as a complement. I think the reason for the name change at NIH is a kind of message saying, 'Don't choose between us and alternative therapies; that is, don't reject our way.' Thankfully, these decisions are still in the hands of each patient.

"There is, I think, a very subtle empowerment that is attendant to putting the definition of alternative and complementary into the hands of the patient, in our case in the hands of women who make that decision, as opposed to having the definition be in terms of what is accepted practice in conventional medicine *at the moment*. It also makes much more sense than designating a therapy itself with one of these terms, only to have it changed as attitudes toward that therapy change within conventional medicine. It used to be, for example, that nutrition, supplements, acupuncture, lifestyle issues, and some mind-body approaches were considered alternative. Now, at the very least, they are considered complementary and will soon, I think, be part of conventional treatment. Vitamin E and acupuncture are already entering the regime of chemotherapy treatment in some cases, for example.

"So I adopted four major objectives. The first was enhancing my immune system. Obviously the breakdown of my immune system had permitted me to get cancer. There was no question in my mind that the primary objective of whatever health enhancement plan I could do for myself would have to involve my immune system. The corollary to that and the second objective was avoiding exposure to carcinogens. Thirdly, I needed to adopt a lifestyle in support of health and well-being; that is, I needed to really look at my lifestyle and eliminate things which did not support my health. More than just not doing things that are detrimental—it meant designing a lifestyle that would support me. A big task. Even though I had thought that my lifestyle had never been particularly unhealthy—except for smoking, which I quit just before my forty-first birthday—obviously it was not healthy enough, and I would have to look more critically at my habits. The fourth and final objective of my health plan was to monitor for recurrence.

"Monitoring for recurrence is a major problem because of my dense breast tissue. Apparently for those of us with dense breast tissue—and this is something I think a lot of women don't know—the mammogram is often unreliable. Sonograms can be useful if you already feel a lump and want to check if it's a cyst. But this whole detection issue is problematic. I would urge women to ask their doctors whether they have dense breast tissue and how likely it is that a malignant mass will be detected, or that she might be at risk for microcalcifications (which are detectable, although they are controversial in terms of whether they are life-threatening or not). Understandably, physicians don't want us taking any chances, but until I see some research that shows that yearly mammograms have no long-term adverse effects, I consider having one a trade-off since effectiveness is limited.

"In any case, mammograms—and in the case of finding a specific lump, sonograms—are tools that can be used, but they are limited tools in the sense that they only monitor or only find a cancer that is already there. I wanted to be able to detect a cancer before a lump appeared. I talked to my oncologist and others about tumor-marker blood tests, and the general consensus seemed to be that these were also very unreliable.

"A few months after my surgery, I heard about an M.D.—a pathologist/professor and breast cancer researcher—who was doing something called a skin window as a way to measure the response of the immune system against a patient's cancer. The idea with the skin window is that it is measuring what is called antigen response. Antigen response is the body's ability both to recognize a cell as a foreign entity and to marshal its forces to come to the rescue. One wants a positive response. This is called cell-mediated immunity. I chose this technique—which is not new, but seemed a very rational approach to me—as my main avenue for monitoring for recurrence.

"So I'm doing a lot of things. I'm changing my lifestyle; I'm monitoring for recurrence; and I've changed my diet. For exercise, which is most difficult for me, I have adopted a rather strenuous program of Iyengar yoga, which I love, except that I have a very difficult time maintaining a daily practice. Actually, that's my most pressing change-of-habit issue: incorporating a daily practice of an hour of yoga.

"There is also for most of us, I think, a strong spiritual dimension to confronting breast cancer. This is one of the benefits of the disease—I think a good number of women will confirm this view. I began to practice yoga for physical reasons and it became an opening for me to pursue other so-called mind-body therapies like meditation. These became the opening through which I began an exploration of self—asking just who was this person living with and possibly dying of breast cancer? I also spent a week in Thailand with an energy healer who taught something called 'Universal Energy,' which is a means of healing others as well as oneself. This also includes meditation. This experience prompted me to delve into some reading on energy healing, which, in turn, led me into physics, of all things. Not being at all scientifically oriented, this was and continues to be a struggle for me, but at some level it does provide an expanded understanding which I know can be of help if I am able to develop it. It is amazing how similar the language of physics is to the language of the so-called New Age spirituality (Eden 1993; Hawking 1988.)

"To recap, it was the science that led me out of conventional and into alternative therapies. It was the science which exposed me to what I refer to as national breast policy. *National breast policy* is the term I have coined which refers to the standardized framework within which breast cancer is diagnosed, staged, and treated. National breast policy is the decision-making framework for the treatment of breast cancer derived from the statistical results of the many clinical trials that have been and are being undertaken to determine the response of the disease to various forms of treatment. This is in some ways a very inexact science, with a multitude of variables operating. The problem is not so much that there are many variables, but that there are not enough variables applied to an individual's recommendation. The treatments are prescribed wholesale; they are based on the results of studies of treatment protocols in which some significant number of women with some similar characteristics may respond, in a limited number of studies, in a significant, and sometimes not-so-significant, percentage of the time.

"For the most part these studies do not produce overwhelming and unequivocal evidence for the effectiveness of most breast cancer treatments—at least they are not convincing to me. But under national breast policy what's been shown to be of limited benefit for a limited number of women is then prescribed for all women within very broadly defined groups—like those with positive lymph nodes, for example.

"National breast policy is based on how we are alike, not how we are different. This is one of the fundamental flaws of the current treatment for breast cancer. Certainly, there are women who are helped and whose lives are extended by chemotherapy, but the problem is that we do not know exactly which women chemotherapy helps and which women it does not help. The variables are not discrete enough to determine who is going to be helped, and so many patients die despite the treatment. With a conventional therapy as toxic as chemotherapy is, if one is not helped, one is by definition harmed by it because it decimates the immune system. There is no question that it is an inherently harmful therapy.

"During the time I was looking at all of the research studies and trying to make a decision about radiation, I couldn't understand why science could not come up with some kind of treatment that was inherently supportive of the immune system rather than inherently destructive of it.

Every therapy in the 'conventional arsenal,' as it is termed, is toxic and damaging. This seems to me to be another fundamental flaw in the current cancer strategy." When we spoke with Holloran in early 1998, she remained in good health.

Advice to Other Women

"The most important suggestion I have is for women to do whatever is necessary to have confidence in your treatment—to ensure that your head, your emotions, and your therapy are all going in the same direction. For some, like me, this will mean doing a lot of questioning of treatments before deciding what to do. For others, this will mean going ahead with whatever is recommended without delving into the studies, the statistics, or the latest information.

"We all have a different way of dealing with this, and my personality and background makes me very inquisitive and somewhat skeptical. Others may not share this approach, so I would say that the first thing is to find the right balance for you. For women who want to know more, I would say: First, begin to understand your pathology reports. These are the basis for a strategy that can be as individualized as possible. Then talk to your doctors about the treatment that is recommended for you and ask about the applicability of the most recent research to your particular case; things are changing very fast now and new studies are released almost daily. Many of them could help to refine your treatment strategy or help you make more informed trade-offs. Look at how many pathology factors were taken into account in the studies. Discuss the efficacy or effectiveness of a particular therapy over time, take a look at comparisons with a group that did not receive the therapy, and look very carefully at long-term effects and, above all, survival. If, for example, the research showing efficacy of a treatment is based on a sample of node-positive women and you are node-negative, or if your cancer is well differentiated and the study does not take this factor into account, then the applicability of the treatment's success in your case is questionable. Find studies in which the patient sample most closely resembles your situation—your pathology, your menopausal status. Get someone to help you interpret what the statistics might mean for your case, and remember that the statistics can never definitively predict the course of your particular case. And look at probability from both sides—that is, the chances that something will happen and the chances that it won't.

"Most importantly, if you elect to have chemotherapy or hormone therapy, adopt a corollary or complementary program that will enhance the immune system and support health. I think that any therapy that has adverse effects on the immune system must be complemented with a program that has a strengthening and enhancing effect on the immune system. Another important thing to do is save your tumor material. Before surgery tell your surgeon that you want this tissue. Most hospitals save this in paraffin blocks as well as on the set of slides which are used for your diagnosis. You should tell them you want all your slides and blocks. This may help you later to determine the response of your cancer against a variety of potential treatments, assess your DNA information, possibly even run new tests, and a variety of other uses.

"For early-stage breast cancer patients, my recommendation would be to go very slowly. Take time to interview doctors—surgeons and oncologists—and get the best; don't just stay with the first person you see because it seems easier or less stressful. Lumpectomy surgery is a good choice for many women, and you should look carefully into whether it's appropriate for you. Ask about survival rates between mastectomy and lumpectomy as they apply to your case. Find out the latest studies on radiation therapy that apply to your case. If you feel better about having a mastectomy, that is probably the best for you, but you need to know what the options are first and something about what those options mean in terms of survival. Also get your doctor to explain the difference between recurrence and survival. It's survival that is most important to us as patients, so be sure to focus on that issue, not just on recurrence.

"I have real reservations about the lymph node surgery—the axillary dissection that is part of the standard recommendation for surgery. I would suggest that women find a surgeon who has experience with a limited, sampling surgery which takes about ten lymph nodes, for example, rather than the full axillary dissection. If a biopsy shows a small tumor and the initial pathology shows a slow-growing cancer with well-differentiated or even moderately differentiated cells, and other pathology factors indicate a relatively good prognosis, I would suggest looking for a surgeon who is doing a new procedure which removes only the sentinel lymph node. If I had to do it again, I would have this surgery.

"On the other hand, if I were facing an aggressive cancer and chemotherapy was very likely to be recommended whether or not cancer was found in my lymph nodes, I would consider skipping the lymph node surgery. If you have decided to have chemotherapy, then the only reason to have this surgery is to reduce the 'tumor burden' on your body. The idea here is that the less cancer the body has to fight the better. But it's a major surgery—and it's still controversial whether surgery promotes the spread of cancer—and often surgery has long-term complications like pain and swelling in the arm. There is even an organization of people who have had this problem—it's called lymphedema—as a result of their surgery, so you know it must be a significant problem. There are always trade-offs. If you have decided on chemotherapy, I would strongly suggest using alternative therapies to help build your immune system before, during, and after treatment. You can do this with supplements, herbs, and various forms of mind-body therapies along with feel-good therapies like Shiatsu massage (be careful of massage just after surgery and deep massage in general), aroma therapy, and even flower essences for those who want to try one of the more esoteric remedies.

"My own philosophy developed rather early on—that is to say, in the months following my surgery. I adopted the basic Hippocratic oath of 'First, do no harm.' For those with early-stage breast cancer, we have the luxury of time. I am using the luxury of time to put together a program that will permit me to use the least harmful therapies first and the most toxic therapies last. That is, the last resort becomes the first resort. That would be my recommendation for early-stage breast cancer: to take the less toxic road. Looking into the literature, one will find, as I did, scientific support for taking that path for some women.

"How to deal with one's oncologist or surgeon when deciding to take an alternative route is a very difficult issue. I told my oncologist that I was uncomfortable with radiation, and, finally, that I was not going to do it. I told him that I was going to try Iscador, that I wanted an anchor in the medical mainstream, that I hoped it would be him, that I hoped he could stay with me and if necessary learn along with me about some of the things that I would begin to test and adopt or discard, depending on how I responded to it. His reaction—and I think I had an exceptional oncologist, so I would think this is probably the best that one could expect—was that he would 'turn a blind eye' to what I was doing, and he would just try to support me and give me what he knew best. In some ways, oncologists are singularly unprepared to help us with health. They are, after all, steeped in disease—it's their world and a pretty narrow world at that. I realized that I was asking too much, and I think we do ask too much of conventional physicians, who know nothing about alternative therapies. Medical school doesn't teach them this. They have no training or knowledge in nutrition, much less in herbs or other health systems such as Ayurveda, Chinese traditional medicine, or naturopathy. They don't know about specific alternative therapies; they're just not educated about them, and, frankly, they are seldom inclined to learn about them. I guess quite naturally, most are quite defensive on the subject. To ask their advice can be counterproductive. It's unfortunate, but we just cannot depend on their knowledge in this arena; in fact, often they give us a lot of misinformation on alternatives. There are very authoritative sources that one can turn to, like Ralph Moss. Taking a cue from mainstream medicine, when you want the most thorough and detailed information—ask the specialist!

"It's also difficult to talk to doctors about research—about what various studies show about treatments. I practically drove myself crazy trying to understand the implications of research studies, and the one thing that struck me was that none of the studies provided a simple, clear-cut, unequivocal answer. The success rates of various treatments were often less than I had anticipated, plus it was almost impossible for me to figure out why a certain treatment worked for some women in the group and not for others. Of course I came to realize that no one knows the answer to this question—no one ever knows exactly who will benefit and who won't. This is something I would advise all women to keep in mind.

"The best advice I could give to other women is to look at the science—get specific references for journal articles that provide the kind of information you want, get enough information about your own case to see where you fit into the studies—and talk to doctors and others who are knowledgeable; ask hard questions, and then take your own advice. Your intuition is important and should never be discounted. In breast cancer there are no answers that are right for everyone. There is a lot of information, for both research and referral, on the Internet including Medline, an information-and-reference service available through the National Institutes of Health; Oncolink; breastcancer.net; and the *New England Journal of Medicine* breast cancer site, which can help you find the information you need. There are also good sites for alternatives like <www.altmed. net>. A good surgeon and oncologist can also point you to relevant research studies. The essential ingredient for the most positive outcome is, I think, to take responsibility for your own health. This is easier if your intellect and your emotions are both leading you in the same direction.

"Of course, the same level of research is not available for alternative therapies. One of the reasons that conventional practitioners don't know anything about alternative therapies is because for the most part the studies have not been done. So when our doctors say there is no evidence that these therapies work, they may be, in fact, correct. What they don't usually say is the more accurate statement that the studies have not been done to determine the effectiveness or ineffectiveness of most of these therapies. It's the difference between a partial and a complete truth. This is something all patients need to understand—how to get the whole truth from your doctors. It's one thing to say that something has been shown to be ineffective, which implies that the studies have been done. What doctors should be saying is that they don't know whether or not a therapy is effective. Usually their implication is that the studies have been done. There are various kinds of studies, too. Often alternative practitioners will do studies, but for some reason their methodologies are questionable or there is some other reason given why the results are not valid. There is a lot of arguing back and forth about methodologies.

"I would suggest that a woman get a friend to be her partner to help ask the questions and do the research. Take your partner with you to doctors' appointments and make a list of questions ahead of time. Your partner should write everything down while you just listen. It is very important to select the right person to help you with this; otherwise, it can create more stress. I can say from my own experience that it is almost impossible to remember what doctors say when you are in a state of high stress. Also, keep a notebook every day with absolutely everything in it—

names, phone numbers, resources, things to do, appointments—everything. Get on the Internet, lurk on various forums online, and look for medical studies, new therapies, and alternative medicine. Get a few books: *Choices in Healing,* by Michael Lerner; *Breast Cancer? Breast Health!* by Susun S. Weed; *Breast Cancer: What You Should Know (But May Not Be Told) about Prevention, Diagnosis, and Treatment,* by Steve Austin and Cathy Hitchcock; *Cancer Therapy: The Independent Consumer's Guide to Non-Toxic Treatment and Prevention,* by Ralph Moss (he also has a newsletter)—these can get you started. It's also a good time, if you can, to change your diet. Go off dairy fat, sugar, caffeine, and alcohol for a start. Drink green tea and eat cruciferous vegetables and soy products. And exercise! This is kind of the short version of a longer strategy that can be refined later. I think any successful health strategy must include a spiritual (I'm not talking about religion) component as well. I accessed this through yoga, which I believe to be the best starting point for many women."

Opinions on Cancer Research and Publicly Supported Cancer Organizations

"The Office of Alternative Medicine, housed within the National Institutes of Health, was a move to retain and contain the power of breast cancer research, and alternative research in general, within the research institutions that now control that agenda. The name of this office has recently been proposed to include 'complementary,' I suppose because 'alternative' was too radical a word—first, because it was already in use and had been defined outside the bureaucracy, and second, because it implies a rejection of mainstream treatments.

"The increasing demand for alternative therapies is redirecting more attention and money from conventional cancer therapies and the cancer establishment in general. This is threatening, so the response has been to try to take control—this includes controlling the patient, controlling access to treatment, controlling information, and controlling the investigation and evaluation of alternative therapies. In the end I think this is going to prove to be unproductive or counterproductive. Unfortunately for the United States, I think leadership in the field of alternative therapies will come from Europe—Germany is already far ahead of us. The irony is that, in the end, the U.S. research and pharmaceutical establishment will not only miss the health opportunities that these therapies will offer but will miss the economic opportunities as well.

"The research inquiry is too narrow, and I think basically we're not looking at the right box. No matter how rigorous the methodology and how much money is spent, if the right questions are not being asked, the right answers will never be discovered. There is a great saying attributed to a Sufi named Sam Lewis: 'The only reason we don't find solutions to our problems is that the answers interfere with our concepts.' I think this is precisely where conventional cancer medicine is stuck right now. Accepted practices are stifling the creativity of science.

"With respect to cancer organizations like the National Cancer Institute, I would say they have little credibility with respect to alternative therapies or, as they refer to them in reports, 'unconventional' therapies. One of the most egregious examples of bias and misinformation—even disinformation—can be found in NCI's publication called *Cancer Facts* (the phrase itself is almost an oxymoron), in which all alternatives are briefly described, then debunked as having 'no evidence' that they are effective means of fighting cancer. There are no references to any studies that might be the source of this 'no evidence.' Usually they describe their own very unscientific review of cases or studies of the therapy. Often this is followed by a description of investigations by various branches of the federal government for things like false advertising or sending material across state lines, and these reviews usually conclude with references to some bureaucratic body that pronounces that the therapy has no value. There is a boilerplate about the dangers of using alternative therapies that accompanies each therapy description. It's worth looking at these just to get an idea of the caliber of thought that goes into these NCI publications.

"There are some alternative organizations that I think are very useful—such as Ralph Moss's diagnostic analysis service Healing Choices; People Against Cancer; CanHelp, a cancer information, research, and options service; and the Cancer Treatment Centers of America. I called them and received some very good information on alternative cancer treatments. I particularly valued finding, when I was first diagnosed, the book by Michael Lerner called *Choices in Healing*. It was the most well-researched and beautifully balanced book on the theme of choice, which is really where I think the rubber hits the road with breast cancer and perhaps other forms of cancer as well. We patients should be helped to be fully informed, and we should be free to make a supported choice about our treatments.

"Finally, on a personal note, I have found my forays into the alternative world to be an exciting adventure, one I never would have embarked on had it not been for my diagnosis of breast cancer. I have met many wonderful and interesting people, and I've discovered many things, including much about myself, along the way. I think most of us who have been diagnosed with breast cancer feel that this is in some way a personal wake-up call, and that something is required of us. It is something different for everyone, but it moves many of us to travel down a very individualized path, and for those of us in this book that path includes alternative as well as conventional medicine."

References

Austin, Steve, and Cathy Hitchcock
  1994 *Breast Cancer: What You Should Know (But May Not Be Told) about Prevention, Diagnosis, and Treatment*. Rocklin, Calif.: Prima.
Bailar, John C., III, and Heather L. Gornick
  1997 "Cancer Undefeated." *New England Journal of Medicine* 336(22): 1569–74.
Eden, James
  1993 *Energetic Healing: The Merging of Ancient and Modern Medical Practices*. New York: Insight Books, Plenum Press.
Fisher, Bernard, Stewart Anderson, Carol K. Redmond, et al.
  1995 "Reanalysis and Results after 12 Years of Follow-Up in a Randomized Clinical Trial Comparing Total Mastectomy with Lumpectomy with or without Irradiation in the Treatment of Breast Cancer." *New England Journal of Medicine* 333(22): 1456–61.
Fisher, Bernard, Madeline Bauer, Richard Margolese, et al.
  1985 "Five-Year Results of a Randomized Clinical Trial Comparing Total Mastectomy and Segmental Mastectomy with or without Radiation in the Treatment of the Breast." *New England Journal of Medicine* 312(11): 665–73.

Hawking, Stephen

    1988 *Brief History of Time.* New York: Bantam Books.

Lerner, Michael

    1994 *Choices in Healing: Integrating the Best of Conventional and Complementary Approaches to Cancer.* Cambridge, Mass.: MIT Press.

Moss, Ralph

    1992 *Cancer Therapy: The Independent Consumer's Guide to Non-Toxic Treatment and Prevention.* New York: Equinox Press.

Vaidya, Jayant, and Indraneel Mittra

    1997 "Fraction of Remaining Normal Life Span: A New Method for Expressing Survival in Cancer." *British Journal of Medicine* 314(7095): 1682–4.

Weed, Susun

    1996 *Breast Cancer? Breast Health! The Wise Woman Way.* Woodstock, N.Y.: Ash Tree.

thirteen

Barbara Joseph

A Doctor Combines Chemo and Macrobiotics

Barbara Joseph, M.D., is a board-certified obstetrician and gynecologist, and she is the author of *My Healing from Breast Cancer: A Physician's Personal Story of Recovery and Transformation* (New Canaan, Conn.: Keats Publishing, 1996).

Her Story

Dr. Barbara Joseph felt the lump in her breast only eight weeks after giving birth to her third child. "It was clear during the initial weeks of breast feeding that one can't really tell what is going on in lactating breasts because they are so engorged. At eight weeks things had settled down and I noticed a large lump. Some part of me was hoping that it was a lactation-related lesion." She had a sonogram and the results were suspicious. A mammogram added no useful information, so she decided to have the lump biopsied. "I knew that if it was malignant, it was very aggressive to have grown so large, so fast. I went up to Yale and had a biopsy.

"It was the classic story of the doctor telling the patient that it was nothing, and then the nothing went on to a dreadful something over a couple of days: from 'Oh, it's not life-threatening,' to the discovery that I had enlarged axillary nodes that were also likely positive for malignancy. Things were looking pretty grim. I continued working up my case. I went for a chest X ray. There were questionable lesions on my lungs.

"Here I was, a doctor, walking myself through this in disbelief. I began to get medical opinions. My medical oncologist recommended that I have chemotherapy first (neoadjuvant chemotherapy). This had been tried in Italy with some success in women with locally advanced breast cancer. It allowed women to avoid very disfiguring surgery. However, that wasn't the reason I wanted to do neoadjuvant chemotherapy, if you can say that I wanted to do it at all. The reason was it made sense to me. As I obtained additional opinions, I consulted with Dr. Susan Love, who was very helpful in clarifying things for me. It was great to work with a physician who was very systematic and intelligent, and who also valued my input."

Joseph got several opinions regarding optimal therapy. Immediate radical surgery was one choice, and there were other options. She decided in favor of the neoadjuvant chemotherapy approach because it made sense with her advanced disease to treat the systemic aspect of the disease first. "Some women, unfortunately, think, 'Cut it out—just do the surgery. Get it done and let me get back to my life.' I try to cut through that myth in my book. You can't get back to your life because no life will ever be the same after cancer. So I did chemotherapy in conjunction with various complementary approaches and treated the systemic aspect first, rather than just treating my breast. All diseases are really imbalances of the body and its immune system, not diseases of isolated organs.

"As Susan outlined it to me, the treatment could go in any number of ways. I might not be responsive to the therapy, in which case I would then consider doing surgery if the mass continued to grow. Or, if it remained the same, I could just see what happened over a couple of cycles of chemotherapy. Or the tumor mass might start to respond, in which case the plan was to do six months of this therapy because that's what was considered standard therapy in the literature. (The regime was CNF, or Cytoxan®, Novantrone®, and 5-fluorouracil). So I went ahead and did it. My oncologist thought Novantrone® was slightly less cardiotoxic than Adriamycin®."

At the same time Joseph began to explore complementary therapy for her stage III breast cancer. She did this in part because she felt "an inner need to participate" in her treatment and recovery. She had also heard stories about the macrobiotic diet, and she had read Anthony Sattilaro's book (Sattilaro 1982). "It just intrigued me, and I began to investigate it. I started to eliminate junk food from my diet, started reading and working on creating a macrobiotic diet. It's interesting how things happen. I went up to a nutritional counselor, who I thought would give me all this macrobiotic information. Instead, he said that he thought that in my case breast cancer was a very emotionally related disease. I didn't walk out with the recipes and drinks that I thought I would. Yet, that became another important component that I followed through with: the emotional aspect of cancer and healing. I did at a later point go for a personal consultation with Michio Kushi, and I did get those macrobiotic recipes. We absolutely need nutrients for optimal immune function."

She found out about Bernie Siegel, M.D., and attended one of his workshops. "I felt very inspired and empowered sitting with a hundred other people who were in similar circumstances. He said so many wonderful things: that we're all mortal and we're all going to die, and that's okay; that's the human journey; and to stop working/living in fear and just start living authentically." She also read Lawrence LeShan's *Cancer as a Turning Point.* His message and others similar to it made sense to her because they provided a framework for her to release her fear and get on with recreating her life. "Cancer is a multifaceted disease, and one of the ways we set ourselves up, immunologically, for this disease is by refusing to release our emotions. I feel that we have just so much energy, and when it is tied up in a lot of emotional baggage, then it's not available for our immune function."

As a result of her cancer, Joseph confronted long-standing emotional problems from her youth, such as the death of her mother. "Having just given birth, here I was, the mother. The night that I found out I had cancer and couldn't feed Oliver was the most painful night of my life. I ended up seeming to fuse with my mother, and I didn't want to. I was sitting with these breasts that were so engorged; it was so painful. And it was unbearable emotionally.

"I was told, 'You can't feed your baby, and you have cancer.'

"I was thinking, 'What is this?' and then somewhere out of that I said, 'I'm not my mother. I'm not giving up right now. That's not my story.' I didn't want that story, so I was going to create a different story—a different life."

As part of the emotional and spiritual side of her healing, Joseph also saw a therapist and joined a support group. She found her children especially inspiring, particularly in terms of helping her to live in the moment. "I decided that no matter what, I wasn't going to leave my children with the legacy of a mother who went silently under. I was going to actively participate and do whatever I could. Going into their rooms at night was just so wonderful. I never appreciated little kids until I had my own. Just being with them brings you into the moment, because that's where they live. They don't have a past and they don't have a future; they just have now. They want it now and they're living it now. If you really are with them, you're in the now because there is no other place. It's very mystical. Healing can't take place in the past, and it can't take place in the future. The more you immerse yourself in the moment and free yourself of all your baggage from the past and all your future projection, you slow your body down enough to heal. Being with my kids and just slowing down was powerful."

Three months after her diagnosis (that is, by the third month of neoadjuvant chemotherapy), she had made substantial changes in her diet, was going to the support group, and was spending more time with her children. At that time, "it became obvious that the tumor was nearly half its original size. It was no longer a six-centimeter mass; it was more like a four-centimeter mass. I was on the path. The time was rolling around when I would go back to Dr. Love. She said something about coming halfway through just to see how things were progressing. One morning I said, 'Hey, wow.' All of a sudden, those big nodes in my armpit were no longer there. Originally they were walnut-sized nodes and then they were gone. It was amazing. I was definitely responding. She said at our original consultation, 'Yes, I have seen some cases where the tumor was completely gone after six months.'

"I said, 'Yeah, that's where I want to be. It's a possibility.' That was what I was aiming for.

"Six months later Dr. Love said, 'Gee, if I hadn't known that you had cancer, I wouldn't have thought that there was anything there.'"

However, there was a thickened area where the original biopsy site was. "It was impossible to tell if a tumor was there or not. Dr. Love recommended that I have a lumpectomy. There was some discussion of whether or not to surgically remove my nodes. I was against it. In my case it made no sense to have the axillary node dissection because I had already had the most aggressive chemotherapy and the nodes weren't physically palpable. Why would I want to dig around my armpit looking for microscopic metastases? I had already done the most aggressive therapy. My oncologist said that the chemotherapy might be extended or changed, but I thought, 'How much chemotherapy can a person take?' Then I thought, 'If there's no tumor in the breast, then there's a very good chance the axillary node dissection would be negative.'"

In Joseph's case, the lumpectomy proved negative. "There was no residual tumor. Then I had to make a decision about stopping therapy, which was difficult. My oncologist thought that the cancer was aggressive and I should have more chemotherapy. There's no endpoint because no one knows how much is enough. There are studies, but every case is different. My oncologist felt my case was so aggressive that I should have more chemotherapy. I signed on. I was afraid to say no." Besides the additional chemotherapy, Joseph accepted radiation after her lumpectomy. "Eventually my body rebelled. My white blood count dropped to dangerously low levels and I was hospitalized with viremia. Chemotherapy was thus terminated."

Meanwhile, she pursued a strict macrobiotic diet. "I was cooking seaweed and all those foods that were new to me. I lost so much weight, all my fat stores. Overnight my kitchen changed." She remained on a strict macrobiotic diet for two to three months. For years afterward her diet centered on grains and vegetables, including sea vegetables, legumes, and an emphasis on soy foods with very little animal food. She continues to eat organic unprocessed whole foods today.

Joseph also developed and followed an exercise program of walking around the track three or four times a week. "Of course, when you're on treatments, all your body wants is rest, and that's the best thing that you can do." She had read the Simontons' book *Getting Well Again,* and she built into her daily routine a time to meditate. She also stopped working. "I was lucky because I had the resources not to work. Some people aren't able to do that, but I think there is always room for modification of lifestyle.

"That's another thing—the women who do too much. This was my third kid in four years, and I had a full-time practice. Cancer just completely stopped me in my tracks. What was I doing? How much can women give? There's a lot written about women who can't take care of themselves, but they take care of everyone else. It is the metaphor of the breast, the organ of nurturance, turned against us. We take care of everyone but ourselves."

Overall, Joseph emphasized the mind-body connection and how she tried to live in the here and now. "Cancer was an experience of getting closer to real living and the preciousness of life. I think the result of feeling close to death was that I had less fear of death after having cancer. I have my own notions about what life is all about and how we evolve spiritually. I think on some level that we help each other along. In writing this book, I was changing my way of thinking from the medical model of 'What's your symptom/disease? Here's the drug/cure,' to 'How can we learn and evolve from this experience? How can we heal our lives?' I see cancer as part of my spiritual evolution. I can be a resource for women in similar circumstances. I can validate these principles to others."

Does Joseph wish she had done things differently? "I had a very advanced cancer and was schooled in conventional treatments. I couldn't have chosen to ignore surgery/chemo/radiation. That wouldn't have made any sense to me, as to who I was and the stage of the disease. I think that the best we can do here in America right now is to use what we do have and complement it and modify it on an individual basis. I think that the best we can do is to use the technology, not to overuse it or think that it's better than other approaches." However, she added, "You can't get away from the fact that you need to feed your body properly and prioritize self-care. There's no shortcut in that." As of early 1998, she remained in good health.

Advice to Other Women

Barbara Joseph's main advice is for women "to calm down." She explained, "Anything that the body has done in terms of creating cancer is really a message. The input your body is receiving is not conducive to creating health; you need new input. You must make changes.

"There is a great Chinese definition of insanity: you do the same thing over and over again, and you expect it to turn out differently. In other words, if you eat the same way, think the same way, do the same things, and then take this conventional treatment and expect to go on with your life exactly the same way as it was before, how could your body not come up with cancer or some other degenerative disease? You have to take cancer as a message. Your body is not functioning properly because the input is wrong. Look at the input—your diet, the emotional struggles of your life—and be honest with yourself. For this life, this may be the last chance you get. Take it seriously, but don't forget to have fun along the way.

"Listen to the message of your body, and let the dreams come through. My subconscious was overflowing during my illness. I had constant dreams. I would go to bed each night and images would pour through. I would write some of it down and try to understand it. Powerful messages were coming through. I think people, if they slow down enough and ask for this, will receive guidance. I think there is a story in everyone's life. There's no situation beyond our ability to resolve.

"I have included exercises in my book for women to slow down and listen to themselves. That's the most important thing. No one knows you better than you. There is no doctor who can examine your breasts better than you can. There's nobody who can say no to a therapy better than you can, or yes to it. You know if it's right.

"My book gives women something to stand on. So many women go in to the doctor and are afraid to say what they really feel. If it doesn't seem right to you, and you have it in print, you could say, 'Hey, look, this worked for this person. And maybe it's okay to say no to a procedure that has such negative consequences.' Maybe you don't want edema in your arm and maybe the information that could be gleaned from the procedure ultimately will not be that helpful. Maybe we *can* say no."

Joseph discussed in more detail the confusion surrounding axillary node dissection. She underscored the fact that the procedure is done for staging and then to help decide whether or not to do chemotherapy after a lumpectomy or mastectomy. "The rationale is that if there are tumors in the lymph nodes, women should have chemotherapy. Does it really make sense? No, it doesn't make sense, because there are women who have metastatic tumors and negative lymph nodes. I see the lymph nodes as helping to filter and to eradicate the cancer. It doesn't make sense to me that if you have a tumor in a lymph node that it means you absolutely need to have chemotherapy. It doesn't all follow.

"If a woman has negative nodes, then her doctor may say, 'Okay, well, we did the surgery. You have a tumor in your breast, nothing in your nodes. You may have radiation, then you're done.' Then the NCI recommended chemotherapy for all women regardless of their node status. That meant all stage I women should have chemotherapy because 20 percent of women who are stage I would otherwise die of metastatic disease. But what about the 80 percent who don't need it? What is the cost physically, emotionally, and economically of administering chemotherapy to all of them? It became this big political issue—whether stage I, node-negative women should have chemotherapy. And then what was the point of doing node dissections? That is why I urge women to think it through. If your doctor is of the philosophy, and if you believe, that no matter what the stage every woman should have chemotherapy because breast cancer is a systemic disease, then I don't see a point in doing lymph node dissection."

Regarding radiation, she commented, "Radiation has nothing to do with systemic disease. It's only a local treatment. It reduces local recurrence. Across the board any woman having a lumpectomy for breast cancer is told to have radiation following it, so that the rate of local recurrence would match that of women having mastectomies. The problem is the long-term side effects from the radiation, which itself is a carcinogen. There are reports of leukemia and higher rates of secondary cancers in women who have had chemotherapy and radiation. Conventional treatments are very immune-suppressing. There are some women with very small tumors who can definitely do without the radiation. And no studies have ever been done on women who decline certain conventional treatments, but do make the long-term changes in diet, lifestyle, and their emotional and spiritual lives that I talk about in my book."

Joseph commented that her personal decision was not well-informed. "I really didn't understand all the long-term effects of treatment. I think that we need to do a lot more looking. We need to do what I did—tremendously improving on diets and lifestyle, and doing our emotional work. We need to look at the women who do without radiation but do build up their immune systems in terms of recurrence and long-term outcomes. I just don't see any of that happening right now. I just don't see any answers, even from the studies that are being done with diet. There's no control over food quality. That's such a big component of the food equation. You don't see these studies with women talking about using organic foods as compared to those using nonorganic foods."

Opinions on Cancer Research and Publicly Supported Cancer Organizations

Joseph did not go to any publicly supported organizations for help. "In general I think organizations are corrupt. Ralph Moss's exposé [1996] of the cancer industry says it all. Some of the people who are running Memorial Sloan-Kettering and who are deciding where research money goes are industry people, petrochemical and tobacco executives. I can't even touch that. It's just too immense; there is just so much money involved. We need to be aware of these influences."

Dr. Joseph also had some comments about research on food and supplements. "I'm sure the food studies in progress will point us in a direction, but I don't think they'll have the impact of my recovery story. I radically altered the quality of my food, and that made an unbelievable difference. The principles of macrobiotics are wonderful: clean foods, local and seasonal foods, fiber-rich foods, and lots of green, yellow, and sea vegetables with all their healing components. Respect for nature is important. The scientific community just isolates nutrients and then does studies on them. It's so absurd. Food is dynamic and whole.

"The vitamins in food act in concert. You just can't isolate beta carotene, for instance, and measure its effect on lung cancer, then say, 'Well, it doesn't work.' I think you've got to go for it all. You've got to do the whole thing. Women have to completely change their diet; in fact, they have to change their way of being in order to heal. It's this quick-fix mentality that doesn't work, when one says, 'Well, I'll just take supplements and that will do it.' Actually, I think there's healing power in whole foods that can't be isolated. A healing diet is a time-consuming proposition. You can't go to your local food mart and say, 'Hey, now I'll go to the natural section and buy stuff there.' It means shopping in different stores, taking your time with meal preparation, blessing your food, and eating with gratitude. People say that they want to get better, but I think that in order to get better, you really have to invest in it."

She added that she wasn't taught about nutrition or supplements in medical school. "Medical school focuses on acute care, not prevention.

Years ago doctors used food. 'Let food be your medicine; let medicine be your food.' That all came out of medicine. But then we got carried away with technology and we got away from what health really is."

Although she applauded the creation of the Office of Alternative Medicine, Joseph recognized that "they get a minuscule amount of money." Regarding the problem of evaluating alternative and complementary therapy, she concluded, "I'd be dead if I had to wait while they validated many of the methods I utilized. Yes, it would be interesting to devise the right studies, but you'd be wasting your energy trying to convince the powers that be, because they're not interested in it. The cancer industry is not health oriented. Read books like Moss's *Questioning Chemotherapy* before you decide whether or not you need chemotherapy. There are many options. There are lots of things out there for people who are not doing well. Unfortunately, there's no central data bank. Never forget that you are the ultimate authority in your case. Take your power back and rejoice in who you are and what you are here to learn."

References

LeShan, Lawrence
   1994 *Cancer as a Turning Point*. New York: Plume.
Moss, Ralph
   1995 *Questioning Chemotherapy*. New York: Equinox Press.
   1996 *The Cancer Industry*. 2d ed. New York: Equinox Press.
Sattilaro, Anthony, with Tom Monte
   1982 *Recalled by Life*. New York: Avon.
Siegel, Bernie
   1986 *Love, Medicine, and Miracles*. New York: Harper and Row.
Simonton, O. Carl, Stephanie Matthews-Simonton, and James L. Creighton
   1978 *Getting Well Again: A Step-by-Step Guide to Overcoming Cancer for Patients and Their Families*. New York: Bantam Books.

fourteen

The Wake-Up Call from Your Body

Dixie Keithly, now sixty-six, is retired and does a people-sponsored (volunteer) radio program in California that features people who have reversed their prognoses of "terminal" or "chronic" conditions with alternative therapies. A free catalog of the program may be obtained from Your Choice Your Health by calling 800-990-7332.

She also fields calls from all over the United States from patients wanting information on alternative therapies. At the time of the interview, she was president of the Northern California chapter of the International Association of Cancer Victors and Friends in San Jose (408-448-4094).

For balance she run-walks four miles four times a week and swims a half-mile two times a week. She claims to be 90 percent vegetarian and 95 percent organic in her eating habits, and she drinks only distilled water.

She manages five rental units and treats her renters as though they were family, a technique that is not found in any books, but which she says is the only way she can do it.

Her Story

Dixie Keithly began her story by acknowledging that at age fifty-six she would have a few drinks and some cigarettes before going to bed at night. "That was the habit I was into. I am really glad now that the cancer came along, because it brought that ritual to light. Otherwise, I would be a shriveled up old prune by now."

Although Keithly did smoke and drink somewhat, she generally ate what she considered to be a healthy diet. She read Adelle Davis's *Let's Get Well* long before she had cancer, and the book influenced her enough to try to maintain a healthy diet. "Health became my hobby, and I kept learning all I could. It still didn't save me. All I knew was that I was eating a whole lot better than everyone else I knew."

She also had some very difficult romantic relationships that increased her stress. One of her boyfriends was involved in crime and another was physically abusive and an alcoholic. "Later I read that it takes close to ten years for a little cancer to grow, and stresses like that help trigger those things. So that was a high degree of stress, then you add the smoking and the drinking and the family history."

Six people on her mother's side died of cancer, including her mother, who was dead by age forty-seven, even though she had a mastectomy and radiation treatment. Keithly was only twenty-one when her mother died, and her trip back to the Midwest to take care of her mother during her last months of excruciating pain and emaciation left a lasting memory. "Thirty-five years later the medical establishment was about to do to me essentially the same thing that they had done to my mother. In 1987 they were about to perform a double mastectomy and lymphnodectomy." Though Keithly added that two people on her father's side had also died from cancer, she stated, "I don't believe the 'it's genetic' attitude which was being touted." She feels cancer has more to with familial ways of living: what people eat and drink and their activities and ways of coping with life.

In 1987 she suffered from irregular vaginal bleeding. She was fifty-six years old and thought she might be going through menopause, but the doctor told her to come in for a checkup. He gave her a D & C and offered to put her on hormone therapy. "I was somewhat leery about it because nutrition had been my hobby. I told him that the hormones cause cancer and he said, 'No, they don't. Besides, we can cure cancer but we can't cure osteoporosis.'" He waved the estrogen replacement therapy prescriptions at her and told her to take them when she was ready.

Keithly interviewed two women in their eighties who liked the hormone treatment, so she decided to try it. Three days later she started bleeding. Her doctor told her to finish the month out before discontinuing them, then to call him after she had been off the hormones for a month.

Five days before she was supposed to call him, "I found a little indentation on my breast. It felt like the eraser on a yellow pencil, but smashed. It had irregular edges and was hard. I called the doctor because over the years I had previously had three biopsies and I had become so cavalier about biopsies that I would ask about my watch instead of whether the lump was benign or malignant. This time the doctor tried to aspirate it, and nothing came out, which seemed to him to be a bad sign." The lump was removed, and she was diagnosed with lobular carcinoma.

To try to gain more information, she found a lab technician who let her look at the tissue. "I couldn't see a thing. I don't see how they can tell because I didn't see any difference." Although the doctor was suggesting a single mastectomy, Keithly eventually decided to have a bilateral mastectomy because "the doctor explained that the cancer was the type which jumped from one breast to the other. I agreed to that because I said, 'You take one breast and I will be having mammograms every six weeks for fear that it is in the other breast. I will go crazy.' I agreed wholeheartedly for them to take both breasts. In fact, I suggested it, and everyone was very happy with that.

"I am very pragmatic. I have saved the lives of little animals growing up on the farm, nurturing and bringing them back to health when the adults didn't want to touch them. I have also killed animals. When there were too many cats, I knew what to do. I was just that pragmatic. You need to take my breast? Okay, well, take them both."

Prior to the surgery, however, she also investigated alternatives. Unfortunately, most of the people whom she called had used conventional therapies, so they were not helpful. Another step toward alternatives occurred when a former boyfriend brought her a library book on alternative therapies. "The book described such things as nutrition, chiropractic, and acupuncture and stated that the AMA tries to drive them out of the country. That didn't move me because I thought, 'I knew that.'

"But my girlfriend put me in touch with Walter, who turned around his death sentence of six months and had lived five years. He said, 'Call Yolanda Fraire. She's the best hormonally-induced–cancer doctor in the world.'" After other phone calls and discussions with a patient in Sacramento, Keithly thought to herself, "I can afford to go to Mexico. I'm going to check this out. It's my life. I get to choose." Going against the admonitions of friends and family, she went off, alone, to Mexico.

In Mexico Keithly worked with Yolanda Fraire, M.D., who had been the director at the Hoxsey clinic for many years. Harry Hoxsey was the founder of the famous Hoxsey herbal formula. He battled continuous persecution by the American Medical Association during the middle decades of the century.

Keithly read his book *You Don't Have to Die*. "It tells about the terminal cases he cured and how the AMA never stopped persecuting him. It told of how he would carry around a roll of bills to bail himself out of jail. It had pictures of terminal patients he had cured. He won one of the biggest lawsuits against the AMA, and all they did was come after him harder and harder." Keithly chose Dr. Fraire not only because of her affiliation with the Hoxsey formula but because Walter recommended her. Although Fraire had only a small suite of offices, Keithly was impressed by her approach.

"Dr. Fraire explained, 'We believe in detoxifying the body. Every clinic has its own way of doing it, but we use the Hoxsey Herbal Tonic. Then, we feed the body the healthy foods that it needs. It knows what to do; it has been doing it for millions of years.' Now that is a very simple statement that rings true. When a doctor cuts you, who does the healing? No matter what they put the magnificent body through, it's the *body* that figures out how to heal it."

In addition to the Hoxsey Tonic and diet, Dr. Fraire's treatment for Keithly included pharmaceutical products such as staphage-lysate, an immune system stimulant; an antifungal vaccine; nystatin; and isoprinosine, an antiviral agent. "I went on an anticandida diet so I wouldn't be overburdened with yeast. I douched with a very, very weak solution of Lysol. Also, every three months I did a seven-day fast with just bottled grape juice. She wanted me to drink spring water, and a friend of mine said, 'What spring?' so I used distilled water and didn't tell her. That supposedly counteracts the herbal tonic. I didn't understand chemistry, so I didn't allow it to disturb my herbal tonic. A friend told me about colonics because she was in the Gerson therapy and those people love to do enemas five times a day because they were so toxic. Well, I never got that toxic. I was still well when I got there. I was way ahead of the usual cancer patient who goes to Mexico. I didn't need to take extreme measures."

Her dietary change involved no alcohol, tobacco, carbonation, sugar, salt (or substitutes for sugar and salt), red meat, tomatoes (because they counteract the herbal tonic), or vinegar. She was allowed to eat fish and some chicken and turkey, as long as it was white meat and without the skins. "Later Dr. Fraire said to me that her diet isn't too strict because she found that if it is too strict, people won't do it at all. As far as extra vitamins and minerals, she said that if I could afford to continue taking them, it was fine. She left that up to me and said that I already knew what I was doing in that area." Keithly did take many supplements, and the doctor added thymus extract to help build up T-cells. Keithly continues to refine her supplements every year and has become 90 percent vegetarian.

When Keithly got home, she felt somewhat overwhelmed by the regimen. She called Walter. "He told me that it *would* get easier and gave me a woman's number who had been through it. That helped a lot. He often expressed how proud of me he was because so many patients would come back from Mexico and leave their 'protocol' on the floor of the motel, because they don't want to take responsibility for their health." As in many of our other interviews, the key to Keithly's long-term survival seems to be her ability to stick with a program.

After three months Keithly returned to the clinic. The doctor told her, "Now, if you want to have the surgery you can. We have improved your immune system enough so that the cancer won't spread throughout your body."

"I made an awful face and said, 'No. I've changed my mind!'

"She smiled and said, 'Good, because we can accomplish the same thing; it's just going to take a little longer.' So I never had the surgery.

"I had wanted to get rid of my breasts, the pragmatic little witch that I am. And Yolanda was a good enough psychiatrist to know that if I felt that was the only way to stop the cancer, she would not stop me. She's also one of the rare doctors who will combine Western medicine with the complementary/alternative therapies. She's not territorial about this being the only way to go. There she sat, saying, 'Now you can have the surgery,' but I had outgrown the idea. How did I do that? I don't know.

"The therapy for breast cancer can be three years, five years, or whatever. I have continued to see her because I trust her and it was cheaper to have my X rays and lab tests done in Mexico, to fly there, stay in a motel, and see her than it was to have a checkup in California. I kept receipts on everything. I am on the tail end of the treatment right now, ten years later.

"I take one-half of one teeny-tiny little pill which is called methyltestosterone. It is my antiestrogen pill for an estrogen-induced cancer. From 1987 to today, I have remained on the methyltestosterone. The pill itself is about the size of two pinheads. Then I cut it in half, which isn't easy. I'm no longer on any other pharmaceutical products. I dropped the Hoxsey Herbal Tonic, too—it made my breath smell like iodine. I stayed on the Hoxsey for about five years.

"My trips and treatment in Mexico cost me the same as my Blue Shield Insurance premium for the same five-year period! (They did not cover alternative treatments.)

"Three years into my treatment I had an opportunity to go on a safari to Africa and asked Yolanda if I could go. She okayed the trip, stating that I could skip part of the protocol but listed what I should be sure to continue taking.

"This would be my second trip to Africa, all because of what I had said to myself after my mother died: that I would take good care of myself, have regular medical checkups, and if they ever found cancer, they would get one shot at it and then I was going to Africa. I had decided that seeing the animals in Africa would cause a spontaneous remission, and if not, well, at least I would have seen the animals of Africa before I died.

"I later heard such plans are called a 'life script,' and strangely enough they affect one's life. When I was in my early forties, I heard a program where the man said the animals were being killed wantonly and the political situation was so bad that Africa would soon be a closed continent. I wouldn't learn until many years later that the brain is a computer. All I knew was that my brain went, 'Africa, Africa,' and I went to a travel agency and booked my first safari, never questioning it for a moment. I had a wonderful time.

"Now thirteen years later I found I was going on another safari; this time it was a first-class trip. I had never spent so much money on myself. But this was part of what I discovered during my recovery. I learned that I was worthy of love and being treated well. I had (like most women) always put others first and took what was left. Now I was coming through, taking my place in the sun. I deserved the best! Subsequently I went on a trip to Hong Kong, Outer Mongolia, and Siberia with two other women. What an adventure! A week after returning, I met an old high school boyfriend in Salt Lake City and hopped onto his Gold Wing Honda motorcycle, and we cruised through the Grand Teton and Yellowstone National Parks. Yahoo!

"You've heard of self-fulfilling prophecies. You could say that I wrote a script for getting cancer. However, I don't think so because I didn't have a fear of it. I just wrote my little script and figured people could break their necks falling out of bed, so why worry about cancer? In fact, when I was diagnosed, that was my attitude: 'It's just a virus; I'm going to give it my best shot. Either it wins or I win.' I never had that outrageous fear that the doctor would love patients to have so they would immediately jump onto the operating table. I was willing to do that, but not out of fear . . . just ignorant pragmatism."

At the time of the interview in early 1997, sixty-six-year-old Dixie Keithly was busy: "I run four miles four days a week, manage five pieces of real estate, am president of a chapter of Cancer Victors, work for the reform party, and am an alternative therapy hot-line. . . . Oh yes, I do a one-hour radio program two times a month for patients who have reversed their 'chronic' conditions or 'death' sentences with alternative therapies.

"Nearly every day someone says, 'I love your energy.' I feel cancer was my wake-up call to treat my body better. I am moving on a spiritual path to become the best possible person I can be, as well as a happy, healthy example for all to emulate." When we spoke to her in early 1998, she remained in good health and good spirits.

Advice to Other Women

When patients call Dixie Keithly, she tries to find out the diagnosis and what has occurred so far, how they happened to call her, what their anxiety level is, and the kind of help they want. She warns that is it very confusing to decide what alternative route to choose and that each survivor loves her own doctor or clinic. As for many of the women we talked with, Keithly admits that advice is difficult to give because everyone is different.

"To demonstrate how powerful their thoughts are, I give this example. Just imagine that your doorbell rings and a man is there with an Uzzi and a sock over his head. Would your biochemistry change? Now, the guy tears the sock off and says, 'April Fools.' Does your biochemistry change again? If he says, 'Oh, shit! Wrong apartment,' does your biochemistry change again? Now you want to chase him down the hall and kill him, right? Every thought you think changes your biochemistry. And it is my impression that you want to keep your biochemistry as close to neutral as possible. With a car in neutral, you can push it backward and forward. If the cells are bathed in all their nutrients, and all the stuff that is inside the body, and they're in neutral, they can do what they learned to do over a million years. But if you are uptight or suffering from unresolved anger, pain, unresolved emotional issues with your family, your job, etc., you have to find some way to get these things resolved so you can have this neutral chemistry. Then your body is just going to do miracles with everything that's good for you that you eat and do. That's one of the things that I hit on."

She also suggests books, places, and doctors, and she may refer them to other patients. She has met women who seem unable to take charge of their disease, particularly because of pressure from family members. "I didn't have a husband who said, 'Oh, that's ridiculous,' or children who said, 'Mother, Mother, you must have the surgery. We don't want you to die!' I have heard this from patients. I have them all ready to save their breasts and not have the surgery. I give them videos and books and all kinds of things that will make them feel real good about the choice.

"Once, after a few days I called one to get my videos back for a presentation in Monterey. I asked if she looked at the videos. She said, 'No, I'm leaving for the hospital. My children think that it's best.' My heart sinks. It's as if the patient suddenly becomes very old and turns herself over to her children, giving up all power and responsibility."

Keithly adds that in addition to taking charge, an important part of healing involves forgiveness. "Forgive anyone who you have ever been angry at, and allow yourself to be forgiven, too. That's part of getting that biochemistry in neutral. Minerals, raw foods, enzymes, and oxygenating your body are also very important. People who survive are those that leave no stone unturned. When you decide to get well, you grab any information that's out there and see how it works and resonates with you, and go for it."

She says, "I call getting cancer a WAKE-UP CALL. When your body aches, or has been diagnosed with some scary thing, is it saying it needs to have a part cut out or to be poisoned with chemicals or radiation? I don't think so. I say it is the body's call for help. Pick up the phone and say, 'Thank you for calling, body. I know I haven't been treating you very well. Help me keep my mind open so I can learn what I have to do to treat you better, because I live inside of you. You are my life. I love you.'"

Keithly tried a support group and attended a meeting prepared to tell the story of how she got involved with alternative therapies. Instead, the facilitator asked her, "If alternative therapies are so good, why aren't more people using them?" Being new to the alternative approach herself, Keithly was not prepared to defend the unorthodox approach to cancer. (Keithly says if you asked her that question today, she could talk for two hours.)

She came away from the meeting feeling angry at the way they treated new members who have recently lost their breasts and/or their hair. The meeting was held in the basement of the hospital. She feels that the setting "contributed to the 'spin' of the entire meeting."

Keithly's colorful description of the experience was that she felt the response she got would be similar to a Muslim woman walking into a Catholic women's group and saying, "Now let me tell you about our heaven." Keithly commented, "No open-hearted compassion here, not when these women have already been through the surgery, chemo, or radiation. Nope! Saying these approaches are not necessary is heresy. Stone her."

Opinions on Cancer Research and Publicly Supported Cancer Organizations

"I'm disgusted with them. They should all be audited, as they are primarily money-generating empires (for salaries for their hierarchies) which have a powerful conflict of interest. The need for their organization would cease to exist if they told people the truth, or the money was directed in an area of research such as prevention and immune support. No organization, no job. Very simple.

"So instead we hear, 'Send money. We are on the verge of discovering a cure!' I've heard that for forty years.

"I like what Eleanor Roosevelt once said: 'I support the organization which is eliminating the need for that organization.'

"I read about a young woman who was thrilled to be employed by an eminent researcher, only to discover that he 'spun' the results of his experiments so he could get more research funding. Then I met a woman in real life who had lived that exact same experience. I now have a jaded view of 'science,' because it seems whoever pays for the research gets the results they want. We hear about it every day on the news.

"From my 'alternative' perspective, I have discovered that if a person gets access to good information and is willing to put the time in (eighteen hours a day), they can turn around 'incurable' cancer of all kinds. Such people have been interviewed on my radio program.

"The fact that our tax dollars are supporting the *suppression* of practitioners who can turn these 'incurables' around is the most appalling aspect of all. Here is the scenario. An AMA doctor complains about an 'alternative' doctor (competition) in his area. The gestapo arm, the FDA, (often without due process) crashes in the door of the unsuspecting doctor, his staff, and clients with guns at the ready. They confiscate his computers, client records, supplies—whatever they want. A court battle ensues. After possibly six years the doctor is found to be innocent. He WINS! But he is broke; his practice is vanished. Mission accomplished. With the unlimited taxpayer dollars, they crushed a healer who was merely in competition with the AMA CLUB.

"I don't like any publicly supported cancer organizations that focus on cancer therapies. I call their numbers to hear what they have to say, and they're all marching to the same tune, just like the AIDS people. They've become hierarchies for raising millions of dollars which they use to pay outrageous salaries. The type of research that will be funded is tightly controlled, and they don't want answers because their foundation/charity would become obsolete. There is a whole book on the subject called

Unhealthy Charities (by Bennett and DiLorenzo). Another book I recommend is *Assault on Medical Freedom,* by Joseph Lisa. He says that the American Medical Association puts four thousand pieces of literature into the media every week to make sure we stay where we are supposed to stay in our thinking . . . such as 'pharmaceuticals are the answer to every problem.'

"Doctors not only don't know but they are taught misinformation. They used to take out babies' thymus glands. Who needs a thymus gland? Then they realized that those kids got terribly sick later. And of course, they took out every uterus, back in my day. Now, it's mammograms. I dutifully had mammograms every fifteen years. One part of my brain knew that this was radiation and it was *not good*. But I didn't know what else to do. Now they're saying we should have one when you're forty and then do it after your menopause. They're still arguing about it. It's another big business. They smash your breast and radiate it. Not smart! Not for me!

"Here is another thing getting cancer brought to light. I had never felt that I was very bright. But I began to look at myself differently. I realized my best friends were all very high up there, you know, the Mensa-type IQs. I had been comparing myself to them all these years. Now enough time had passed and I realized I had assets those friends didn't have.

"With all their intelligence they were not as happy, not enjoying their lives as much as I, no, not even as healthy as I, in spite of cancer. I had the gift of being able to enjoy my life and I had common sense (which is uncommon). I was sharing and caring and generally got the same in return. Among those friends, one died of cancer (you couldn't tell him anything). One I call 'my Alcoholic.' (He caused me to discover I had a heart and brought me books on alternative therapies, and for him I shall always have deep feelings.) We are still in contact and, though he has been 'dry' for over ten years, life continues to be a struggle for him. Another went through alcoholism and came through it, but has had a life of serious struggle; and the last one kind of looks at me as if to say, 'How did you do it? You are serene and financially comfortable; you get to travel; you have many friends . . . with your limited mental facilities.' Her life is a constant struggle, in spite of the great brain.

"So now I appreciate the gifts I have. And I enjoy working for political and social issues which I believe in, and I long for ways to teach people how to care for our planet as well as their own bodies . . . which goes hand in hand.

"People call me to talk about their cancer, then say, 'You've spent so much time with me. Can I send you a check? How can I thank you?' And I say, 'Your appreciation makes my endorphins dance. What could be more wonderful!' That's an injection of longevity, happiness, and energy. I am validated, oh joy!"

References

Bennett, James, and Thomas DiLorenzo
    1994 *Unhealthy Charities*. New York: Basic Books.
Davis, Adelle
    1965 *Let's Get Well*. New York: Harcourt, Brace.
Hoxsey, Harry
    1956 *You Don't Have to Die*. New York: Milestone Books.
Lisa, P. Joseph
    1994 *Assault on Medical Freedom*. Norfolk, Va.: Hampton Roads.

fifteen

Teresa Kennett

Everything Counts

Teresa Kennett is a former patient of Dr. Burzynski. For the last two years she has operated a referral and support service for people seeking alternative treatments for their cancer. She has been making jewelry for a living and is currently working on a master's degree in psychology. She is also a writer.

Her Story

In 1984, following the birth of her daughter, Teresa Kennett was diagnosed with stage IV non-Hodgkin's lymphoma at San Francisco's St. Mary's Hospital. "Being diagnosed with cancer came as quite a shock. I was in good health, working fifty hours a week, and had just experienced a beautiful natural birth at home. My husband and I were both devastated by the thought that I may not be around to take care of our daughter.

"In the very beginning, I panicked and didn't perform an extremely thorough search of the various therapeutic treatments." Kennett didn't look into everything but just gathered whatever information sounded the best to her. "I wasn't in a frame of mind to be very discriminating with my evaluation of the treatments. Yet, I felt that I had to take responsibility for my own healing. Even though it is becoming an overutilized term, 'taking my power' truly reflects my feeling of taking control of my health.'"

Surgery was performed on Kennett in an attempt to excise the tumors found on her MRI scans. "The oncologist said I would be treated with chemotherapy as soon as I recovered from the operation. But during the operation, they saw that the cancer was too far advanced, and they merely removed a biopsy sample. They immediately informed me to stop breast-feeding my daughter. I was also told this was an unfortunate situation because the cancer was a slow-growing type of lymphoma with a limited response rate to conventional treatments, in particular chemotherapy." Kennett was shown the statistics on chemotherapeutic response rates on the type of non-Hodgkin's lymphoma she had, and they were dismal. "I don't remember the specific information, but I was shown a bell curve and basically told the chemotherapeutic response with this type of lymphoma was extremely low." These statistics would be pivotal in her decision not to pursue traditional treatment.

Kennett's next step was to obtain a second opinion at the Stanford University Medical Clinic. At the clinic, there were three active protocols for non-Hodgkin's lymphoma. The first protocol was for an intravenous form of three chemotherapeutic agents; another was for the oral route of a slower and longer course of the chemotherapy; and the third was for nontreatment with intervention only on a compassionate plea basis. Justification for the third protocol was that slow-growing lymphomas allow patients an extended period of asymptomatic, good quality of life prior to the necessity for treatment. "I chose this third option and over the next eight months began monthly visits to the clinic for the continual monitoring of my lymph system."

For Kennett, these visits to Stanford Clinic were extremely tedious in an emotionally negative way. "Walking into the clinic was like walking into the land of death. People looked so bad, and the atmosphere was just charged with fear and depression. I finally came to a point where I couldn't stand being in that environment and stopped the monthly monitoring visits."

Between mid-1985 and the end of 1986, Kennett made the decision to stop consulting with mainstream doctors and explore nontoxic cancer treatments. Prior to being diagnosed with cancer, she was bedridden with a severe case of poison oak. Her dermatologist recommended cortisone treatments, explaining that otherwise the poison oak would run its course in about a month. "I had heard about the negative effects of cortisone and did not want to start the treatment. Somehow, I thought I could deal with the poison oak through other methods." It was during this period that Kennett was given a copy of *Creative Visualization* by Shakti Gawain. "I was already open-minded about metaphysics and visualization, so it wasn't unusual for me to read the book." After a week of visualizing the poison oak going away, it was gone. "This incident with poison oak had a major impact on my perceptions of the healing process." As soon as Kennett was over the shock of being diagnosed with cancer, she started looking for help in the area of alternative medicines.

"Not being a scientifically minded person, I made my early decisions surrounding alternative therapies based on my own belief systems, past experience, and anecdotal information." Regarding Kennett's choices among the various alternative medicines, scientific research and statistical results did not play a major role in her decision-making process. "I felt as though I was in a completely different universe when I was examining the alternative medicines." Over the next two and a half years, she found out about the different alternative treatments mainly through her own research. "I also had the good fortune to have family and friends who provided me with articles and books." In her investigation of the alternative cancer treatments, Kennett found that the information on the various treatments was mostly anecdotal. "In retrospect, there didn't appear to be as many choices as there are today. The books continually described the same treatments, and these were the options I eventually pursued as treatments."

Kennett attended a Menlo Park program, which allowed her to begin dealing with her emotions. "The ability to change my beliefs about the possibilities of my healing was at the core of everything that has happened to me." She believes the healing she experienced could not have taken place without these changes to her belief system. "I feel as though the evolution of my beliefs has continued gradually throughout my healing process."

Between 1984 and 1986, Kennett tried a number of other nontoxic cancer treatments. Her next step was to travel to Mexico for a three-week course of daily treatments with peptide therapy at St. Jude's Medical Clinic. After the peptide treatments, she worked with an American physician whose therapeutic regimen consisted of a high-dose combination of vitamins, including vitamin A and laetrile. After a negative reaction to the vitamin A, Kennett moved on to other therapies, including Dr. Emanuel Revici's lipid treatment, macrobiotics, and Dr. Stanislaw Burzynski's antineoplastons. She continued her healing process through vitamins, a natural diet, homeopathic remedies, herbal therapy, and radical psychotherapy.

"I tell you one thing—everywhere I went, I met people who were doing well with the alternative treatments. Some of these therapies were recommended by the numerous professionals I worked with during this period. The homeopathic physician whom I consulted provided me with the recommendation for Revici's therapy." Kennett remained on Revici's lipid therapy for approximately nine months. The macrobiotic diet option was through a referral to an Oregon nutritionist. "The nutritionist informed me of Burzynski's antineoplaston treatments and strongly suggested I contact his Houston clinic. Her recommendation was based on the fact that several cancer patients she was working with were having remarkable results with the antineoplastons."

It wasn't until Kennett started Burzynski's antineoplaston treatments that her cancer went into remission. "I was on the oral form of antineoplastons from the beginning of 1987 to the beginning of 1988, then was on the intravenous form until April 1989. All told, the treatment period with the antineoplastons was two years but generally I feel the effective part of the treatment was the second year."

In 1987 Kennett began daily treatments with forty-five capsules of antineoplastons. "The first thing I experienced with the oral dose of antineoplastons was a tremendous increase in energy. The burst in energy was incredible for me because I was weighing 90 pounds and my normal weight was 105 pounds. I had to quit working because of my weakness and fatigue." At this point in the course of her disease, Kennett had developed large tumors throughout her abdominal area. "I was on the oral form of the therapy for several months, and there was really no change in the size of the tumors. But I felt much better and my blood work continually improved over the course of my treatment.

"During the summer of 1987, I began taking Cytoxan® as an adjuvant therapy only because it was recommended by Dr. Burzynski." Kennett experienced hair loss, amenorrhea, and periodic bouts of nausea while on the Cytoxan® therapy. "I stayed on the Cytoxan® therapy for approximately one month but just couldn't bear the side effects." In the autumn of 1987, her MRI scan results showed no changes with the tumors, and she immediately began an intravenous form of the antineoplastons. "It was nice that my insurance company paid for the catheter, but it still wouldn't pay for the treatments." Kennett began self-medicating per Burzynski's prescription/recommendation with a nightly intravenous drip, and she gradually built up to a one thousand-cc dose of the anti-neoplastons.

During the course of the second year, Kennett remained on the one thousand-cc dose of antineoplastons and traveled every six to eight weeks to the Houston clinic for her MRI scans, blood work, and physical examinations. "Every MRI scan, except one, showed the continual reduction of the tumor masses until finally there was nothing on the scan and my blood work results were normal." Kennett stopped the antineoplaston therapy two and a half months after her clear MRI scan and has remained in remission the past seven years. In March 1996, prior to attending a Washington rally for Dr. Burzynski, the result of her MRI scan was clear.

While she was on the antineoplaston treatments, Kennett wanted to consult an oncologist for a baseline scan and follow-up throughout the course of her treatment. Her husband at the time was a news cameraman who had met a highly respected oncologist through his work. "The oncologist agreed to take me as a patient, which was great because he was somewhat more open-minded than most of the oncologists I consulted over this period. However, with the research of Tom Elias, a journalist who was writing about Burzynski's antineoplaston therapy, this oncologist stated that he believed my recovery was a result of spontaneous remission and not the antineoplaston therapy. The journalist, Elias, called the American Cancer Society and inquired about statistical data on spontaneous remission rates in cancer patients. He was informed by the ACS personnel that those statistics were not kept because the rate of spontaneous remission was almost negligible." And yet, according to Kennett, scores of Burzynski's patients interviewed by Elias all experienced "spontaneous" remissions.

"Early on in my remission period, I went through a phase where I was so sick of macrobiotics and the various restrictions that I started drinking Margaritas and eating regular junk food. It was the most healing thing to just let go and have a good time. I really think I needed to go through this change and continued to remain well during this time." Here again, Kennett stresses the point that a patient's belief system and emotions are crucial in the healing process. "I personally hold the belief that my emotions are intimately connected with what happens to me physically. If I am dealing with them in an ongoing, dynamic way, it helps me in feeling my best and I continually build from there."

Currently, Kennett is maintaining a wellness program consisting of attention to diet, exercise, vitamins, creative visualization, and psychotherapy. She is consulting with an orthomolecular physician, who provides her with a comprehensive monitoring system. "The physician has worked with a number of Burzynski patients and has commented on the dynamic nature of our immune systems. He gave me several different tests, extensive blood work, and recommendations on my vitamin and dietary regime." She is following the Zone diet (Sears 1995) and takes fairly moderate amounts of vitamins C and E, a multipurpose supplement, essential fatty acids (EPA and DHA), acetylcholine, bromelin, and zinc. "Even though I didn't have cancer anymore, I still wasn't feeling tip-top until I adjusted my diet. It wasn't until I starting the Zone diet that my energy level increased again.

"I started walking when I visited my parents for a summer holiday, and I have continued this daily exercise routine." Kennett either exercises on a power rider machine or through outdoor activities. "Since August 1996, I have been walk-running daily for an hour when the weather permits. I am continuing with visualization, and it has almost become a way of thinking." Kennett has learned to be with intense emotional states through therapy and meditation, and she feels this has also been enormously instrumental in her physical well-being. "I did some very radical therapy while I was sick and recently I have been doing traditional psychotherapy. It has been fantastic. It has helped me so much." As of early 1998, she remained in good health.

Advice to Other Women

"I would say, first of all, most people who are first diagnosed with cancer are in a complete state of shock." Kennett became dependent upon her circle of friends and family. "It was as though I regressed to a two-year-old and wanted my parents to take care of me emotionally." She was extremely frightened and encounters this same emotion in her work with patients who are facing a cancer diagnosis. "I think you have to acknowledge that you are in a vulnerable state. The tendency is for patients not to question their physician's recommendations."

Kennett suggests the first important step is to gather support from family and friends and to ask for help. "Feeling supported by people is very important in your healing process." She also suggests questioning the recommended therapies as the most appropriate treatment for you. "Just don't take the first piece of advice you receive. I felt rushed into making decisions when I was first diagnosed with lymphoma. Luckily enough, I was someone with a slow-growing cancer and I had the 'luxury' of more time than most people. Even so, the oncologist rushed me into having surgery and the possibility of chemotherapy. I felt as though I was on a bullet train to the world of chemotherapy and ultimately my death. I have met many patients who have gotten well using conventional treatments, so I'm not judging what's right for others. I shouldn't say, 'many patients' because the majority of patients who chose conventional treatments at the time of my diagnosis are not living today. You must recognize that you are ultimately responsible for your healing process and the choices that you make. I think if people can feel some sense of agency and efficacy in their health, it is tremendously healing."

Opinions on Cancer Research and Publicly Supported Cancer Organizations

"The Cancer Control Society was an extremely helpful resource for providing lists of patients who were evaluating nontoxic treatments. Also, it's wonderful for creating forums where practitioners and patients can discuss different therapies. Another organization which was extremely helpful in my healing process was CanHelp of Washington State." CanHelp assists patients by helping them sort through the myriad choices surrounding cancer therapies and matching them with efficacious treatments. "I didn't use their services extensively but spoke briefly with the organization's director. Our conversation was helpful because the number of therapies available to cancer patients is overwhelming." The only support group Kennett attended was a three-week group session focusing on creative visualization.

Kennett also provides insights into frustration and outrage with the Food and Drug Administration and its actions toward Dr. Stanislaw Burzynski. "I think it is criminal that the FDA is bringing these interstate commerce felony charges against Dr. Burzynski. If he is convicted of transporting antineoplastons across Texas state lines, he could be in jail for a very long time.[1] It would be such a great loss to humanity if he couldn't conduct his research. I just can't imagine the possibilities for healing if he can be allowed to continue his antineoplaston treatments. I am outraged and frustrated that the FDA is trying to control the lives of Americans this way. As Americans, I think that we should have access to promising nontoxic treatments for supposedly incurable diseases.

"Dr. Samuel Epstein recently conducted a press conference, and he quoted a statistic that was shocking to me. He said that there is only a 5 percent permanent remission rate in the United States for all cancers treated with chemotherapy, radiation, and surgery. To me, a 5 percent remission rate is just not enough. Dr. Burzynski's antineoplaston therapy is a successful treatment and I know there are other promising nontoxic treatments. It makes no sense to me that patients are getting well with Burzynski's antineoplastons and they aren't permitted to use it."

Kennett is currently working with Burzynski patients in the organizational role of managing a phone referral service. "People call me and I provide referrals to Burzynski patients who are in remission with their type of cancer. I also talk to them about treatment options and how to get started with the antineoplaston treatment." Kennett wants to expand her ability to help patients by talking to them about other nontoxic cancer treatments. "At times, for whatever reason, the antineoplaston treatment may not be an appropriate therapy. And sometimes people are prohibited from obtaining the antineoplaston treatments by the medical establishment. The FDA is requiring that with most types of cancer, people must fail two forms of conventional therapy before starting the antineoplaston treatment. So most of Burzynski's patients have already been through conventional treatments before they are permitted the antineoplaston therapy. I think it is rather extraordinary that people who have been given

1. After the interview, in the spring of 1997, Dr. Burzynski was acquitted of all charges, and subsequent government action against him was settled out of court in early 1998.

up by the medical establishment have had so much success with Dr. Burzynski's antineoplaston therapy."

References

Gawain, Shakti
  1993 *Creative Visualization*. New York, N.Y.: MJF Books.
Sears, Barry
  1995 *The Zone*. New York, N.Y.: Reagan Books.

sixteen _____

Charlotte Louise

Cancer as a Spiritual Voyage

Charlotte Louise, former actress and fashion model, is a long-term survivor of lung and ovarian cancer. She is the founder and director of the Cancer Survival Workshop and author of *Cancer Survival Workbook.* Charlotte Louise has earned certificates in drama therapy, hypnotherapy, and master neurolinguistic programming. As an advocate for innovative cancer care, she has made many appearances on WNBC-TV News, *The McCreary Report, Geraldo, The Barry Farber Show*, and *The Gary Null Show.* She also testified at the 1993 congressional hearings, sponsored by Congressperson Susan Molinari, titled "Cancer Treatment: New Directions for the 1990s." She has an audiocassette tape called *The Inner Smile* ($15), which "teaches how to circulate healing energy throughout the body, organ by organ." She has also written the *Cancer Survival Resource Workbook* ($30), which provides "tools to develop a survival strategy." The tape and workbook, as well as information about her and her workshop, can be obtained by writing to her at 14 Fifth Avenue, Suite 4B, New York, NY 10011, or calling 212-777-0111.

Her Story

In 1980 Charlotte Louise, an actress and fashion model, was diagnosed with oat cell lung cancer and oat cell cancer in the right ovary. At the time she knew very little about cancer or alternative medicine, although she had heard about the Simontons (1978). She commented, "I knew that

168

there was some kind of body-mind connection that wasn't being addressed in conventional medicine."

From the beginning Charlotte Louise was not satisfied with the information and options that she was given: "The way I was being handled by the medical profession just wasn't making sense to me. For example, before the tests came back confirming that it was indeed oat cell cancer, the doctor wanted to schedule my operation because he had to go away for a golf tournament. He wanted to slit me down the middle and look at all my organs. I said, 'Look, I'm a show girl. I can't possibly continue my life if you slit me up the middle like that.' They just looked at me as if they were thinking, 'Well, that's no concern to us. You really don't have much time to live anyway, so what difference does it make?' My own integrity was never an issue with them."

Although she declined the offer for the radical exploratory surgery, Charlotte Louise did accept several of the conventional treatments that were offered to her. She had a complete hysterectomy followed by three rounds of chemotherapy. "Then they wanted to radiate my brain, and I was against that. I said, 'Why do you want to do that?' They said either 40 or 60 percent of the cases metastasize to the brain and you die a horrible death. It was just doom and gloom and terrible prophecy. In all the research that I've done, the one thing that most strongly determines whether the patient outlives the prognosis is the way the doctor delivers the diagnosis. It's very important for the doctor to be hopeful and provide some positive tools. When I was first diagnosed, my gynecologist who did the surgery told me I could take vitamins and help myself, and he gave me hope. With that I was able to feel hopeful and go ahead.

"But even he wanted me to sign a permission form so that when they went in to look, if they found cancer, they could do a hysterectomy right away. I didn't want that. I was willing to let them go in and look, but I wanted to be able to consider whether I was going to have a complete hysterectomy or not. Literally, as he stood in the hospital room, he turned his back on me until I gave in and agreed to a hysterectomy. So I signed the paper, but the next day when I got to the operating room, I said, 'I know I signed that, but here I am: I want you all to witness that I do not want a hysterectomy.' I don't know what internal intelligence was telling me that there was only one ovary involved and everything else was all right. Everyone agreed, but when I woke up I had a hysterectomy."

We asked her if she had sued, and she answered that she thought none of them would have substantiated her claim. "There was no choice, and I was angry about that."

Concerned about the side effects of chemotherapy, she was determined not to lose her long blonde hair, which had become a trademark of her career. She saw a chiropractor "who did something for me that proved the mind-body connection. I explained that I was a show girl, actress, and fashion model. Probably my greatest weakness was my vanity, but it was also my greatest strength because it stopped them from cutting me open and disfiguring me from surgery. When it came to chemotherapy, the type of chemotherapy that they wanted to give me and gave me was the kind which would cause me to lose all my hair. I told my chiropractor that I didn't want to do that, and I wanted him to hypnotize me so I wouldn't lose all my hair. He said he would do that, and he did something called calaxis—I was awake and consciously involved in the process. He told me, too, that the most important factor in healing was the will to live. I knew that there was a body-mind connection, and I had a strong will to live, especially because I felt my twelve-year-old daughter, Siobhan, would be devastated without me. One proof of the body-mind connection was that I didn't lose my hair. He also demonstrated the body-mind connection through muscle testing and kinesiology. So I did have some proof. Every time I went into my oncologist's office, he would pull my hair and say, 'Is that a wig?' but it wouldn't come out. I did lose some hair, maybe ten to fifteen percent. After the third round of chemotherapy, it started to get slightly thin, especially around the front of the temples. Every other woman I know who had that type of chemotherapy not only lost all her hair, but also lost her eyebrows, eyelashes, and other bodily hair. So to me that was a very strong proof, a demonstration."

During her rounds of chemotherapy, Charlotte Louise began to see a nurse-psychotherapist. "I got her to get some figures because nobody would give me a picture of the true situation in a way that I could comprehend. She told me that less that 1 percent survive from this type of lung cancer, most of them are dead within six months, and all are dead within two years. The picture for ovarian cancer wasn't very good, either. I decided that they didn't have a very good track record and that I could probably do better on my own.

"That's when I started first with the Kelley program for nutrition. It was based on metabolic typing, which I found to be the key to the effectiveness of the program." She had a very good chiropractor who was able to guide her on the program, and she found that the individualizing emphasis of the Kelley program was particularly attractive in comparison with the across-the-board dietary recommendations of some of the other dietary programs (see Kelley 1969).

Charlotte Louise stayed on the Kelley program for about two months while she was finishing the chemotherapy. "Having established myself on the Kelley program, I felt ready to leave chemotherapy. I then went to Emanuel Revici, M.D., and replaced the chemotherapy with the Revici therapy. I did both the Kelley and Revici programs at the same time. I called up Kelley and told him about Revici, and told him I wanted to go on Revici's protocol and asked if they would be compatible, and Kelley said, 'I love it.'

"I stayed on Kelley for quite a while, maybe six or nine months, then I started switching around. I did Chinese herbs for a while, and I did Bernard Jensen's detox program (Jensen and Bell 1981). He's a chiropractor and I think a doctor of nutrition and an iridologist. The program I went on was tissue cleansing through bowel management. I did the Jensen program because I still had residual chemotherapy in my body, and I wanted to cleanse myself of all the toxins."

Ms. Louise drew on a number of alternative healing modalities as part of her pathway toward long-term cancer survival. In addition to the programs and therapies already mentioned, she tried Russian baths, acupuncture, Shiatsu massage, and sessions with a native Mexican Indian shaman. She made her decisions in an intuitive way: "I prayed. I'm a Buddhist. People were telling me to go to Boston to go see Michio Kushi (macrobiotics), and other people were saying I should eat raw vegetables. People were trying to be helpful, but I got so many suggestions that I started to feel powerless. So I chanted, 'Nam myoho renge kyo.' I said, 'I don't know if I'm supposed to live or die, but if I'm supposed to live, please lead me to what I need to know.'"

So, in response to our question about the role that science played in her decision-making process, Charlotte Louise answered that in a sense her experience with her hair and chemotherapy was empirical proof that allowed her to find alternative therapies credible. "I set up a test and it worked." Likewise, she knew from the statistics she had seen that for her type of cancer the long-term prognosis was very poor under conventional therapies. However, her process of choosing among alternative therapies was not guided by scientific research. In fact, she said, "It was exactly anti-scientific. I had to have the faith to make that quantum leap, to admit that I know that science doesn't have an answer for me here. I knew that I wasn't dependent on science; I was dependent on my source of health, the divine power of the universe that I'm connected to. I'm going to do every-thing I can to reestablish a clear connection. So I started receiving clear signals about how I was supposed to be living my life, how I can get rid of toxicity, and how I've allowed it to enter my life on every level—spiritu-ally, culturally, matrimonially—and in every relationship: my child, my mother, with my home environment, with my physical being, and my health. I felt that I had been sacrificing myself, that I was selling myself out. I had to turn that all around. I had to look at every way I was making my life toxic—at the emotional level, the spiritual level. That's how I did it."

We found the idea of "emotional toxicity" very intriguing, and Char-lotte Louise commented that she had to work out and resolve several problematic relationships with key people in her life, including her for-mer husband, her mother, and her daughter. "I had to reexamine my needs and where I wasn't really meeting my needs. Also, at one point I had to examine what needs I was fulfilling by getting sick and how I could fulfill those needs without being sick." She had to work through her own "victim mentality" with respect to the abusive patterns of her relationship with her former husband. Her mother was also a source of strength: "I talked to my mother and she said, 'They're wrong. You're not going to die.' That's what I wanted to hear. She had that fighting Irish spirit and I wanted to plug into that. My attitude was 'In-your-face, brother—I'll prove you wrong.'

"So I set out to reframe that whole experience and to think of this as a test. It was like what you hear on the radio: 'This is a test. It's only a test.' I reframed it as a limited mythic journey test, where they set it up and it looks so terrible, but if you just adopt the right attitude and go through it, all the terribleness dissolves and you come out with the prize. I figure it was like one of those stories where you walk through fire and the fire burns off all the dross material, and you come out pure gold. This is part of my journey as a spiritual being toward enlightenment, and I have lessons to learn in it."

She has been healthy since the early 1980s. "When I go for an X ray, they don't believe me when I say I had cancer. If I didn't have my original X rays and tissues, they would tell me I was lying."

Advice to Other Women

When women come to see Charlotte Louise about their cancer, her main concern is "to empower them in their choice of alternatives, if they want to make that choice. What I also hear is that friends and relatives want them to make those choices, even when it is outside the person's belief system. The person also has to take charge, to want to take an active role. A passive role plays into the standard medical model, but an active role is for people who are willing to go out on a limb and choose alternatives. They are people who don't need someone else to be a path-blazer for them or who have to have it proven with statistics in trials and double-blind studies. If you want to take charge, if you've got a fighting spirit, or if you want to claim your power back, then alternatives are the way to go." She quoted a passage from Carolyn Myss's book *Anatomy of the Spirit,* which she highly recommends: "For alternative therapy to succeed, the patient must have an internal concept of power, an ability to generate internal energy and emotional resources, such as a belief in his or her own self-sufficiency."

Charlotte Louise now runs the Cancer Survival Workshop. The sessions are open to men as well as women, and they consist of six small-group sessions that meet once a week. "It's really about assessing our needs and taking a good look at where we're supporting ourselves, where we've given away our power, how our dreams got lost, and how to reconnect with those dreams. We look at stress and how it affects our brain, our glands, and our hormones, and how that creates abnormal cells and lowers our immune defensive functions. Then we look at how we can reverse the effects of stress by handling it differently and reframing the issues in our lives.

"We touch on nutrition by giving a very general outline of the subject. We refer people to medical doctors who do metabolic typing because I think that's the most helpful way to approach nutrition and supplements. It has to be an individualized program. Very few things are right for everybody across the board." She clarified that when she refers to metabolic typing, she is talking about more than classification of people into types related to the sympathetic and parasympathetic nervous systems. "It's genetic coding in the blood, and there is a whole range of types." She mentioned the work of Peter D'Adamo, M.D., as an example of this approach (D'Adamo 1997). "It has nothing to do with Kelley, but I found that they dovetail perfectly."

Charlotte Louise studied crisis intervention at New York University and drama therapy at the New School for Social Research, and she applies some of this background in her workshops. "It's a crisis intervention model: assessing needs, finding your own inner support system or resources, finding your outer support system, creating a wellness plan, then referrals and help implementing the wellness plan. I don't do a psychological support group; instead, it's empowerment and looking at your life. We use cross-cultural techniques to go through each of these stages, such as closed-eye meditation exercises to help deal with fear, guilt, and forgiveness and to awaken and mobilize your own healing energies. I draw on ancient Chinese Taoism, shamanism, modern neurolinguistic programming—everything I can find to support and empower people through those stages. We use the creative arts to connect more strongly with your own inner being."

Charlotte Louise added, "In terms of advice for women, I'd say make a list of the ten or fifteen things that give you the most pleasure, and don't limit it, make it as far out as you want. After you make that list, make sure, every day, to include something from that list in your daily life. With me, it was going out and giving myself dance classes and voice lessons every day. It was something I previously wouldn't give myself permission to indulge in. I said, 'If I'm going to be dead in six months, I might as well live the life I've always wanted to live.'" When I compared this idea to Lawrence LeShan's proposal (1994) that patients should look at their lives and ask whether they are "singing their song," Charlotte Louise answered, "That's really part of it, but more profound than LeShan is the book I mentioned by Carolyn Myss." Again, she highly recommended Myss's book to all cancer patients.

Opinions on Cancer Research and Publicly Supported Cancer Organizations

When Charlotte Louise was diagnosed with cancer and fighting the battle for her life, she did not draw on information or support from cancer organizations. One of the problems is that the organizations were less developed and diverse than they are today. However, even today most cancer organizations remain very conservative on the topic of alternative and complementary therapies. "After I got well and started doing my workshop, I tried to contact different organizations to see if they would be interested or open. The only positive response I got was from SHARE. I think at the beginning SHARE was hesitant about alternatives, but they've since relaxed and opened up. I was on a panel there of long-term ovarian cancer survivors—ten or fifteen years, past statistical expectations. Each woman, as she told her individual story, said, 'Now I don't advise this for everybody, but I did not do what they told me to do.' It was interesting that SHARE put together a panel of long-term survivors, and the truth came out."

Charlotte Louise said that she could not think of any other major cancer organizations that were open to alternatives. "I found that most organizations are politically tied up with conventional therapies. Cancer Care in New York is so tightly married to drug providers and conventional doctors that they'll talk to me, but with extreme disdain, and they don't want to know about alternatives at all. Now Cancer Care in New Jersey is not that tied in, and they were very open to finding every way you could help support yourself while on conventional therapies. For example, they were more willing to consider the question, What other things could you do to help yourself?

"At first I thought I was going to be offering support to people who wanted to do alternatives, but there are so few that I had to broaden the outreach to supporting people who have cancer, no matter what their choices are. I work to make them aware that there are other things they can do to support their healing. I try to cooperate with whatever choice they make and not go against the doctors or whatever conventional treatments they take. In my heart of hearts I often think that it's not going to do them any good and it's possibly even going to do them harm, but unless they ask me that question, I don't feel that it's my job to persuade them. My job is to mobilize whatever healing energies they have and support them in their choices, and when they ask me for information, to be a good resource."

Overall, Charlotte Louise believes that dramatic reforms are necessary in both the medical profession and the government regulatory structure. For example, on the topic of the poor humanitarian skills of many doctors in the cancer field, she commented: "I found nurses to be the greatest help because they naturally have a holistic approach when it comes to healing. They're also with patients all the time at the hospital, whereas doctors see patients much less frequently. Somehow because of their training they're really not available, especially on an emotional level. This is a generalization and there are wonderful exceptions, but I'm just saying that it would be helpful for medical schools to change the way that doctors are chosen. I think only a certain type is accepted, and it's not the type that has humanitarian skills; it's the type that has cool analytical skills. The people already in power are the cool ones, and they're who are choosing who gets into medical school and what the curriculum is, and they keep repeating it. I think there has to be a big shift."

She would also like to see reforms in insurance coverage and in the Food and Drug Administration: "Alternatives are really the lowest-cost item among the different healing modalities. Some insurance companies, such as Oxford, are covering more of the alternatives. I found that what drives up the price of alternatives is when the doctors have to start hiring lawyers to defend themselves against government prosecution. To me, this is the greatest travesty going on in the health care field today. They're trying to take away our freedom of choice, and they're persecuting doctors who offer choices. It reminds me of the old attitude of a hundred years ago when women didn't have the right to vote and they were very paternalistic toward us. Men would say, 'Oh, we really have to protect you for your own good so that you don't make decisions that are harmful. There are people trying to take advantage of you.' It's still like a parent-child relationship. It's very disempowering and it keeps us victims." Clearly, Charlotte Louise is providing an important contribution to the movement for alternatives that offer empowerment.

References

D'Adamo, Peter
  1997 *Eat Right 4 Your Type*. New York: Putnam's Sons.
Jensen, Bernard, and Sylvia Bell
  1981 *Tissue Cleansing Through Bowel Management*. Escondido, Calif.: Author. (Rte. 1, Box 52, Escondido, Calif. 92025).
Kelley, William Donald
  1969 *One Answer to Cancer: An Ecological Approach to the Successful Treatment of Malignancy*. Grapevine, Texas: Kelley Research Foundation.
LeShan, Lawrence
  1994 *Cancer as a Turning Point*. New York: Plume.
Myss, Carolyn
  1996 *Anatomy of the Spirit*. New York: Harmony Books.
Simonton, O. Carl, Stephanie Matthews-Simonton, and James L. Creighton
  1978 *Getting Well Again: A Step-by-Step Guide to Overcoming Cancer for Patients and Their Families*. New York: Bantam Books.

seventeen ———————————— Matilda Moore

A Chemist on Grapes, Nutrition and the Bible

Matilda Moore, M.Ed., is a chemistry teacher, recipient of a
National Science Foundation award, and an Ed.D. candidate.

Her Story

When chemistry teacher Matilda Moore went for a gynecological examination in April 1991, she wasn't surprised with the results. "I was an incredibly busy person and neglected the testing that should have been done. The next thing I knew, it was fifteen years before I'd had a pap test. I had been having a little trouble, a kind of burning sensation in my lower abdomen."

Moore's gynecologist diagnosed her with cervical cancer. "He wasn't sure whether or not the cancer had metastasized because the cervical canal was so inflamed. Unsure of its staging, he thought it was either stage II or III cervical cancer. He was noticeably more upset than I and called in his nurse to show her. I don't know; maybe he'd never had to give someone that diagnosis before.

"I asked him the typical questions, 'What are you telling me? Is the prognosis so bad that I need to go home and write out my will? Can you take care of it in the office?' He seemed to think it was bad, and wasn't very encouraging about the chances of a good recovery.

"I had done enough of my own research to know what my choices were among the conventional therapies. I knew my gynecologist was going to talk about surgery, and if I didn't need chemotherapy, probably at least some radiation. When I asked him, 'What kind of treatment are we looking at?' he responded, 'I don't know; it depends on whether or not it's invasive, and I can't tell how extensive it is because of the inflammation of your cervical area.'"

Moore's gynecologist wanted to schedule a conization. "I said, 'Fine, you can do the conization in thirty days, but I am going to pursue other options.' It wasn't that I didn't believe what he was saying, but I wanted to go home and try alternative therapies. He didn't understand my reasoning and became offended by my choice of options. He said, 'Okay, I will give you the name of someone else for a second opinion.'

"I said, 'No, I am fine with your care, but I want to go home and try nutritional therapies. I'll be back in a month.'

"He said, 'You shouldn't wait.'

"And I said, 'Well, that is fine. That is your opinion. I'm going to do this.'

"It wasn't a big leap for me when my gynecologist said, 'You've got this, and we've got to operate.' It really wasn't a quantum leap, so to speak, for me to say, 'No, I am going to do some alternative things.' He wasn't too happy with my choices. I outlined to him what I was planning to do, and he said, 'It won't work.' And I said, 'Well, we will see.'

"I guess the strangest thing to me, when the doctor gave me the diagnosis, was this mental or psychological feeling of having absolutely no control over something. As I look back on it, one of the strongest things that alternative therapies offered me was the feeling that I was still involved in the process. It wasn't something that was happening *to* me; I could still make some choices. I wasn't just some nonentity out here; I was intelligent enough to read and figure things out as much as anybody else.

"So I went home and spoke with my husband. He was wonderful throughout my experience. When I got home that afternoon, after being diagnosed, he asked me, 'Well, what do you want to do? I will support whatever your choice may be.'

"I had a lot of pressure from other family members and friends who thought I was going to just sit there and die. That was not my intention at all. I just wasn't willing to turn that decision over to someone who I thought wasn't as capable at making it as I was. That is pretty much what I think of the medical profession when they make decisions without the patient's being involved in the decision-making process. I think they are getting better, but for a long time decisions were made by medical professionals about you and not with you.

"In particular, my parents weren't happy with my decision to use alternative therapies. My mother had breast cancer in the mid-1970s and chose allopathic therapies. She had a radical mastectomy, and the cancer reappeared in nine months. They performed surgery again, this time an axillary node dissection followed by massive amounts of chemotherapy and radiation. My mother is still alive, but her health has never been good since the conventional treatments. I am convinced her diminished lung capacity is caused by the radiation. Three years ago, my father died of prostate cancer. He also chose allopathic therapies, but not the most radical treatment. Instead, he simply had the radiation treatment and not surgery. He lived for twelve or thirteen years after his diagnosis. As you can see, cancer is genetically close to me."

Twenty years ago, Moore began studying dietary laws from the Old Testament, and that experience sparked her interest in nutritional therapy. "I studied the rituals and the laws that God had given the Hebrew people on cleansing and activities to prevent disease. I started comparing these rituals and laws to those within different religious sects that have much lower cancer rates. I concluded from my research that lifestyle and nutrition are very important parts of your well-being.

"At that time, twenty-some years ago, you never heard of any allopathic practitioners talking about nutrition. The focus of medical science was only on a small part of this enormous body of knowledge. The things that we may or may not understand also influence what happens in the physical body.

"When I started studying nutrition and other therapies, it seemed to me that you could blend the two. You could put scientific knowledge and ancient practices together and come up with a science that was also an art of healing, of having health. It is a mental state or lifestyle for me; it isn't something that you could just segregate from everything else; it's a state of being."

Moore continued to educate herself on alternative therapies by reading and attending seminars and workshops. "I had previously read Johanna Brandt's book, *The Grape Cure*. Evidently, Brandt had been diagnosed with cancer and used the grape diet outlined in her book. Supposedly, she followed the diet, and afterward the cancer was reportedly gone. I went to several health bookstores and finally tracked down the book, reread it, and did a lot of praying."

Although pressured to choose conventional therapies, Moore chose to begin her grape fast and kept a log of her experiences. "I ate nothing but grapes and drank distilled water for twenty-three days. After the first eighteen hours, I had this awful headache, which was a sign to me that I had a lot of toxins in my system. The headache is known in naturopathic circles as a detoxification headache. I had had the experience before when I was a chemist working with nitroglycerin. It is the same type of headache—one in which your whole body hurts.

"The headache lasted into the second, maybe the third day, and then I was fine. I actually worked throughout the 'fast.' At the time, I was teaching science to eighth-graders." Moore had also just completed her master's degree and was a department chair and team leader at the middle school. "I was busy but still had the energy to continue with my obligations. I didn't try any other therapies during this period; I wanted to focus exclusively on the grape fast.

"At the end of the twenty-third day, I started to feel hungry for something else. To me, the hunger indicated that my body was in need of additional nutrients. I went off the grape fast and starting eating more fruits and vegetables.

"I had been a vegetarian since the early seventies, because I had become convinced that animal products, especially meats, weren't to be eaten. They were full of parasites and weren't to be put in my body. I ate mostly raw fruits and vegetables, but when I came off of my fast, everything I ate was raw."

Moore had made up her mind that when she completed her fast she would look into conventional therapies. In May 1991, after a month on her fast, she called her doctor's office and scheduled an appointment. "I told him what I had done, and he said, 'Well, evidently you just had to do it. It's not going to make any difference.' However, when I went back for the examination, my gynecologist found that the cancer had been localized. I kind of laughed at him, saying, 'I guess it doesn't work?'

"His reaction to my progress after the grape fast was rather funny. He was flabbergasted because he had already said, 'That stuff doesn't amount to anything.' Interestingly enough, he is my age, and I know how much nutrition he has learned from medical school. My stepson is also a physician, and I have looked at his nutrition book. It is put out by a pharmaceutical company. I wonder what their agenda is . . . let's be serious here.

"My gynecologist and I proceeded to talk about my different options, and eventually I went ahead and had a conization to confirm the cancer was localized." Moore also had a partial hysterectomy. "I was in my early forties and I wasn't planning on having any more children. It wasn't a major thing to me, not as major as if I had been twenty. The partial hysterectomy was scheduled for the second or third week in June, and my gynecologist performed the surgery. After the surgery, I continued to remain on my diet of raw fruits and vegetables."

In terms of other alternative therapies, Moore did some juicing and periodically fasted. "My lifestyle habits have always been within this realm. It wasn't like the people who go on the Gerson therapy, who have to undergo an enormous lifestyle change. It has been a gradual change for me over the past twenty-five years.

"And, of course, I was much more spiritually focused during this time. I am from a very conservative lifestyle and type of religious understanding. I haven't been able to do any type of meditation or anything in the spiritual realm that focuses on something other than God. Many 'New Age' or mystical forms of meditation seem to uplift the self, and they are just not for me. When I speak of spiritually pulling things together, I am speaking of pulling it together through a deep communion with the Father. I went through an awakening of a deeper awareness of how things relate to one another and what the bottom line really means to me."

Moore has become more and more convinced that internal cleansing is critical. "In the book *Fit for Life,* Harvey Diamond talks about 'Natural Hygiene,' and I have finally put it together that it must be a holistic cleansing. It is spiritual, physical, mental, and emotional cleansing. I pulled together the spiritual, physical, and emotional. It is almost like moving into another phase of awareness. Life is not two-dimensional; you don't go live on a rock somewhere."

Moore continued to have problems and chronic lower abdominal pain. "I didn't have my ovaries taken out when I had the partial hysterectomy, but they did shut down and I was put on hormones." She went back to her gynecologist after a year and told him of her continuing problems. "He did a laparoscopy and found out that it was endometriosis. It's really interesting, if you think about it, because the body tries to rejuvenate itself. What I understand about endometriosis is that it is uterine cells, and the hormones that the ovaries are producing contribute to the growth of these cells."

In the summer of 1993, Moore went through another surgical procedure to remove the endometrial cells along with her ovaries. "The only thing I remember about the surgery was that it was scheduled for a Wednesday, and I went home on a Friday. I was sore but felt great and very strong. In a week I was back at work. When I look back on it now, I have had symptoms of the endometriosis since my teenage years. I don't pay attention to things that are inconvenient unless I am thrown flat on my back. I mean, if they get in the way because it hurts so bad, then I do something about it."

Moore continually examined and educated herself on various therapies through literature and attending seminars and conventions. "I didn't know as much when I was first diagnosed, but the seminars and conventions are more accessible now. More people are becoming interested in alternative therapies. Even medical doctors are joining hands with alternative people.

"I haven't read Bernie Siegel's books, but I bought one, *Love, Medicine, and Miracles,* and sent it to my stepson. Siegel has written several books on the power of love. My stepson is a medical doctor and totally ignores anything that he thinks isn't physical or scientifically provable. He wasn't raised that way; his father is very spiritually oriented, so maybe it was his way of turning his back on it. I have read Dean Ornish's books on diet and heart disease. Ornish's colleagues thought he was a heretic when he said that with diet you can reverse heart disease. I believed it twenty-five years ago, but I am sure Ornish had an uphill battle."

Moore also found Andrew Weil's book, *Spontaneous Healing: How To Discover and Enhance Your Body's Natural Ability to Maintain and Heal Itself,* very much in line with her understanding and beliefs on conventional and alternative therapies. "It really excites me that we might be able to turn some medical doctors out who would be comfortable having some other arrows in their quivers. I find it a shame that we can't marry the strengths of the two and come up with something better. In fact, I don't call it alternative any more. I prefer to think of it as complementary, because the two understandings of health and healing work hand in hand.

"I don't know if my choices among the complementary therapies were conscious decisions. I just don't think that I said, 'I have everything laid out and I choose this one.' Overall, I think the time that I spent studying and learning about nutritional aspects of health helped put me in the position where a pathway developed for me. It wasn't totally passive and/or totally active; it was intuitive. Pasteur described similar circumstances when he stated, 'Chance favors the prepared mind.'

"I believe the complementary therapies made my gynecologist uncomfortable enough to think about them. It's wonderful if they did that. I hope my insistence to try a naturopathic approach made him so uncomfortable that he isn't able to forget about complementary therapy easily. I do think in some measure he was receptive to them because he plays classical music in the operating room while he operates. He does that because he believes that it is more healing to patients, even though they are totally out. When he performed my surgery and asked if I had any other questions before the surgery I replied, 'Yes. Would you please play Vivaldi for me?' And, just as the anesthesia was kicking in, I heard him put Vivaldi's 'Four Seasons' in the CD.

"I tell people all the time that the whole situation, the cancer diagnosis, is one of the best things that has happened to me. It was a blessing; it really was. And I am thankful for that attitude; it's not something that I talked myself into having. It is just in my heart and gut to be that way. I am thankful because I see the difference in my whole perspective that has resulted—the thankfulness that such an experience creates within you, that it *can* create in you. Things don't bother me as much as they did in the past. I mean, what is going to happen?"

Advice to Other Women

"I have had a few people call me for advice. They are individuals who know that I am willing to help anyone, but it is a time when the patient must be the one to initiate things. Being diagnosed with cancer was an anxiety-ridden experience for me in the beginning. When people tell me they are diagnosed with cancer and ask for advice on how to handle the diagnosis, I tell them the only battle I had was the mental one—that was *the only* battle.

"We are conditioned by everything outside of us to think that cancer is an insurmountable obstacle that has been put in our paths; i.e., this 'thing' is going to get you. What I began to see is that cancer can become your god. Because the cancer is all that you think about, it controls your life. Well, what is that? If you think about something all the time, and it controls your life, then what is it to you? It is a god. And then I realized, 'Oh, this is terrible.'

"I would never tell somebody else which therapy to choose. I wouldn't even say not to do conventional therapy. For me, it was not right, especially radiation and chemotherapy. I honestly believe you are doing more damage to your body because you are putting poisons into your system. They may kill the cancer, but if you destroy the body, what difference does it make that the cancer was killed?

"I would advise individuals to listen to their inner beings and find the answers from within when choosing between alternative or conventional therapies. I would tell them, 'You need to do what you are convinced that you have to do, what is right for you.' But be convinced of it. If you can, back off and relax. Let the Truth lead you, even though that is so difficult to do when your own mind is bombarding you with all the traditional beliefs about cancer. Your thoughts are your own worst enemy. If you can, be quiet long enough to actually hear the Truth that is within you. It's tough, but that is where the spiritual part comes into play. You just have to get into that quiet, silent place and hear from God."

Moore also believes communication skills are a necessary part of the process. "By communications I mean not so much talking as listening. Regardless of the realm on which you speak, anyone will tell you that we don't know how to listen anymore. That is the biggest problem in communication. We need to be better listeners, especially on a spiritual realm. We are so busy. Who has time to sit down and listen and hear? I am convinced that if we are able to do that, to listen and to hear, we will know the Truth. I don't think it is necessarily hidden from us or that we have to peel away the layers to see it.

"I would also advise individuals to access whatever resources they can find that will help them. Use whatever you can get your hands on, however you can get it. I even got information from the American Heart

Association because it is all part of doing your research. Nobody has the whole answer. Holistic or complementary people don't have the whole answer. But you can get pieces of it, and the more pieces that you can put together, the more of the whole you will get. You need to educate yourself and be more open. For various reasons many people can't accept learning more on their own; some are too scared to think differently than the doctor. If that is all you can do, do it."

At the time of the interview, Moore was writing her doctoral dissertation in educational administration. In the process she has acquired an extensive background on educational curriculum and instruction. "Back in the early 1980s, I completed a correspondence course in naturopathic medicine. That was probably the basis on which I built my own mental library about complementary medicines. My desire is to be able to merge my educational curriculum and nutritional background together and to be of some service to others. I believe the key to any new pathway in life is education.

"We've got to understand that things *need* to be different before we are going to be any different. We need to use those kinds of techniques to actually teach people how to live. Maybe God will open the door to allow me to work with people, like Andrew Weil is doing, in a way that I could use my expertise to serve."

Opinions on Cancer Research and Publicly Supported Cancer Organizations

Moore believes changes will occur with cancer research. "The reason I think this is because so many people are aware of it now. The nutritional supplement industry has gotten big. That is the only reason, though, because now we are talking money. The industry is so big that the conventional industries now want a piece of it. If you have a treatment accepted, the FDA moves in, more than they have already. Insurance companies are going to try to get complementary, holistic therapies under their control. It has gotten to be too big a business. If you go back to the early 1900s, when the split happened between allopathic and naturopathic medicine, the Carnegie Foundation was behind that. Why were they behind it? Economics. We are talking big bucks, zeros behind numbers that I don't even understand.

"In the summer of 1991, I was at Hope College in Michigan; I had received a National Science Foundation Fellowship for the summer to study advanced chemistry teaching. One afternoon a chemistry teacher from another part of the country and I were in the lab talking about cancer and cancer research. It turned out that he has a friend who is a biochemist doing cancer research. He shared with me what his friend told him — that at that time we could cure cancer, but there is no money in curing it. This information didn't surprise me because I had suspected it, but it did put things in a different perspective.

"If you stop and think about it, it is a shame, but the bottom line is the economy. If you want to look at the big money makers, just look around you. Who has the big buildings? Who makes all the money? You have the insurance companies, pharmaceutical companies, doctors, hospitals, lawyers, and funeral homes. All these types of people and institutions make money off the calamities of people. Big fortunes are not made from people who are healthy.

"I believe, especially here in the United States, that we are barely chipping away at the surface because we are also in bondage, not just in spiritual or religious things but in everything that we do. We are so inhibited, so bound up, not just with what we don't know but with what we don't feel comfortable exploring."

Moore has not consciously accessed publicly supported cancer organizations. "I have never accessed them directly, but sometimes I have picked up material from them at the bookstore or health food store. I have occasionally gone to some of their sponsored meetings. I have also attended the conventions sponsored by the Cancer Control Society.

"My dad told me something interesting after he was diagnosed and treated for prostate cancer. He called the American Cancer Society and volunteered his time to talk to people who had been diagnosed, anything that he could do. He contacted the ACS several times and asked to help, but they never called him back. I thought it was really sad because that is a time when people need each other, and it might help to know that there is somebody else who has been there. Maybe that person will say one little thing that I can hook onto that might be my lifeline."

References

Brandt, Johanna
  1995 *The Grape Cure*. Hastings, N.Y.: Society of Metaphysicians.
Diamond, Harvey
  1986 *Fit for Life*. New York: Angus and Robertson in association with Warner
    Books.
Ornish, Dean
  1984 *Stress, Diet, and Your Heart*. New York: Holt, Rinehart, and Winston.
Siegel, Bernie
  1986 *Love, Medicine, and Miracles*. New York: Harper and Row.
Weil, Andrew
  1996 *Spontaneous Healing: How to Discover and Enhance Your Body's Natural
    Ability to Maintain and Heal Itself*. New York: Fawcett Columbine.

eighteen

The Marathon Olympic Tumor Eradication and Prevention Program

Susan Moss is the author of *Keep Your Breasts! Preventing Breast Cancer the Natural Way* (1994). In its fifth printing, it is available at independents and all chain stores as well as health food stores, and it can be ordered from Re:Source Publications, 4767 York Blvd., Los Angeles, CA 90042. She also has a video available at 800-231-1776. Moss has spoken in numerous public forums, including the First World Conference on Breast Cancer in Kingston, Ontario, in July 1997.

Her Story

At the University of Nevada Susan Moss majored in art and psychology, and she helped to establish a suicide prevention center with Dr. James B. Nichols. She considered a career as a psychologist, but her artistic side won and she became a painter. However, her background in psychology, as well as her father's long-term interest in holistic health, was important to her when she began her process of healing.

Moss began her battle against lumps and tumors when she experienced a lump in the lymph nodes of her neck. Other symptoms included shortness of breath, loss of appetite, and extreme fatigue. Her doctor advised her to give up acrylic paints because of the fumes, and she followed his advice. "My dad bought me a juicer and I did the carrot juice, and I rubbed lemon on my neck and ran a lot on the beach. I also discovered visualization."

Moss's undergraduate background in psychology was helpful to her practice of visualization, which she modified into a more powerful form: "There was a newspaper article about Dr. O. Carl Simonton that described his method of working with cancer patients using visualization. They would visualize aggressive attacks on the cancer cells using sharks or some other metaphor for the white blood cells. I would turn on the radio, get some loud rock music going, and visualize little men in white coats going down into my neck with a rope and then tying the rope around my lump. I would pull it out of my neck and through my mouth to the beat of the music. I did this twice a day—this very aggressive, energetic visualization. I found that if you combine exercise with visualization, or if you combine chanting or meditation or prayer with visualization, then you have a very powerful tool that you would not have with visualization alone. In other words, if you expend energy while you're doing visualization, if you put your energy behind visualization as well as your force of mind, then you have a very powerful tool. I think this is something I discovered that I can pass on to others: when you do the visualizations, you don't do them passively. I don't believe meditation is quite as good as chanting, because when you're chanting you're expending some vocal energy and you're using a spiritual approach."

Her doctors gave her a year to get rid of the lump. "They said, 'If you don't get rid of this lump in a year, we're going to operate and take it out.' So I did get rid of it in one year." That appeared to be the end of the story. However, eleven years later Moss's doctor discovered a lump in her breast and a tumor in her uterus. Moss had her first mammogram, which was very painful. The result was negative, but her doctor insisted that she see a surgeon. She refused surgery and she also refused a needle biopsy because she was concerned that the needle would puncture the protein sheath around the tumor and cause cancer cells to spread. As she wrote in her book *Keep Your Breasts! Preventing Breast Cancer the Natural Way*,

Lumps, bumps, and tumors which the body grows are symptoms of illness and/or the degeneration of the body. Cutting these symptoms off won't always work. The cause of the problem is not being attacked. My problem involved more than just a lump in my breast and a tumor in my uterus that could be surgically removed. Surgery would not magically change the conditions of my life. Whatever problems I had in my life—my diet, my environment, my emotional and business life—would still exist after surgery. (1994: 15)

Although she did not accept further medical intervention, Moss agreed to return to the doctor after two months for an additional exam. During this time she developed MOTEP (Marathon Olympic Tumor Eradication and Prevention Program), which she has described in detail in her book.

How did she have the courage to challenge medical authority and take the risks that she did? "I've never believed in authority figures. I think most artists are like this. We question authority. I do go to the doctor, and I am supportive of going to the doctor. I'm not antimedical at all. But I believe in questioning what they recommend that we do. I think they're very good at diagnosing. But a doctor is only a helping person. He can't cure you or make you well. Your body has to do it. For instance, if you broke a bone, they can put a cast on it and that would help, because your leg wouldn't move and the bone would reset itself, but your body has to do the healing. So doctors to me are not authority figures; they're partners to work with. I always listen to my doctor, but I always weigh what he says and the second opinion is always my opinion."

How did Moss put together her program? To begin, she drew on her previous experience with a lump. "I did evaluate my past experience, and I also checked out a lot of books from the library on alternative medicine. I got books by authors like Michio Kushi on how the macrobiotic diet helped patients with cancer heal themselves. Another book was about visualization; another was about psychological problems. So I decided I needed a whole program that encompassed everything. Certainly nutrition can help. You can get well, for instance, just doing the carrot juice. I've heard of people getting well from cancer just doing that. Beta carotene is a powerful force in healing the cells."

Moss's program is therefore much more general than a modified diet with carrot juice. MOTEP has twenty basic steps that include dietary changes, psychospiritual interventions, a daily exercise routine, ways of de-stressing the body, nutritional supplements, saunas, and elimination of toxicities from the diet and environment. She went on a semivegetarian diet that was low in fat and had some fish, no meat, no dairy, and few eggs, plus fresh-juiced carrots and oranges every day. The diet was high in foods that contain amygdalin, one of the active ingredients in laetrile. (A list of those foods appears in the appendix to her book.) The psychological interventions included visualization, positive thinking, laughing, group therapy, having a strong will to survive, having a strong belief in the program, ending an unhealthy relationship, and building good relationships.

Moss used a number of supplements: "I used flaxseed oil, and I also used vitamin C and the B vitamins and vitamin E. I take calcium and now I've added echinacea and horsetail. I never tried shark cartilage, but I did eat shark. I grow aloe vera in my yard, and when I come home at night I rub it on my face because it takes away a lot of the day's weariness. I did use flaxseed oil on my breast and also a half cut lemon topically. I had a diet with mostly vegetables and fruits and juices and whole grains (such as barley and brown rice), some fish and nuts, and then I underate for a month, because that gives your body a chance to throw out the garbage."

Regarding the coffee enemas made famous in the Gerson program, Moss commented, "Well, my parents like to do enemas. My dad is in his eighties and my mom is in her seventies, and they're healthy. It's just a personal decision. I didn't do any enemas because I believe if you eat what I call a detoxification diet, your body throws out the garbage. My body does clean itself out better now. I don't keep waste products in. My body is really clean now. In fact, I got rid of all my cellulite and I got rid of all kinds of allergies. When I say 'clean,' I'm not talking about showers that we all take in America. Americans don't think much about detoxifying their body and cleaning it. When you eat whole grains like brown rice and barley and lots of vegetables and fruits, they scrub your insides clean. When you're eating foods loaded with fat and with no fiber—ice cream, sour cream, hamburger, white flour, white sugar, baked goodies, whatever—this is food that's not going to nourish your body. It's going to block the arteries and stifle the cells. If you overeat meat and dairy products, you have a real problem in clogging your body up. That's why it's good once a week to go on a detoxification diet where you do mostly juices, maybe some fruits and vegetables, and let your body clean out."

Moss emphasizes that nutrition was not the only aspect of her program. "Chanting and meditation work so well because they calm you down, and your body starts to repair itself." Chanting was therefore important to overcome stress. "When you're under stress, your body manufactures certain hormones, like adrenal steroids or corticosteroids, which are used for fight or flight. If you're under long-term stress, you're shutting your immune system down, because you're manufacturing these hormones which endanger your immune system. That's why you need to do detoxification. Also, if you have too much fat in the body—even an extra five pounds—it's a hardship on the body. If your body is clean, your immune system can work more efficiently and get to those cancer cells. One researcher says we have over eleven hundred cancer cells in the body every single day. As long as the immune system is functioning properly, you're not under stress, and you're not overweight, then your immune system will fight and destroy those cells."

As her self-therapy progressed, Moss encountered a period when her breast became inflamed, hot, and very hard. She could not even raise her left arm, a condition which she believed meant that the cancer was being cleaned out by her axillary lymph nodes (the ones in the armpit). Moss states that she was suffering from inflammatory carcinoma, a rare but deadly category of breast cancer that is diagnosed from the symptoms alone. She later found out that Max Gerson, M.D., had an interpretation of this type of "flare-up." He viewed it as part of the healing process. Moss also mentions that the famous bacterial vaccine of William Coley, M.D., produced a fever that contributed to the effectiveness of Coley's toxins against some types of cancers. "Fever is the real healing technique that the body uses—healing and inflammation. Western medicine often tries to suppress that. We give antiinflammatories and something to get the fever down, but this is not always the best idea, because it's the body's way of healing itself."

Five days before her two-month appointment with her doctor, the uterine and breast lumps disappeared. Moss believes that giving herself a deadline was an important part of the psychology of the healing process. "I think the body does work with a deadline. I tell women if you miss that deadline, then set another one, because your body will listen. My body is very obedient! I said, 'You've got to get rid of these tumors in two months, Body, and that's it. Otherwise, you're going to lose everything: you're going to lose your breast, your uterus (you're going to have a hysterectomy), and you're going to lose your studio and your house because you don't have health insurance.'"

At a checkup a year later, Moss learned that she remained tumor free. "It only took me two months to heal myself, but it took seven more months to get well. That's what people don't understand. They don't comprehend that when you get rid of the tumors—whether you take them out surgically or you get rid of them yourself, which is a new concept— that you aren't well yet. Tumors are only a small part of the disease. Your whole body is degenerating. So I spent the next seven months building my body back up. I did that through weight-lifting, swimming, getting rid of stress, changing my life, better relationships with people, diet, vita- mins, and self-healing." When we spoke with her in early 1998, she remained in good health. As she commented, "I have been tumor and cancer free for seven years."

Advice to Other Women

Moss has become a public figure, a leader in the patients' movement to develop better, nontoxic therapies for breast cancer. She has appeared on national television and radio, and she has spoken to many women with cancer. Her message is a simple one—help the body to heal itself—and she is a living example of her message. It is interesting that although she lives in southern California, she did not go to Tijuana for treatment in one of the alternative clinics there. "I believe that the body heals itself. You don't have to go anywhere or spend any money to do it. The body heals itself for free. It's the gift that we have from nature. The body does- n't charge. The body will do the best job that you can get anywhere in the world. All you have to do is detoxify and de-stress the body, and be patient and watch what happens. You don't have to spend a nickel. In fact, you can save a lot of money by going on my program. You'll stop buying so much meat and dairy products."

Although diet is a very important aspect of her MOTEP program, Moss warns against therapeutic approaches that are focused only on diet, supplements, herbs, and metabolic approaches. "It's not only what you put in your mouth; it's what you put in your head that is important. If you restrict your program to just what you put in your mouth, it's proba- bly not going to be as effective as looking at your whole life. The idea of taking the tumor out surgically is what I call a Santa Claus belief. When I was four I learned that there was no Santa Claus. When I was in my for- ties, I learned that taking the tumor out didn't stop the cancer. In my friend Kimberly's case, the cancer returned in the chest wall where her breast used to be. So this is what I call waking up and discovering that cancer is a systemic disease, that cancer is not the tumor. The tumor is only one small symptom of a disease that affects every part of you and that is affected by every part of you—spiritually, mentally, physically, with the diet, the exercise, the visualization, and your relationships."

She notes that cancer and depression are often linked. "There's a very strong link between the immune system and depression. When I talk to a lot of women now who are fighting the disease, all of them speak of being depressed for a number of years before they found out they had cancer."

Moss also thinks it is important to clean up one's personal relationships. "The cells are only a reflection of us. We are only a reflection of our cells. If you have destructive relations with others, that's going to be reflected in your cells. We know that the cancer cells relate very destructively and parasitically with respect to the normal cells, using and abusing the normal cells."

Moss therefore emphasizes the importance of taking a self-inventory and a close look at one's entire life. "Lawrence LeShan [1994] looks at that a lot. He believes that cancer patients are not 'singing their song'; they weren't doing what they really wanted to do. They had a life of self-sacrifice to others, and this bred a lot of resentment. Negative feelings are very hard on the immune system. Jealousy, resentment, anger, and other kinds of negative emotions that you hold within your body eat away at you. So it's not just what you're eating; it's what's eating you. Often when these patients change their lives and start doing what they want to do, or at least spend some hours doing what they want to do (such as playing the violin), they get well."

As an artist who also studied psychology, Moss believes that art and science need to come together in the healing process. "I don't believe one precludes the other. Being an artist and being a scientist are very similar in some ways. They both try to look at the facts and come up with a creative solution. I think we separate science and art, and I don't believe they should be separated. The art of healing has as much to do with a creative art as it has to do with the science and technology that we've set up. Doctors don't know that much about the human body. It's still a mystery as to how people get cancer and heal themselves. I attempted to take some of that mystery out by showing people what the disease really is and how they can go about preventing it, and if they get it, God forbid, how they can go about getting well and live through it. Then, if they live through it, I show how they can prevent getting it again (recurrence). Even the people who have used conventional medical therapies have told me that my book has been a tremendous help in getting them through this. Not only do they change their diet, but they start looking at their lives—doing what they want to do with their lives, not feeding themselves negative thoughts all day."

References

Kushi, Michio
    1981 *The Macrobiotic Approach to Cancer*. Garden City, N.J.: Avery.
LeShan, Lawrence
    1994 *Cancer as a Turning Point*. New York: Plume.
Moss, Susan
    1994 *Keep Your Breasts! Preventing Breast Cancer the Natural Way*. Los Angeles: Re:Source Publications.
Simonton, O. Carl, Stephanie Matthews-Simonton, and James L. Creighton
    1978 *Getting Well Again*. New York: Bantam Books.

Going To Mexico to Regain Medical Choice

Pat Prince is a long-term American Biologics, S.A., patient and a cancer support group person. She has become a patient representative for American Biologics, and her E-mail address is <pat@mexia.com>.

Her Story

On April 1, 1977, Pat Prince was diagnosed with breast cancer. "My doctor told me that it was an encapsulated cancer, an early stage. I also had bleeding of the colon, and he could feel a mass in my abdomen about the size of an orange, but I was only diagnosed with the breast cancer."

Prince had received prior radiotherapy in the early 1960s for a rare spinal vascular condition. In her words, "My blood vessels were enlarged like varicose veins inside my spine and were pressing against my nerves and I was losing use of my arms and legs." She was given radiation therapy, and her spine up to her brain stem received the lifetime limit of radiation. "The first year after that, I was in the hospital five or six times for three or four weeks at a time. I was in the hospital more than I was out, just for dehydration from the radiation. Also, it burned me so badly that I could hardly move. At the time, they couldn't pinpoint radiation like they can today. It was a five-inch strip down my back. Of course, it hit every major organ in my body. It burned me to a crisp. I am still scarred with this big wide strip running down my back. In fact, in the summers when I start to get into the sun and get tanned, the strip comes up real dark down my back.

"The treatment weakened me so that I couldn't even turn a door knob. I was so weak that I could hardly feed myself. There were days that I couldn't feed myself right afterward. In the first year it was the dehydration, then it was the pain and other things. It stopped my pancreas from producing enzymes, and I had to start taking this powdered mixture of pig-pancreas enzymes. I had to take it any time I took a bite of food in order for it to be digested. It affected my lungs and intestines; it affected me wherever the radiation hit me. Then they told me it would be five years before they knew whether it would help me. It did. Within five years the pain had lifted, and it did shrink the blood vessels. But it was just agony to go through the radiation."

Because of her prior radiotherapy, Pat Prince was not a candidate for radiation treatment for her breast cancer. Although she was offered chemotherapy and surgery, she decided against both: "I had such horrible side effects of the radiation in 1963, and if chemotherapy is anything like that, I would rather die. Also, I am not brave enough to face life without my breasts.

"I didn't know of anyone who survived these conventional treatments for very long. Also, at that time my doctor didn't have anybody on alternatives or just wouldn't tell me about them. I felt as though I was going to die anyway. So since I was going to die anyway, why not try something that might help me? I knew the conventional therapies weren't going to help me. If I tried something that might have helped me, if I saw that it wasn't going to help me, then I would have time to come back to the United States and try something that would. I just couldn't lay my body down to be mutilated, burned up, and then die such a horrible death. I had seen my friends die this way, and I just wasn't strong enough to go through it."

Prince had a friend who opened up the door of alternative therapy for her. "I had a friend who went to Mexico for laetrile treatments in 1975 for breast cancer. She was doing fine, and in fact she is still doing fine. And when that happened to her, I said that if I ever got cancer, I was going to go to Tijuana. Otherwise, it probably never would have occurred to me, just like it doesn't occur to a lot of people today to do things other than what their doctors tell them. We have grown up in a society where whatever the doctors say to do, you just do it (although I have seen a shift happening over the past couple of years)."

Prince added that she still had some fears about going to Mexico for treatment. "I had no idea if I was doing the right thing. I wanted to come home. I didn't know what to do. I really wasn't going for what they had there; I was really running away from what they had here. That is the only way I can describe it. I was running away from what they had here. And I really didn't know what I was getting into there. So when I got there and saw the doctor, the hospital, and clinic, how modern and scientific everything was, and also that you were treated like a real person, I knew my prayers had been answered.

"I went straight to Mexico and didn't have any conventional treatments: no chemotherapy, no radiation or surgery. It was called laetrile therapy then because the media and law enforcement officials zeroed in on laetrile. Possession was a felony offense in those years."

Prince first went to the Contreras clinic, where Dr. Salvador Rubio was her doctor, and in 1984 she went to the American Biologics clinic to continue the same therapy. She "found out that it wasn't just laetrile therapy. That's only 10 percent of the total treatment. It was more a total therapy of balancing the mind, the body, and the spirit, as a trinity, the way we were created. And I was treated that way, too. I was very surprised with the personality of my doctor and the rapport we developed. I have heard the same thing said by others who have gone to the clinic. I just felt like his friend, you know, that I would talk and he would talk to me. I never felt this distance, this doctor/patient distance. He never set himself up to be better or smarter than me, and that was impressive to me. At that time it seems that with cancer patients even doctors would stand a little farther from you than they did before. And you really need that closeness. He told me from the very beginning that I wasn't coming there to die but was coming there to live. They didn't give lessons on death and dying; they gave lessons on living.

"I was put on a strict diet. It was a healthy diet, the same diet that God gave to his people in the Old Testament, practically word for word: natural foods, white fish, nuts, grains, seeds, fruits, and vegetables. He told me the easiest way to describe the food we are talking about is to avoid any foods that man has tampered with. The dietary regime included the juicing and coffee enemas from the Gerson diet. I met Charlotte Gerson; she is a very, very dear friend of mine now. In fact, they used to take us in vans to the Gerson clinic, where we would go to listen to Charlotte Gerson's lectures. We ended up including some of the Gerson diet in the diet that was worked up by our clinic. What is so ironic is that when the National Cancer Institute came out with the anticancer diet several years ago, you would think that they copied it word for word. It was the exact diet we were put on at the clinic. It was the same diet that God put the children of Israel on in the Old Testament.

"About half of my food is raw, then the next best is steamed, and cooked is next. I just try to make my diet of as many natural foods as possible. No prepared foods, no frozen foods, and very rarely will I eat beef. For the last couple years, I have barely eaten chicken or fish, mainly because I have lost the taste for them." Prince did try the macrobiotic diet during the 1980s, and she even went to school to learn about it. However, she did not feel that the diet was right for her body. "I have known a lot of people who have gotten wonderful cures on the macrobiotic diet. I am the last person to say that it doesn't work, because I know it does. Just like the Gerson diet works for some people, and the laetrile treatments for some. No one has a panacea."

At the Mexican clinic Prince also received many vitamins and minerals, including daily injections of vitamins A and C. She noted that some people also consider laetrile to be a vitamin, because laetrile is derived from amygdalin, which can be found in foods. Some people even call laetrile vitamin B-17.

"The alternative doctors and clinics that I have been to over the years—actually I would rather use the term *complementary* because *alternative* signifies something 'other than' or the opposite; I would even use the term *integrative*—they all draw from all over the world the things doctors are using as natural. So you may be getting different modalities from several different countries that have been found to work for your particular condition."

In addition to the therapeutic diet and substances, the program at American Biologics included biofeedback and visualization. "I visualized that I was a healthy person and that the cancer was getting smaller. I learned to relax my body so it could heal itself more physically. I also detoxified my body through fasting and coffee enemas. I still fast periodically with spirulina, and even the USDA has declared it the most nutritious food in the world. I take the spirulina and fast from two to three days every couple of months. I also do the coffee enemas to keep my liver detoxified."

Prince added that the spiritual dimension was important to her recovery. She distinguished between becoming a "spiritual" person and being "religious." She commented that before she understood the difference, "I wasn't on a one-to-one relationship, friend-to-friend relationship with God, which I believe with all my heart is necessary. It had a big effect on my recovery and keeps me that way."

She stayed at the clinic for three weeks, the standard length of the first visit. "I was feeling very ill; I was bleeding through my colon. The American doctor wanted to do an exploratory surgery of my colon, but I didn't want to have that done, either. I didn't want them to do a biopsy on me in Mexico, so I said, 'If there is cancer in the colon, what will you do?'

"They said, 'Pretty much the same as what we are doing.'

"I said, 'Well, forget it. I'll just take my chances.' It may sound off-the-wall, but it made sense to me that if you are going to build up your immune system and build up your body so that it will take care of itself, then why go with these aggressive things, if you already know you have cancer somewhere?"

After returning from Mexico, she stayed home for three weeks. She still did not feel well, principally because of her digestive problems. She then returned to the clinic for another three-week stay. "When you get home from something like that, you're just sort of on an island by yourself. Nobody understands what you're doing or why you're doing it. People think you are nuts for going to a different or foreign doctor. All those negative influences around you are hard on you when you are fighting for your life."

Upon returning, she stayed on the program. "When I returned in November 1977, my test results were negative. Everyone at the clinic was so relieved and overwhelmed by how well I was doing. Then Thanksgiving and Christmas came along, and I sort of did what a lot of people do. I just took my medicine until I was well and then went back to what I was doing before. Before I realized it, the first of the year, I was taking my vitamins once in a while, and I was eating and drinking like I did before. I got off of my biofeedback practice and other things. Around April 1978 I started to really feel bad. Then in May or June 1978, I started to get a lot of pain in my side. I went back to the clinic, and they did bone and liver scans on me. They found two spots on my ribs, on my right side, and also what they call 'hot spots' in my liver, which you could only determine if it was cancer by a biopsy, and I am against anything invasive to my body. I mean I had become very against it by then. I asked the doctor again, 'If it is cancer what will you do?'

"And he said, 'We will intensify everything and treat that particular thing.'

"So I said, 'Okay, let's do it, rather than invade my body.'

"What they did at that point was to put me right back on the total therapy that I was on from the very beginning, which included intravenous laetrile every day. I stayed in the clinic five weeks until my blood work and everything started to look better. By the fall of 1978, my scans were a lot better. They weren't cleared up, but they were a lot better, and I was not having any of the bone pain or anything after that. Now, what that was, I can't say because I wouldn't allow them to diagnose it. All I know is that it went away with the therapy.

"The doctor was very serious with me at that time. He told me, 'For a lot of people, once they are in remission, it's like breaking a limb off a tree. Once you strip it, treat it, and it heals, and the leaves come back, you just don't go back the next year and hang a child's swing off the end of that limb. That is the way your body is. If you do hang that swing, you will break it off completely. Most people who do this don't come back the second time, and you won't come back the third time.' He was mad at me, a little bit. You can't do it, you have to realize it is like a broken bone. If you go back to an environment that has created this, you are going to create it again. So since then I have been a good girl and have been fine.

"I worked really hard on the stress and got into a biofeedback program. I worked with a psychologist on my thought processes. And I really worked hard on my spirituality, where I put things more into God's hands. As for the physical part, I threw out of my kitchen those things that I couldn't have. I started to do everything naturally, and put the whole family on it. They all went into shock. It was a real experience to cook healthy foods and not have the kids know they were eating healthy foods. It was about six months later that I went back for a full checkup and then another six months for the next checkup. In the meantime, I kept taking everything that I was supposed to. You might say, I just started devoting my life to my life. It was about a year and a half before all my tests results were negative.

"I have never been back to a U.S. doctor since my initial diagnosis. I have just seen too many people who, when they go to the doctor, they get all these prescriptions and I don't see them getting well. They get over the symptoms that they all have and before long, they've got it again. I know very few people whose doctor tells them anything about nutrition, puts them on any vitamin or mineral program, or even just teaches them how to take care of their own body, physically, mentally, or spiritually. I just don't feel like taking that kind of chance with my life. I would rather just get on an airplane and go back to Mexico, if I don't feel exactly right. Now, if I had an emergency, I wouldn't have any choice. I'm not a doctor and I don't have a right to criticize a profession that I am not schooled in, but I am just talking about the way I feel inside myself. If it is right or wrong for someone else, it's not for me to judge, but for me if you really don't believe in what you are doing and you don't believe in your doctor, then you've got two strikes against you from the beginning.

"And I have just not been able to establish that belief given the things that happened to me with the radiation. In fact the specialist told my husband that I got an overdose; they didn't turn it off when they were supposed to. My doctor told me at that time, that with the amount of radiation I got at that time, I was more than likely to get cancer within fifteen years, if I lived that long. My husband never told me that until after it happened."

Prince has continued to add different elements to her program. For example, she has tried several of the herbal teas that may have anticancer properties.

As of early 1998, Prince was feeling fine and planning to travel throughout North America and the Virgin Islands, sharing her story of survival. She was working on two books, *Surviving: Being Alive* and *Ponderings*. She also "graduated" from her square-dancing class.

Advice to Other Women

Prince began this topic on a cautionary note: "I don't feel as though I am in a position to advise somebody, but I can tell them what I think I would do or what I feel is the main thing that everybody has to do. That is to look into an integrative program and find a doctor that will go along with you. Cancer Centers of America are wonderful, and they are in all the major cities. I would always choose integrative over the conventional therapy because for many, many years people have survived without the conventional therapy. Investigate what your doctors want to do with you and find out how it works. Then, investigate everything else and find a doctor who will work with you on it."

Of course, that advice implies taking control of one's illness. Prince emphasizes the importance of having an active attitude. "I think we have to take charge of our own lives. I know of people who will go to a natural clinic and they expect it to be like taking your car to a mechanic and saying, 'Fix it. I'm going somewhere in it tomorrow.' It doesn't work that way; you can't do it that way. You can't use that clinic, that doctor, or that particular treatment as a jump-start on a battery."

She also emphasized the importance of individualized treatment: "I think we need to seek and find what is best for us. I remember one doctor saying, 'There is no truth in medicine or science because what is true today won't be true tomorrow.' Our bodies are constantly changing with the environment and our age. Old things are being rediscovered that are good for the body. And I think we have to make those searches on our own. Through prayer and meditation, we can learn to pick and choose and find out what is best for our bodies. We just have to take our lives into our own hands. We just can't put it into someone else's hands other than the Lord's hands." (To be clear, Prince is not advocating home treatment, but an active role in the partnership with a caring, open-minded, competent doctor.)

Prince's focus on developing an individualized program has another benefit. It allows patients to have the hope that they can beat the odds. "I look at everything more on an individual basis, the way I feel and everything. I don't feel like any type of statistics have to do with me, because I am on my own. I feel as though if one person has ever made it, if one out of a thousand made it, I could be that one. And I don't like to put myself in any type of statistical measurement, because it's just not individual."

Prince also emphasized the importance of adopting a strategy of building up the body through healthy food and lifestyle. "With the people I know, the ones that eat, drink, and think cleanly, it is amazing how their bodies have responded to it." Part of that healthy lifestyle involves exercise. She thinks that in the past, such as when most of the country lived and worked on farms, people were able to eat diets that were high in fat because they exercised more. She added, "Having an active lifestyle helps to maintain a healthy you. What I do is walking and bicycling. I keep my own yard and garden and do a lot of exercise pertaining to maintaining it. I have always been pretty active. I am sixty-three years old and I climb trees with my grandchildren. And their mothers are too old. I run and play with my grandkids. I'll play ball—whatever someone is doing, I am in the middle of it."

Prince added that a spiritual or intuitive source of inner strength gave her the courage to think independently: "It is more intuitive. I think that if we are destined to find something, we will find it. There are people I know, that I have met, that have gone into this type of thinking and have said they were spiritually guided to do it. I do think it is an intuition inside of us to persevere. Not just lay your body down into somebody else's hands. Look into everything, then sit back and give your body some time to digest it and make your decision. Whatever you're doing, believe in it with all your heart and know that it's not a death sentence. It's just a big boulder in the road that we need to climb up over and keep going.

"I think we have grown up in a society in which through the media, our parents, friends, we learn to believe that what we need we get from an outside source. Actually, I believe everything that we need in our lives is from the inside. And if we get still enough, and absorb enough, our answers will come from the inside, emotionally, physically, and spiritually. And if someone gets quiet long enough, they know where they are. They will know where they are spiritually; no ministers will have to tell them. They will know where they are emotionally and physically. Most of us know what we need to do; we just don't do it. We tell other people what we need; we just don't do it."

She also recommends Leo Buscaglia's book *Living, Loving, and Learning*. "He is the only one who is talking about how to improve your life and how to have a better lifestyle. He's also the only one I read that gives you any permission to be angry, depressed, or in despair. He is the only one I read who says that those emotions are as much a part of life as love, joy, and peace. You aren't going to get into the love, joy, and peace mode and float off into utopia. That's never going to happen. He says it's okay to be depressed, to be in despair, that Olympic athletes have days when they don't want to get out of bed. That doesn't mean that your disease is worse. Just know that this is going to pass. The only thing that is wrong with that is if you get caught up in that and stay in that mode. And he gives an analogy in the book of a man hitting his thumb with a hammer. After hitting his thumb, no one thinks he is a baby for sucking his thumb because he just hit it with a hammer. He has a right to suck it. But if he is sucking it four days later, then there is a problem. So that's the way to look at it. If we have depression, we are depressed because we're depressed. Norman Vincent Peale made me feel guilty if I was not feeling good all the time, but Leo Buscaglia gives us permission to feel that way, and step over it, get over it, and keep going."

Opinions on Cancer Research and Publicly Supported Cancer Organizations

Prince thought that the value of most publicly supported cancer organizations was limited to getting information about conventional therapies. For information on alternative, complementary, or integrative therapies, she mentioned the National Health Federation, the Cancer Control Society, the International Council for Health Freedom, and the International Association of Cancer Victors and Friends. She also mentioned the numerous alternative medicine newsletters and magazines that are now available, and she suggested using the Internet. "It is amazing what is on the Internet for natural medicine. It is just amazing what you can learn, and they can put you in contact with other people and what they are doing. You get in one of those chat lines and say, 'I've got cancer and would like to do something natural, what have you done?' You will be surprised. I have a website on the Internet for American Biologics (<www.abmex.com>) and I get responses from all over the world every day. I play a very active role as a spokeswoman for American Biologics. I believe in it 100 percent."

Prince was also a victim of the regulatory politics during the days of the suppression of laetrile. We close with her anecdote: "In 1980 I was crossing the border with my laetrile and I was stopped by the U.S. Customs. I was arrested and charged with a felony. It was a horrible experience. It was about eight o'clock at night and they happened to open up my trunk and found the laetrile. They arrested me and made such a big deal, like I was a heroin or cocaine dealer. They called in two special agents from the U.S. Treasury Department and interrogated me for seven hours, until three o'clock in the morning. And believe me, the pictures on television about the little room with green shades and the people taking turns with the interrogation are true. They fingerprinted me, mugshot me, and asked me if I wanted to call an attorney. I didn't have an attorney; I didn't even know one. They let me go at 3:00 A.M. They confiscated my car and all my personal belongings. They gave me my driver's license, social security card, and a dime out of my purse to make a telephone call. They wouldn't let me use the phone in the U.S. Customs Office. I had to go out on the street and hunt down a pay phone at 3:00 A.M., to call someone to pick me up. Hopefully, that one dime would do it. I did call somebody and he picked me up. It was a boy from the laboratory and I just happened to know his phone number, because I didn't have a way to get a number of anybody. He came down, picked me up, and took me home.

"At my arraignment, the federal prosecutor told my attorney that he was recommending that I be held without bond. I had never been in a courtroom, let alone a federal courtroom, and didn't know what was going on. My attorney went white, and I asked him what it meant. He said, 'It means you aren't leaving this courtroom.' The judge eventually let me go on my own recognizance and set the trial for a month later. During that time I couldn't leave the state of California. In the meantime, my attorney plea-bargained with the prosecutor and I pleaded guilty to a misdemeanor. I got three and a half years of supervised probation. It wasn't pleasant.

"I went back and forth to the clinic. What was strange was that my probation officer was a U.S. Customs agent who had an office at the border. During that three-and-a-half year period, I couldn't cross the border, either way, without his permission. I didn't try to bring any more laetrile back. I accessed it through other means because it was saving my life. I told him, 'You'll never stop us' and 'I didn't do anything wrong.'

"He said, 'You broke the law.'

"And I responded, 'Yes, I may have broken the law, but I didn't do anything wrong. What I am doing is not a threat to human life; it doesn't constitute a crime.'

"Laetrile is now legal in many states, but the Food and Drug Administration has continued to close down the offices of supplement companies and alternative health care practitioners."

References

Buscaglia, Leo
  1995 *Living, Loving, and Learning.* New York: Simon and Schuster.
Peale, Norman Vincent
  1996 *The Power of Positive Thinking.* New York: Fawcett.

twenty

A Journey from the Personal to the Political

Virginia Soffa, M.Ed., is an educator and writer. She is the author of *The Journey beyond Breast Cancer: From the Personal to the Political* (Rochester, Vt.: Healing Arts Press, 1994), of chapters in *Misdiagnosis: Woman as Disease* (Hicks 1994) and in *Confronting Cancer, Constructing Change: New Perspectives on Women and Cancer* (Stacker 1993), and of articles in the peer-reviewed journal *Alternative Therapies.* She is the cofounder of the former Vermont-based Breast Cancer Action Group and a founding member of the National Breast Cancer Coalition (P.O. Box 66373, Washington, D.C. 20035). During her tenure as an activist, she created the Healing Legacies Arts Registry and produced the first Face of Breast Cancer exhibition in Washington, D.C. She now teaches students with learning disabilities in Long Beach, California.

Her Story

Soffa's experience with breast cancer is narrated in detail in her book, which also provides valuable practical advice to all women with breast cancer as well as to women who wish to become involved in breast cancer activism. She was thirty-eight when she found out that she had breast cancer. A one-centimeter lump was removed, but a second lump remained. Because she was very sensitive to radiation, she wanted nondeforming surgery with no follow-up radiation for the second lump. However, after a long search, she concluded that no surgeon was willing to perform this type of operation in the absence of follow-up radiotherapy. She went on a self-designed program to build her immune system, and after five months the second lump disappeared (as confirmed by a follow-up mammogram about a year later). However, after two years of following a careful diet and practicing a variety of alternative treatments, a five-centimeter tumor appeared at the point of the original biopsy. Because she suspected that her lymph nodes were involved, she elected to have a bilateral mastectomy. She considered chemotherapy and radiation but declined them. A little more than a year later, a tumor recurred on the mastectomy scar near the original biopsy. She again considered chemotherapy and radiation but decided against them. The new tumor was removed surgically, but within the year she had multiple tumors in the lymph nodes near the original tumor.

"When I had my third recurrence, I now had an oncologist, a surgeon, and a radiologist who totally supported what I had been doing. We sat down and looked at my alternatives, and there was no more surgery as an alternative. The radiologist felt adamant about not doing radiation because he felt that it would cause more problems than help. The oncologist had asked me to try tamoxifen, which I did, and because I had such a severe reaction to it, he was convinced that I could not be treated chemically. So here I had three people from a traditional background who were totally on my side, and they said, 'Nothing that we have is going to help you. What are we going to do here?' They all agreed that the neat thing about me as their patient was that when we found the right thing, the cancer was going to go away and they would know that I was cured, because they weren't blasting the system and then guessing and praying that it wouldn't come back. We were actually treating the disease. So once they got to the rationale that I wasn't trying to kill myself, they understood that these recurrences were a marker that I hadn't quite done enough and that I needed to do one more thing. We didn't know what that was until we finally decided that this cancer kept coming back because of the estrogen being produced by my ovaries. We took out the ovaries, and five weeks later the tumors went away, and that's been it." A treatment for breast cancer that has been in use for about a century with mixed results, the oophorectomy worked in Soffa's case, and she remained healthy four years later at the time of the interview.

"I went back to my oncologist last week for a checkup, and he was so cute. This is a man who was educated at Stanford. He's a totally traditional oncologist. He said, 'I'm so happy for you. You made all the right decisions.'

"I said, 'How could you say that? For two years everyone thought I was crazy because it kept coming back.'

"He said, 'Look at you. Look at how healthy you are. You did what needed to be done for you.'

"When he learned that the oophorectomy worked for me, he started offering it to his younger patients right from the beginning. If he can offer an oophorectomy instead of chemotherapy, why not? It's a choice, and many women don't get that choice."

What is it that Soffa did to save her own life? She was very perspicacious about the conventional therapies that were offered to her, and she avoided radiotherapy and chemotherapy (except for a short trial with tamoxifen) because she did not think they were appropriate for her. (Although Soffa is concerned about the overuse of conventional modalities, she does not believe that all women should do as she did. Instead, her message is that treatment should be individualized to include mixes of conventional and alternative/complementary therapies that are appropriate for each individual case.) Soffa also put together—and, equally important, stayed with—an alternative/complementary program that included diet, oriental herbs, supplements, exercise, psychotherapy, visualization, meditation, acupuncture, shiatsu, yoga, and other modalities that were aimed at building up her body and restoring health.

How did she assemble her program? "I started out by speaking to people in the community and finding out who knew anything about this. That led me to a macrobiotic counselor and to a person who gave me cooking lessons. Because the macrobiotic counselor had training in the oriental tradition, it was also a connection to oriental herbs, acupuncture, and all these things that I hadn't ever considered doing. The discussion started at the health food store. I met someone in the aisle there, and they saw all the macrobiotic food in my cart. This woman said, 'I tried that. I have breast cancer, and now they say I'm going to die. I've tried everything.' She did die very shortly after that, but she knew who the local cooking teacher was. The cooking teacher didn't want to give me instruction until she knew what kind of diet I needed. She said, 'You can't do this from a book. You need a counselor to look at your pulses and your condition, and to set up a diet based on your specific situation.' That's when I realized that everything was tailored specifically to an individual's condition. I was coming from an allopathic orientation, where everybody gets basically the same thing and you can buy it off the shelf. I had to be educated that this wasn't how it worked.

"Once people knew that I was using alternative approaches, I was literally bombarded with everything out there. It was literally overwhelming to try to figure out whether the Hoxsey system was what I needed, or the mistletoe, whether I should do ozone therapy—all these things."

To some extent cost entered into her decision-making process. For example, mistletoe was too expensive, even though she had a friend who used it and had not had a recurrence for five years. But Soffa also listened to her inner voices: "At that point the spiritual part of me had become very strong, and I was learning to trust the inner voice. I was meditating a lot, and kind of having conversations with my spiritual guides. I know this is going to sound bizarre, but that's the place I was in then. When something was suggested, I put it on the table. I didn't research it initially, and I'd say, 'Is this something I'm supposed to know more about?' I'd wait, and usually if it was, other people would come to me with the same suggestion, or somebody would call me and give me the name of somebody I needed to talk to.

"For example, the whole macrobiotic thing happened overnight. A friend called me from California. She was a former business associate. I was an interior designer, and I had just moved to Vermont. When she heard I had breast cancer, she called me and told me her story. She told me about how she had discovered the macrobiotic diet and suggested that I look at the book. From that point on, everything fell into place. It was almost effortless. It was what I was supposed to do. Here I was in this strange community, and I met somebody at the health food store in the aisle, and she knew the cooking teacher, and the cooking teacher knew a counselor. Literally, in two days I was all set up to go that way. That's the way most of these things worked. The things that I didn't research I didn't feel called to research, or the path wasn't an easy path."

I asked if her choice to use 714-X involved a similar process. "It did. I was at that point dealing with my second recurrence. I had just had a mastectomy. The doctors told me that my chance of having another recurrence was extremely high and that if I didn't do radiation and chemotherapy, I was probably going to have a recurrence. At that point I felt I needed to do some pharmacological intervention, but I wasn't convinced that chemotherapy was it. A friend of mine who had lymphedema was using 714-X, and somebody else told me about 714-X, and somebody sent me the book about it. Then I found that Gaston Naessens lived just a couple of hours from here, so we called him up and drove up there. We set up an appointment, met with his son, went to the lab. I wanted to see if this was legitimate."

Soffa found an American doctor who would write a prescription for her, but ultimately she was disappointed with him. "He wasn't treating the patient as an individual. He was coming to this as an M.D., with an allopathic orientation, where you see a patient for five minutes and write a prescription. At that point I had been in the alternative therapies program for a couple of years, and I found his manner very off-putting." At the time, she believed that the 714-X therapy might be efficacious. "I talked to other patients in the waiting room who were using 714-X, and some people—especially men with prostate cancer—were having remarkable results." However, in hindsight she is more doubtful. "I don't think it works. I had a recurrence. There were six of us using it. All of them had recurrences, and two of them died."

From her book, it is evident that Soffa also used a number of supplements and herbs, including oriental herbs, shark cartilage powder, vitamins, blue-green algae, Korean ginseng, enzymes, and green tea. I asked how she went about putting together her own program of supplements and herbs. "In the macrobiotic philosophy, they don't believe in vitamins at all, but the diet wasn't enough for me. I was really deficient in vitamin C and I knew it, because they don't have any citrus whatsoever in that diet. So I took vitamin C as a supplement. As for the enzymes and blue-green algae, those were things that friends told me about. I would try something, and if I felt good on it, I continued. If I had a problem with it, I didn't continue. I trusted my system. At that point my system was fairly clean. I could tell if it was doing something or not. Then I learned dowsing, and I started dowsing when I needed vitamins. I had to take a thousand milligrams of vitamin C all along. I think that's one of the things that doesn't make sense about the macrobiotic diet."

Her use of dowsing and inner voices led us to wonder what role science played in her decision-making process. "My initial response to learning that I had cancer was terror, and the only system I knew was the scientific system of evaluating things. I remember so vividly being in the therapist's office and saying to her, 'I want proof that these things are going to work. I want proof that my spiritual guides don't mean that I'm going crazy and that this is for real. You're asking me to make this incredible leap of faith and give up what I have been taught as the basis for making decisions. How am I supposed to do this?' She had guided me to some books written by doctors in which they validated the inner voice. I said to my spiritual guides, 'If you want me to go through these crazy things, I want proof that it's going to work. So I'm going to go to the medical library and you're going to tell me what I need to read.' I was trying to reconcile the educated and spiritual parts of me. I was trying to reconcile two different systems. If I made a mistake, I was putting my life on the line. This wasn't just a philosophical exercise.

"So I was very clear about the fact that I needed substance as to how this was going to work. The time I spent in the medical library reading all the literature on breast cancer got me to the point of understanding that the doctors didn't have a clue about what they were doing and how they were treating this disease. It gave me permission to trust my guides. But I had to go through that whole process. It took quite a while—six or eight months. I'd never been in a medical library before. I had to get over my fears that I didn't know how to read a scientific journal. I didn't know what some of the words were. I had to deal with all of those self-defeating feelings that keep us in some discipline that we are comfortable with. Art was my background. Going into a science library was way beyond what I ever thought I could do. I trusted my intelligence enough that I thought that if I kept reading, it would begin to make sense. Not only did it make sense, but I started to draw some of my own conclusions. I could see that they didn't have the data that they needed to understand what was causing breast cancer, and if they didn't know what was causing this disease, they certainly didn't know how to treat it. Once I grasped that concept, then I could sit back and trust the cosmic information I was getting. I knew that it was just as valid as what was going on in the universities and in the hospitals.

"I walked in and I challenged my doctors. I had conversations with them. They would tell me one thing and I would say, 'No, no. I read that journal. I can tell you what that study said. This is what the study said.' And then they would start backpedaling. They would say, 'Well, you know, it's about this,' and I would say, 'No, no. This is what it said.' They were actually imparting misinformation, and I don't know whether they had come to believe this information or what they were talking about, but the science isn't there for the way they are treating breast cancer. They're not basing what they're doing on science, so why the heck would what I want to do any different? It's just as valid. This light went off in my mind. After about a year and a half I started writing. I wasn't a writer—I was a visual artist—and writing was a big hurdle for me, but I realized that I had this perspective that a lot of people out there hadn't arrived at. The doctors went through this reaction to my writing, saying that I was totally off the wall. Nobody here would treat me. I had to go out of the area. I didn't want to give up having an allopathic doctor to consult with, but it took me a while to find people who would accept what I was doing and not feel threatened or that they were going to end up with malpractice suits."

At the same time that Soffa was studying conventional knowledge about breast cancer in the medical library, she was also reading the alternative literature. "As you know, the books don't cite much scientific literature. It's all people's experience, which is what the doctors discredit. I would call people up. If I read a book by someone and I wanted to see if they were still alive, I would call them up. I would say, 'How was this experience for you?' or 'What did you learn since you wrote the book?' or something like that. I felt at that point that experience was just as valid as scientific research, that these people were just as much experts as the so-called experts." When we spoke with her in early 1998, she was in good health and working as a teacher in California.

Advice to Other Women

Soffa believes that in her case it was necessary to have a combination of surgery and alternative methods. "It was the combination of medical treatment (surgery) and alternatives that healed me. I couldn't have done it just with alternatives." However, she emphasizes that it was necessary to use the alternatives for the body to heal itself. "I guess what I came to was being convinced that our bodies have an innate healing system, and that it needs to be supported."

Regarding chemotherapy and radiation, she said, "Every time I had a recurrence I readdressed whether I would take chemotherapy. I didn't have a closed mind to it forever. I have seen consistently negative results long-term. Every person I know who has had chemotherapy or radiation has had the most virulent recurrence, whereas my recurrences stayed local and were slow-growing. We were dealing with the same cancer. It wasn't taking off and going wild. That's what I'm seeing in other people."

Although Soffa used tamoxifen for a short period of time, she questions the widespread and uniform use of chemotherapy: "It seems to me to be counterproductive to be taking the drugs that the allopathic tradition was offering because they work contrary to the alternative approaches. They actually speed your system up and throw it off balance, so that the natural healing cannot take place."

Regarding alternative or complementary therapies, Soffa also emphasized the importance of individual variation and needs. For example, the high sodium content of the macrobiotic diet is not appropriate for many patients, but in her case it seemed to work. "I have low blood pressure, and I need salt in my diet. I've always needed salt in my diet. In fact, when I'm on a salt-free diet, I get a little lethargic. What I realized is that I got lucky and hit the right diet for me first, but it's not the right diet for everybody by any means. We're all different. I had been battling respiratory conditions and skin conditions my entire life because I was allergic to milk, and I never knew it until I went off it. I felt so good that I can never imagine eating that stuff again. It's been seven and a half years and I'd never go back."

Soffa added that another aspect of an individualized program is that it needs to be flexible enough to change as a patient's needs change. "I had miso soup every morning for two and a half years, but after my mastectomy, I couldn't eat it in the morning. Now I can hardly eat it once a week and I actually crave citrus. I take my vitamin C but I actually crave citrus. It's a question of becoming in tune with what your body needs. I'm very healthy now, in a totally different condition than I was seven and a half years ago. I eat a lot of raw food now, and I couldn't eat any raw food seven and a half years ago. When I eat at home, I eat strictly organic, but obviously when I'm traveling and eating in a restaurant, I'm not able to eat only organic. My system is able to handle it better. I've done blue-green algae for a period, and now I'm not doing it. I did a different combination of vitamins for a while. I just did my first raw juice fast for a week. My macrobiotic counselor didn't advise me doing any kind of fast for that long, let alone juices, but my condition is so different now that I needed to balance the seven years of macrobiotics by doing the opposite. I had a fabulous week and my body got cleansed out, and I feel really strong and healthy. I didn't take any vitamins during that time, and I didn't eat anything else. So I think fasting and probably colonics, if a person's condition allows it, are necessary because some people can't clear their system out fast enough in a normal process; they can't reduce the load on their bodies. The colon is so vital to the healing process. If it's not functioning right, you need to do something to get it cleared out and get it functioning so that your body is giving you clear messages when something is not right. I guess I can't stress enough that it needs to be personalized."

Soffa has also learned that her role as a breast cancer activist is not appropriate for her as a long-term identity. She is now putting the experience behind her and getting on with her life. She has retired from her role as president of the Breast Cancer Action Group. "I realized after a couple of years that I was not a good support person because it kept raising the issue of being so sick all over again. I didn't want to go through that on a daily or weekly basis, so once my book was out, I felt comfortable referring them to the book or to other support groups. I think that the mental-emotional piece is really big. The people I have seen who are dealing with the continuous recurrences and declining health haven't dealt with that. No matter what they've done with nutritional and metabolic approaches, if they don't deal with the psychological and emotional, they keep repeating the same stuff."

Opinions on Cancer Research and Publicly Supported Cancer Organizations

Soffa has played an important role in some of the breast cancer organizations. In addition to cofounding the Vermont-based Breast Cancer Action

Group, she was invited to testify before the National Cancer Institute in 1991, when a number of breast cancer activists went to Washington and formed the National Breast Cancer Coalition. Although she had undergone a mastectomy only a month prior to the Washington trip, the opportunity to testify before the NCI was something she did not want to pass up.

"I said they could throw the gold standard (randomized clinical trials) out the window. It was a farce. It was so funny because there were two reactions. Either they knew it deep down inside and there was no dispute, or they were in shock because they had believed in the system and they couldn't believe that somebody was telling them that their system doesn't work. There was a time when I stood up before the National Institutes of Health and I told them that all they were trying to do was fix women, and that their whole approach to women's health research was totally wrong, and they were sitting there agreeing. And I was saying, 'If you guys agree with this, why the heck are you doing what you're doing? Why were you offering these treatments?'

"One of the issues that I raised when I was in Washington is that there is no cure for breast cancer. This was something that doctors were denying; they were saying that they could cure breast cancer. The patients were the first to say publicly that there was no cure. Now, most doctors will agree that there is no cure for breast cancer. There was a major article in *Atlantic Monthly* where doctors said there is no cure to breast cancer. Five years ago, you couldn't find a doctor who was willing to be public with this news. They were into propaganda. It wasn't until later, after patients came forward, that they knew that the cat was out of the bag. If you just go read their literature, the truth is obvious; anybody can see it. But doctors really seemed to feel some amount of sanctity that a patient wouldn't walk into a medical library and read their journals. It's all there. We have been treated in such a way that the only information we get is what the doctors give us, and the doctors don't give us honest information. I said that to them. What could they say? They knew it!"

We talked for a while about the NCI budget and how some of the preventive medicine budget is going toward research into preventive chemotherapy, and she added, "They call tamoxifen prevention. This is a total joke. I mean, let's give people another kind of cancer. That's what I called it when I was there. I said, 'This is disease substitution. This is not OK.'"

During her trip to Washington the breast cancer organizations met to form the National Breast Cancer Coalition. "We met on the lawn outside the Capitol, and we held a press conference and a protest. Then we all went to a law firm and held a meeting to decide if we were going to form the National Breast Cancer Coalition and who was going to be on the board to set the agenda for the grassroots movement. We were a tiny organization from Vermont with sixty dollars in the bank, and there was no way that it was imaginable we could be part of this. But when I looked at it, I knew that it was the only way. Because Vermont was fourth in the nation in breast cancer deaths, I had gone to my congressman and senators, who are very accessible because it is such a small state. They got on board immediately and wanted to help." In 1992 Congressman Bernard Sanders of Vermont introduced the Cancer Registries Act, which creates a uniform system of collecting data so that better epidemiological research can be done for all cancers.

"I told the board of the Breast Cancer Action Group that we needed to come up with five hundred dollars if we were going to join the national group. I was going to have to travel to Washington or somewhere every month, and we would have to have enough money in the bank to support the travel. When I gave them the report of what went on, they said they would raise the money. Within about two months we had raised about five thousand dollars. I started attending these meetings, and there were activists who were out there fighting for prevention and saying that mammography wasn't prevention. I was so glad there was somebody out there besides me who was saying this, because in my own community I was getting roasted. People were just outraged by the things I was saying, and I found that I was a lone voice here. I found I had sisters out there who had similar points of view.

"But I realized my perspective was quite different. I was the only one of these thirty women who used alternatives. They all used chemo and radiation and went the standard route and didn't question their doctors. I was still a lone voice in this respect. Even in that atmosphere I was still way out in left field compared to the average because I had approached my treatment differently. I had questioned the whole system. I did what I could for two and a half years, then it became an emotional and physical drain, and I had to drop out of that scenario. I was a little disappointed because I had offered my services to the NCI. I said, 'Look, I have used this stuff. Let me come and talk to you about nutrition,' but they weren't open to that."

On the issue of the interest in alternative therapies among the breast cancer organizations, Soffa commented, "They're very traditional. It surprised me, too. I realized that people who are enlightened about fighting the system are not necessarily enlightened about the fact that the system is doing things to them on all these other levels. They just don't get that connection. And there are alternative people who don't realize that there are some parts of the allopathic system that need to be utilized. People get very rigid in whatever they're promoting."

Soffa had also attended some of the alternative medicine conferences. She found the atmosphere of these health expos to be too much like a trade show. "I don't think that the environmental setting of the alternative societies works for me, because most of them are selling you something. They're going to sell you their latest, greatest thing. That's not what this needs to be about. People need to come together on another level. They need to have a philosophical discussion about how and why they have done these treatments, and what has worked and hasn't worked."

References

Hicks, Karen
  1994 *Misdiagnosis: Woman as Disease.* Allentown, Penn.: People's Medical Society.
Soffa, Virginia
  1994 *The Journey beyond Breast Cancer.* Rochester, Vt.: Healing Arts Press.
  1996 "Alternatives to Hormone Replacement for Menopause." *Alternative Therapies* 2 (2): 34–39.
  1996 "Artistic Expression of Illness." *Alternative Therapies* 2 (3): 63–66.
Stocker, Midge
  1993 *Confronting Cancer, Constructing Change: New Perspectives on Women and Cancer.* Chicago: Third Side Press.

twenty-one

Melanie Zucker

Healing through Personal Power

Melanie Zucker is the author of *Cancer Warrior: Healing through Personal Power* (Pinole, Calif.: Dare to Dream, 1996), "chronicling her amazing journey to wellness from breast cancer," and producer of the *Three Keys to Healing* audio tape series. Melanie has been featured at the Professional Business Women's Conference, the San Francisco Bay Area Book Festival, the Whole Life Expo, the National Health Federation, the Cancer Control Society, the Business Women's Success Conference, and the Fourth Tuesday Women's Group; on major radio and television programs; and in various newspapers and magazines. Dare to Dream is located at P.O. Box 315, Pinole, Calif. 94564, 888-DRE-2-DRM or <www.darestodream.com>.

Melanie uses her skills and experience to assist people in gaining more control over their lives, whether they are facing health, relationship, family, work, or financial issues or just want to feel more powerful. Melanie is the founder of Dare to Dream, which offers workshops, speaking, support groups, individual consultations, books, and tapes. She speaks nationwide on the issues of life-threatening illnesses and empowerment. (The italics and headings in the interview were added by the interviewee to the revised, final version of the text.)

Her Story

Melanie Zucker was surprised to be diagnosed with breast cancer in 1990. She was only thirty-five and was known among her friends as a health nut. She was also very athletic: she was a runner, a tennis player, a biker, and a swimmer. She adds, "I had none of the textbook risk factors. It was actually pretty shocking: being that young, and 'healthy' in terms of lifestyle, having no major vices and nothing in my family or health history to indicate that it might happen."

She found out about her cancer "by accident." "I was having my annual gynecology examination. My doctor was examining my breasts and she thought that she felt something on my left side." Her doctor offered to refer her to have a baseline mammogram, and Zucker accepted the offer. "I went across the street and had the mammogram. There was nothing where my gynecologist thought she felt something, but on my right side there was microscopic cancer. It was nothing you could palpate with your hands. So, it was serendipitous in that if she hadn't thought she felt a lump, I wouldn't have gone in for a mammogram, and the microscopic cancer wouldn't have been discovered until much later.

"I quickly discovered I wasn't born into this world with a 'how to' manual for Life. I couldn't turn to chapter 12 to read an easy solution for getting rid of cancer. There was certainly nothing in my formal education that helped me deal with this new life event. And although there was plenty of information on the physicality of the disease, there were no books that addressed my concerns about the *experience* of having a life-threatening illness, nothing to help with the mental, emotional, and spiritual part of my experience.

"Two phenomena were going on simultaneously: cancer and *'the experience'* of having cancer. I've found the people who handle 'the experience' of having cancer in an empowered way get better physical results. How? By being a Cancer Warrior. This means three things: (1) using the power of living at choice, (2) having a belief system for healing, and (3) handling Power Robbers.

"After I heard the three little words *'you have cancer,'* my life began to change because of the choices I made. My first choice was to take a 'complementary' approach to my treatment plan. I did some initial surgery but then chose alternative treatments rather than chemotherapy and radiation. In taking this complementary approach, I was criticized from both sides, with Western doctors disapproving of my alternative treatments ('You're going to kill yourself with holistic medicine,' said one of my surgeons) and some alternative supporters condemning my surgery.

"Because of my choices I was *opposed* by doctors over my choice of what to do with *my body, denied* health plan coverage by my employer and insurance company, *entangled* in the red tape of the medical system, *harassed* by the health department, *badgered* by sales pitches from plastic surgeons, support group organizers, and prosthesis marketers, *confused* by conflicting information about cancer, *deceived* about the safety of implants, *exhausted* by inappropriate demands of the working world, *challenged* on my beliefs, *critiqued* on my healing process, *abandoned* by friends, *haunted* by strange dreams, and *tormented* by my fears."

Her Approach to Healing

"My first step toward healing and staying empowered was to live at choice. Many in our culture don't understand what it means to live at choice. They're too busy reacting to life in ways that others wish them to, whether these are authority figures such as doctors, spouses, friends, the media, or other influential people in their lives. They have trouble determining what *they* believe in terms of healing and what they want to do with their own bodies. Think about it. Do you really live at choice or are you merely reacting to the people or situations around you?

"About this time I read a story about a shaman who could predict when people would die. Several anthropologists traveled to study the shaman, and true to legend, people typically died on or very close to the predicted time of death. What was the shaman's secret? After studying him, the anthropologists concluded the shaman held the power of belief for the village. He also had a ritual of waving a large bone over a person as he was predicting the date of death. The ritual bone waving took the power from the villager and gave it to the shaman. People left the hut believing whatever the shaman told them and died according to schedule, relinquishing the power to create their own life or death.

"There is much bone waving going on within Western culture today. My surgeon was the first to wave a bone at me when she exclaimed, 'You're going to *kill* yourself doing alternative medicine!' Another bone waver was a friend who repeatedly told me, 'If you can only make it five years, then you'll be fine,' completely ignoring *my* belief that I was already cancer-free! Both of these individuals attempted to place their beliefs over mine to rob my power to make my own choices and create my own healing path.

"At that point I began to understand what living at choice was really about, and it became the cornerstone of my journey. I realized that when you truly live your life at choice, the outside world doesn't always support you; therefore, I had to go inside myself and decide I was going to live at choice—no matter what it meant." As a result of her decisions, Zucker faced severe financial problems because the insurance companies would not pay for alternative treatments.

"My second step toward healing and staying empowered was to formulate a belief system for healing. When I discovered I had cancer, I became an information seeker and found having information overload was as bad as having insufficient information. Unless you have a foundation of beliefs with respect to healing and to your body, the information you collect is virtually useless. Decisions won't be made with any degree of confidence unless they're rooted in beliefs. Once I established such a foundation, I was able to move forward and make choices with confidence and power.

"Let me give you an example. I attended the Cancer Control Society's convention last fall, and hundreds of people came by my booth. The attendees were cancer patients or friends, relatives, or caregivers of people with cancer. They were all looking for help. They circled the booths and ravenously collected information. I realized they were all looking for the *magic answer*. One day several people were in tears at my booth saying, 'We came here with the hope we would be able to solve our problem, that we would find information which would lead us to the right plan or right medication. We are *more confused* now than when we arrived!' These people didn't know what they believed about healing. If you haven't developed a belief system for healing, you'll have nothing upon which to make your choices, be they complementary, conventional, or alternative.

"My third step toward healing and staying empowered was to handle Power Robbers, nine different ways people or situations steal your power by victimizing you or pushing your buttons. There are two categories of

Power Robbers: external Power Robbers (those people or situations outside yourself) and internal Power Robbers (the voices inside your head). I handled Power Robbers by first becoming aware how the person or situation was victimizing me or pushing my buttons and then strategizing against them to retain my power. If you don't do anything about Power Robbers, they drain your power. The goal is to conserve and consolidate your power so you can use it for healing.

"By taking these three steps I was able to move through the experience of having cancer in an empowered way. However, fighting to stay empowered wasn't the *easiest* way to get through the experience. Staying empowered requires that you take accountability for every choice you make and every action you take. There's no one to blame when things don't turn out the way you hoped. But there's good news! Being empowered in the face of a life-threatening illness translates into a more positive experience mentally, emotionally, physically, and spiritually. Taken together, that means healing."

Other Healing Tools

Zucker worked with her dreams. "I've always dreamed a lot at night and have found it powerful to record my dreams. Depending on how I experienced them, my dreams became either Power Robbers or tools for empowerment. They were Power Robbers if I allowed them to frighten or threaten me. If I could work with them in a way that helped me along my healing path, they were tools for empowerment. In *Cancer Warrior,* I recount the dreams I had before, during, and after my cancer experience and how I used them to become more empowered. Dreams are a very powerful source of healing. I've helped even those who can't at first remember their dreams learn these skills."

Zucker also used visualization. "Although there are many books cataloging visualizations for healing, I found it most effective to create my own. They were particularly useful when I was at the effect of a Power Robber. Most of my visualizations involved the use of allies or guides which act as bridges between the material world and the spirit world."

On Support Groups

Zucker also had some comments on the value of support groups. She personally did not go to support groups; she relied instead on family and friends. "Support groups can be Power Robbers when a conflict of beliefs exists. I also see the potential for overidentification with cancer, which prevents one from living in the present, with fresh eyes and the possibility something new can happen—like good health and no cancer! You can support someone best by empowering them to make their own choices."

She added that attending a support group should not be a substitute for doing one's own internal psychological work and building a strong personal foundation. "My study of Tai Chi taught me that in life, you have to be like a bamboo tree. Bamboo trees are very deeply rooted into the ground. You can develop your roots by living at choice and knowing your beliefs. Bamboo trees are also so flexible that they will bend all the way over and touch the ground without breaking in a windstorm. You can cultivate this kind of flexibility by learning to manage your power. If you are both rooted and flexible, you, too, can weather life's storms without breaking."

Opinions On Cancer Research and Publicly Supported Cancer Organizations

"Research is good if it gives us information we can act upon to empower ourselves, such as a greater awareness of environmental carcinogens. However, I don't believe 'the cure' is out there waiting to be discovered. Healing is an individual process, one closely linked to our building and maintaining our personal power.

"I question the management of research dollars. Although there is an increase in dollars, we also have chemical and other questionable companies contributing to and sitting on the boards of directors of these organizations."

On the Media

Zucker has substantial media experience because of her work promoting her book and tapes. She found the media to be very focused on the *physical* aspects of cancer as a disease and on the statistics associated with it. In some of her interviews, she was paired with people who "did nothing but recite statistics and talk about the physicality of cancer. That raises awareness about the *disease,* but ignores *healing.* Healing through personal power involves physical, mental, emotional, and spiritual components of the process. Western society is primarily focused on the physical eradication of the disease as opposed to the healing of a human being. We need to broaden our focus."

What's Next

Zucker is another of the active agents for change. It is possible that part of her continued good health can be attributed to her choice to found her company Dare to Dream, with a vision of helping people learn empowerment skills through her book, tapes, speaking engagements, and workshops. "I have in mind three new books. The first will broaden the concept of healing through personal power to illness in general, so those with illnesses other than cancer may benefit from what I teach. The second will focus on personal power in everyday life situations, and the third will take the concept of personal power to children. Other projects include additional *Take Back Your Power* workshops and an expanded audio tape series."

When we last spoke with Zucker in early 1998, she was building a healing ranch in New Mexico.

Conclusions

Many people think that choosing "alternative medicine" as opposed to conventional medicine is an either-or proposition. For most of the women whom we interviewed, the choice is not so clear-cut. The same therapies can be either alternative or complementary, depending on how they are used, a point that Susan Holloran made. Although some women choose to replace conventional therapies with alternatives, others prefer to mix conventional and complementary therapies. The fundamental issue involves medical freedom and control over one's body: the women want to have the information and the right to put together a healing program that makes sense to them.

The appropriate selection of therapies is a very individualized decision. Women want to have the power to make that decision in consultation with a qualified, knowledgeable health care provider. The women we interviewed are not antidoctor, although several had specific problems with some doctors. Rather, they want a better world in which doctors have the right to offer alternative/complementary therapies and the knowledge to do so competently. They also want a world in which patients have the right to choose those therapies.

Finding the Uses and Limitations of Conventional Therapies

Although a few of the women used only alternative therapies, most opted for a combination of conventional therapies with alternative and complementary cancer therapies (ACCTs). Several chose minimal conventional intervention, such as surgery, and chose not to have follow-up radiation and chemotherapy when it was offered. Others, such as Anne Frahm, followed the classical pattern of switching to ACCTs after they had reached the limits of conventional therapies. In other words, there is a variety of ways in which ACCTs may be used, either in combination with conventional therapies or as substitutes for them.

Although ACCTs are sometimes referred to as *nontoxic* instead of by terms such as *unconventional, alternative,* or *complementary,* the concepts of toxic and nontoxic should be seen as forming a continuum. Some of the ACCTs can be dangerous or toxic, particularly when used without supervision by a clinician who understands their scientific basis. Furthermore, the toxicity of conventional therapies varies greatly. In the case of breast cancer, minor surgery such as a lumpectomy is at the low end of the conventional spectrum of toxicity, provided that only a small number or no lymph nodes are removed (large-scale removal creates a risk of lymphedema). Many of the women opted for minor surgical interventions but said no to chemotherapy or radiation therapy. In some cases, such as Cathy Hitchcock's, surgery followed by an intense alternative/complementary program seemed sufficient.

Women who attempt to unlink conventional therapies may face problems with their clinicians. For example, Pat Fogderud's and Virginia Soffa's doctors refused to perform surgery without radiation treatments. After a long search, several of the women were able to find a team of doctors who were willing to work with them on their own terms. Those terms included accepting the patient as an active participant in the decision-making process. From the patient's viewpoint, searching for doctors who are willing to grant women the right to control over their bodies can be exhausting, depressing, and ultimately antitherapeutic. This is one reason why reforms such as the Access to Medical Treatments bill are needed, so that both clinicians and patients have the right to unlink cookbook therapies.

Another issue is that unlinking therapies is usually accompanied by switches to alternative programs. In the case of breast cancer, a lumpectomy with follow-up radiation therapy might be replaced by a lumpectomy with a follow-up nutritional and psychological program. Here the distinction between alternative and complementary becomes fuzzy; a follow-up nutritional (or other) program is complementary to the surgery but alternative to the radiation therapy. Even when patients accept the full conventional package and then use nutritional programs as complementary, they may encounter unhelpful or even hostile responses from their clinicians. Sharon Batt, Matilda Moore, and Anne Frahm all opted for dietary changes as either complementary or alternative to conventional programs, and they all faced clinicians who pooh-poohed the idea. A main reason for that attitude, as Moore pointed out when discussing her physician stepson, is that nutrition is not taught in medical school. The problem suggests another needed policy change: the introduction of a substantial curriculum of nutritional science into the education of health care providers.

Although for some patients minor surgery represents an option that is not very toxic—that is, in comparison with chemotherapy or radiotherapy—some of the surgical procedures currently in place increase the risk of long-term secondary diseases. In the case of breast cancer, one example is the linkage between axillary node dissection and lymphedema. Ann Fonfa and Gayle Black, Ph.D., are leaders in getting the word out to women about the risk of lymphedema from axillary node dissection. Fonfa has also gathered information on less invasive diagnostic procedures, and Black mentioned a gene-based test (sentinel node) that requires the removal of only one lymph node. Both approaches would substantially decreases the risk of lymphedema. As Cathy Hitchcock, M.S.W., pointed out, if a woman has decided against chemotherapy, axillary node dissection may not make sense because its primary value is to determine whether subsequent chemotherapy is necessary. Conversely, as Barbara Joseph, M.D., pointed out, if a woman has already decided in favor of chemotherapy, the procedure may also be unnecessary. The basic problem appears to be that many woman are rushed into making a decision without full information. Gayle Black summed up the current situation as follows: "It's a diagnostic procedure to tell you whether or not you will need chemo, but the insanity of all this is that everybody who has breast cancer goes on chemo. So what is the point of mutilating a woman, who now has this possibility of going through life like me, with a real handicap, when in fact they're going to get chemo anyhow?"

Lymphedema is perhaps the greatest medical problem in the breast cancer field. In general, women are rarely given any information about the risks of lymphedema from axillary node dissection, nor do they have any idea of how debilitating the disease can be. As Black points out, they are also not given crucial information about how to reduce the risk of developing the disease, such as avoiding hot temperatures or lifting. Once women develop lymphedema, few treatment options are available, and women suffer continuous pain.

Axillary node dissection represents perhaps the most pressing problem in cancer treatment for women today. Women should be given full information about the risks of the procedure, its limitations as a diagnostic (not therapeutic) procedure, and alternatives now available. There is also a pressing policy problem: curricula need to be reformed so that health care practitioners understand the dangers of lymph node removal.

Regarding other risks of surgery, there is also a widespread concern that surgery can spread the tumor cells. For this reason some women have avoided even minor surgery. Susan Moss avoided a lumpectomy but eventually faced a situation where the entire breast was hard and hot to the touch (inflammatory carcinoma). Within a few weeks Moss, who describes the process as a "healing reaction," overcame the condition without surgery. Another interviewee, whom we were not able to include here, adopted a similar course of action with less success, and she mentioned that if she had to do it over again, she might have had the surgery and then worked very hard to strengthen her immune system. Surgery may disturb a protective capsule around the tumor and enhance the possibility of metastases, and that question is debated in the alternative cancer therapy community. It may be significant to point to one study that addresses the issue from the alternative community perspective. Gar Hildenbrand and colleagues (1996) of the Gerson Research Organization found that surgery plus the Gerson therapy was associated with a higher survival rate than the dietary therapy alone for cases of melanoma.

Another issue related to surgery and breast cancer is the positive experience of Virginia Soffa, M.Ed., with removal of the ovaries after several rounds of recurrent tumors. A study by the Early Breast Cancer Trialists' Collaborative Group (1992) found that the procedure was of comparable efficacy to chemotherapy. Ralph Moss writes, "This is an extremely important finding that has gotten little attention so far" (1995: 92). As Soffa commented, "It's a choice, and many women don't get that choice."

Regarding radiation treatment for breast cancer, one of the most startling discoveries of some of the women was that adjuvant radiotherapy in premenopausal women who undergo a lumpectomy does not affect survival. To understand the point, it is important to grasp the difference between recurrence and survival. Barbara Joseph explained that radiation therapy was introduced to bring the local recurrence rate following lumpectomies in line with that of mastectomies. Therefore, as Susan Holloran's oncologist told her, radiation therapy is only a local treatment, and it does not affect the systemic aspects of the disease. Joseph adds that radiation therapy is itself a carcinogen that carries with it long-term risks of secondary cancers. It also can lead to burns and scarring, as Pat Prince experienced from radiation treatment for another disease, as well as other health problems, such as lung damage and bone breakage.

The risk in terms of secondary cancer and radiation burns tends to be underplayed, just as the benefit tends to be overplayed. The benefit is questionable: for breast cancer patients, radiation treatment will reduce the risk of local recurrence to the same breast, but the survival rate will not be any higher in comparison with women who do not have radiation therapy and then treat the local recurrence after the fact. It may be more sensible to treat the local recurrence if it occurs. According to Cathy Hitchcock's husband, Steve Austin, N.D., the finding that "women who undergo lumpectomy without radiation have the same life expectancy as do women who follow lumpectomy with radiation" is "now relatively well accepted" (Austin 1996: 45). Subsequent research published in late 1997 suggested that radiation therapy for one category of breast cancer patients may result in a small survival benefit at the five-year mark (Overgaard et al. 1997; Ragaz et al. 1997). The research has several problems of design and interpretation, however (Houston 1997), and it is contradicted by other studies, including one with a twelve-year time frame that showed no survival benefit (e.g., Fisher et al. 1995).

Finally, regarding chemotherapy, the interviewees expressed a wide range of opinions. Some of the women did try chemotherapy with apparent success. Sharon Batt investigated chemotherapy carefully for breast cancer, and she concluded that the experts did not agree and that the "science just hadn't been done." Nevertheless, she eventually decided to go ahead with the chemotherapy, but she combined it with dietary changes and psychological interventions. Barbara Joseph also chose to utilize chemotherapy for her advanced cancer because she viewed it as addressing the systemic aspect of the disease; however, her successful case also involved a full complementary program that she believes mitigated the toxicities of the chemotherapy and had therapeutic effects of its own.

Others decided against chemotherapy. Some shared the perspective of Myrna Gene, who views chemotherapy as a poison. Cathy Hitchcock did not think that the potential benefits of chemotherapy outweighed the potential risks in her case, so she ruled it out. It is possible that new dosages and ways of using chemotherapy will make that modality more effective in the future. For example, Keith Block, M.D., is developing slow infusion along with biological response modifiers such as botanicals that lower the toxicities of the drugs (Block 1997; see also his interview in Hess 1999).

The research on the benefits of chemotherapy is changing rapidly. Claims that chemotherapy may help some patients vary by stage and type of cancer as well as by age of the woman (particularly pre- and post-menopausal status for breast cancer patients). Again, Hitchcock and her husband Austin provide some cautions about interpreting the statistics. For example, in premenopausal breast cancer patients, the claimed reduction of 25 percent in mortality for chemotherapy applies to those who do not achieve long-term survival (usually defined as five years or more) by surgery alone. In this case surgery leads to long-term survival in 70 percent of node-negative women and 40 percent of node-positive women. As Austin writes, "Thus, a 25 percent reduction in mortality would affect only 30 percent of the node-negative patients and 60 percent of the node-positive patients who would have died without chemotherapy. Thus, approximately 7.5 percent of node-negative patients and 15 percent of node-positive patients will live longer as a result of chemotherapy" (1996: 45). He goes on to comment that the increased survival rate is not based on comparison with placebo controls; therefore, some of the benefit may be due to the placebo effect. Furthermore, the 7.5 percent survival benefit is not adjusted for the lower quality of life that results from chemotherapy. Finally, he adds that the benefit of chemotherapy may be only to extend life, not to bring about lasting recovery in many cases.

The ambiguities in the scientific research for chemotherapy and radio-therapy are fairly well documented for breast cancer. However, other women included in this book faced cervical cancer, non-Hodgkin's lymphoma, and kidney cancer. For most types of cancer, there are likely to be ambiguities in the efficacy of conventional therapies (Moss 1995). Rather than pretend that the ambiguities are not there, we suggest that health care practitioners endorse the active participation of a well-informed patient in the decision-making process. The strengths and weaknesses of the therapy should be described, as well as some of the individual life circumstances that might inform the decision (such as a strong personal fear of radiation).

Learning the Science and Questioning Medical Authority

For women who decide to select from the variety of nontoxic therapies, even as complementary approaches to conventional methods, there is soon a bewildering problem: how to choose among the many different possibilities out there? We hoped to learn from these women by asking them what criteria they used in making their choices. We found that their level of background knowledge varied tremendously, even among those who have written books or played an active role as leaders in cancer organizations. Most of the women we interviewed were very new to the whole field when they first learned that they had cancer. In many cases, their choices were shaped by word of mouth and availability.

In other cases the women had a fairly good grasp of the alternative field and were able to make more informed decisions about which therapies were appropriate for them. Some spent a great deal of time reading publications. Ann Fonfa mentioned that she often read about what was being recommended in Europe or China; the comparative perspective provided her with insight into what questions to ask. Virginia Soffa and Susan Holloran were among the women who researched the conventional options for breast cancer and soon came to the conclusion that the experts did not have the answers. Charlotte Louise, who had metastasized ovarian cancer, went more by the poor prognosis that the conventional therapies offered her. Once the women understood the current state of scientific knowledge of cancer etiology and therapy, or the meager-to-nonexistent survival benefit of radiation therapy or chemotherapy for their type and stage of cancer, they were better able to justify charting an independent course. In this sense, learning the science did not entail understanding the intricacies of psychoneuroimmunology or nutritional science as much as learning enough about conventional cancer therapies to know that in some cases they do not offer sufficient benefit.

Women who decide to cut an independent trail for themselves must first get past the problem of hurried decisions. It appears that some of the clinician's pressure for a rushed decision is based less on a concern with better prognosis than a concern with patient compliance. The more time a patient has to make a decision, the more likely she is to begin to do research, talk to friends, and start to ask questions about different options. In other words, more time leads to a more active role in one's treatment decisions. Other factors can increase a patient's ability to participate in the decision-making process. For example, some of the women, such as Melanie Zucker, found it helpful to have a friend go with them for the consultation, or even to tape record it. The presence of a friend or the use of a tape recorder can alter the power relations of the clinical encounter, because it can help capture information that patients may lose due to feelings of shock. Furthermore, some of the women also prepared questions before they met with their clinicians in order to have a more active role in the decision-making process.

The cases of medical abandonment were poignant and sometimes unethical. Charlotte Louise's description of a clinician who literally turned his back on her until she signed the informed consent form was disturbing, but the surgeon's decision to ignore her change of heart regarding her informed consent was shocking. Alice Cedillo merely received a Christmas message on her answering machine that told her she had non-Hodgkin's lymphoma, that it was incurable, and to call if she had any questions. Instances such as oncologists' abandoning their patients because they choose to pursue alternatives do occur, and the implications that such behavior can have on the health of the patient—in terms of its effects on the patient's sense of hope—need to be discussed openly in the medical community. Another policy issue emerges: it is time to question the abandonment of patients who pursue alternative and complementary therapies.

Religion and spiritual guidance played a role for many of the women in making them feel that they could successfully question the standard wisdom. For example, Charlotte Louise chanted and meditated, Myrna Gene listened to her intuition and inner spirit, Pat Fogderud and Anne Frahm were among the women who relied on their Christian faith, and Virginia Soffa listened to her spirit guides in addition to studying the science. Although one might view the role of religion or spirituality in decision making as an irrational factor, a more sophisticated interpretation is that the intuitive or spiritual component helped legitimate a more holistic framework that included coming to terms with the lack of solid scientific information that was available to them.

It is interesting that many of the women had close friends who had similar diagnoses and chose conventional therapies. In other words, many of the women we interviewed tended to form their own "matched pairs." Alice Cedillo and Susan Moss are just two examples of patients who were comparing themselves with a friend who had a similar diagnosis but who chose conventional therapies. Pat Fogderud compared herself with two of her mother's sisters who had the same type of cancer that she did, used chemotherapy and radiation, and did not survive very long. The pairs of friends often shared information, and they each watched the other progress through the different therapeutic choices. Often the friends or relatives who chose conventional therapies were not as successful as the women with whom we spoke; some of them died. For example, Susan Moss's friend Kimberly was diagnosed with breast cancer at age thirty-four. Moss comments, "She had early detection, finding the lump herself, and she submitted to every medical treatment—mastectomy, chemotherapy, radiation, and bone marrow transplant—and was dead at age thirty-eight."

Finding the Uses and Limitations of ACCTs

Several of the women had unsuccessful experiences with individual ACCTs, or they went through various ACCTs until they found one that was helpful to them. Gayle Black is one example. After surgery, she turned to supplements and herbs, then had a course of therapy at two

alternative clinics. Finding only some success with the alternative therapies, she returned to chemotherapy. At this point her use of nontoxic
therapies switched from alternative to complementary: she used various
nutritional supplements and other substances to strengthen her immune
system while on the chemotherapy.

Patients who decide to go to an alternative health care clinic should do
so with open eyes. For example, in Tijuana today there are more than
thirty clinics, practitioners, and hospitals that treat cancer patients with
nontoxic therapies. Some of them are very reputable places with teams of
doctors and good facilities, whereas others are very questionable. Pat
Fogderud, Myrna Gene, Dixie Keithly, and Pat Prince had very successful
experiences in Mexico, and Gene and Prince maintain affiliations with the
hospitals there. However, going to a foreign hospital or clinic is not an
option for everyone, because the cost can be very high. Susan Moss was
among those who advocated working at home with a clinician. As Moss
commented, "In fact, you can save a lot of money by going on my program. You'll stop buying so much meat and dairy products"; another
financial benefit, she added, comes from not "subjecting yourself to hundreds of thousands of dollars of medical 'treatments.'"

Some ACCTs had inherent limitations related to ease of use. For
example, Gayle Black was among the women who did not opt for the
Gerson therapy. Although it is perhaps the best-documented dietary therapy for cancer, the amount of food preparation required was daunting.
Likewise, Dixie Keithly was somewhat overwhelmed when she got home
from Mexico and had to institute her program. Her experience is instruc-
tive: she contacted another patient who had been through the program
and knew what she was going through. His reassurances helped give her
the willpower to continue. That experience suggests that a buddy system
might be useful as a way of increasing adherence to a program. The basic
message of sticking to a total program and not falling off the wagon
comes through many of the interviews.

Some ACCTs also carry with them substantial risks. One example is
therapies that require the use of catheters, or tubes that are placed into the
chest. Alice Cedillo had problems with catheters that involved emergency
room care. Although many patients commented that the risks of radiotherapy and chemotherapy had not been fully explained to them, the

question of informed consent also emerges for alternative and complementary health care providers. It seems that catheters can be very risky, and patients should be made aware of the risks if they are considering a type of treatment that might require a catheter.

Most of the women viewed ACCTs not in terms of choosing a single therapeutic modality from a large field but instead as assembling an individualized, total program. The total program may involve dietary changes, supplements, nontoxic pharmacological products, mind-body interventions, religious or spiritual involvement, and deep introspection into the meaning of one's life and the quality of one's personal relationships. Dietary changes were a key part of the program. Although many of the women encountered doctors who believed that dietary changes have no impact on cancer prognosis, regression, or progression, they often found other doctors who had a more holistic orientation. Most of the women chose a diet that was low in fat, dairy products, and red meat and high in fresh fruits and vegetables.

As occurs throughout the ACCT community, there were differences within the general consensus of a diet oriented toward fresh fruits and vegetables. For example, Susan Moss opted for carrot juice and whole grains (particularly grains with amygdalin), fruits, vegetables, and fish; and Matilda Moore used the grape diet to reduce the cervical tumor prior to surgery. Virginia Soffa and Ann Fonfa are just two examples of women whose dietary programs changed over time. Soffa emphasized flexibility and not getting locked into a rigid dietary program, because the body's needs change over time and in response to health or recovery.

Psychological and spiritual interventions were often important. Several of the women practice meditation and prayer. The benefits of meditation have been documented in the literature. Some women, such as Louise Greenfield, discussed meditation largely in terms of stress management, and stress was indeed an important factor in the life circumstances of many of the women. Others discussed meditation and prayer more in spiritual terms. In either case, several of the women benefited from those practices. Furthermore, conventional cancer therapy has increasingly recognized the importance of a variety of psychological interventions, which in many clinical settings are now an important part of adjunctive cancer care.

Some women also noted limitations with some of the psychospiritual interventions. For example, Sharon Batt questioned the literature on a type C cancer personality, because it could lead to a blame-the-victim psychology that may not be beneficial for a cancer patient to confront along with all the other life problems. Kimberly Eckley found meditation and Tai Chi difficult because she had so much stress that she was unable to clear her mind. Matilda Moore has a conservative religious orientation, and therefore she was uncomfortable with meditation and other practices that focus on something other than God. Pat Fogderud, a devout Christian, also said she was "not into New Age biofeedback, visualization, or psychology." Anne Frahm researched visualization but decided it was not as important as her attitude and state of mind throughout the day.

Some of the women developed psychological approaches beyond the standard ones usually associated with adjuvant cancer therapy. For example, Alice Epstein, Ph.D., distinguished two types of visualization: one was the Simonton style and the other involved working with subpersonalities as she had been taught in psychosynthesis. Melanie Zucker learned how to recall her dreams and then to work with them, and Charlotte Louise did a chanting, Buddhist type of meditation. Susan Moss extended visualization by combining it with exercise and music; one might call it "aerobic visualization" or "creative visualization." Moss also found that setting a deadline for herself—or having the doctors set one for her—helped provide her with the conscious and unconscious motivation for eliminating the tumors.

A strong sense of spirituality frequently provided the women with the strength to blaze an independent pathway. Whether the spirituality was anchored in a strong Christian faith or a non-Western tradition, it contributed to the ability of some of the women to question scientific authority—both for a poor prognosis and for poor therapeutic options—and to have a sense of hope, identity, and purpose. Others mentioned more secular sources of hope, identity, and purpose. Ann Fonfa described herself as having been active in the anti-Vietnam War movement, the civil rights movement, and later the women's movement, and subsequently she became a cancer activist.

Some women also mentioned the important impact of the morale of other patients whom they knew. Teresa Kennett described one conventional clinic as "like walking into the land of death." In contrast, the morale of patients at some of the alternative clinics is often very high. A visit to the Gerson hospital by a team of doctors documented the high morale there, and the doctors suggested that it may account for some of the success of the therapy (Reed, James, and Sikora 1990). Teresa Kennett commented, "I think if people can feel some sense of agency and efficacy in their health, it is tremendously healing."

Advice to Other Women

To reiterate, many of the women emphasized the importance of developing a total program that integrated psychological, spiritual, nutritional/metabolic, exercise, and de-stressing interventions, and sometimes the selective use of conventional therapies. Susan Moss formalized her program and gave it a name, MOTEP, for Marathon Olympic Tumor Eradication and Prevention. Many of the interviewees emphasized the importance of a multifaceted approach. Charlotte Louise had a good metaphor to describe the general process: eliminating toxicities from one's life. She was referring not only to physical toxicities, such as food and environmental carcinogens, but also to emotional toxicities such as bad relationships and stress. Several of the women linked their cancers to problems in interpersonal relationships and their successful recovery to resolving those problems or at least to gaining a sense of control over them. In Susan Moss's terms, "It's not just what you're eating; it's what's eating you."

Almost all the women emphasized adopting a stance of self-control, personal empowerment, or taking charge. Susan Moss stated that she always gets a second opinion, and "the second opinion is always my opinion." Charlotte Louise adds that a passive role is for people who want conventional options; the alternatives are for people who want to take charge. Dixie Keithly noticed that some patients are unable to take control of their disease because their husband or children want them to pursue conventional methods. In some cases the lack of support from family members is too much, and patients give in to conventional treatments even when they may not personally want them.

In Melanie Zucker's terms, then, even well-intentioned people can become "power robbers." Zucker developed a three-step approach to healing that emphasizes personal empowerment. One is "living at choice," which involves "making your own decisions and not letting others unduly influence you." In order to accomplish that goal, the second step involves developing a belief system for healing: patients need to articulate to themselves their own philosophy of healing. Finally, Zucker developed a system of analyzing "power robbers"—that is, people who take away your power.

Susan Moss found that one aspect of taking charge of one's life occurs when patients learn to "sing their song," to invoke the phrase of Lawrence LeShan (1994). Charlotte Louise gave herself permission to do things that she had not done before, such as taking dance lessons. Along similar lines, Dixie Keithly gave herself a trip to Africa, and then she went on adventurous vacations that became part of her long-term recovery.

Taking charge also means having discipline. Pat Prince emphasizes that the active role means continual dedication to one's recovery. As she commented, "You can't use that clinic, that doctor, or that particular treatment as a jump-start on a battery." Moss adds, "You still have to do the work of self-healing." Many of the women cautioned that once they achieved a remission with nontoxic approaches, they could not return to their old lifestyle. Not only does the successful patient seem to develop an individualized total program, but she stays with it even if she modifies it over time.

For Matilda Moore, the overwhelming sense she had in the conventional setting was a loss of control. Conversely, "One of the strongest things that the alternative therapies offered me was the feeling that I was still involved in the process." Gayle Black stated that she chose only doctors who would allow her to do both conventional and alternative therapies; in fact, she interviewed seven doctors before finding one whom she trusted. In her interview she emphasized the importance of finding a doctor who is a friend, but who also is willing to adopt a team approach to healing. Melanie Zucker added that the sense of control does not end with the switch to alternatives; patients need to be just as vigilant about maintaining control when they work with alternative practitioners.

One implication of taking charge is refusing to accept a death sentence. Melanie Zucker compared a poor prognosis with the power of suggestion found among the bone-pointing shamans of other countries. Alice Cedillo suggested, "If you are given a death sentence, just don't accept it. Do everything you can to arm yourself with vital information regarding your diagnosis." Dixie Keithly has interviewed many patients who were given death sentences of incurable cancer and, with dedication and information, have developed programs that led to lasting recoveries. Louise Greenfield was among the women who emphasized the importance of doing research. The more one learns, the more likely it is that one will find rays of light that offer hope. Anne Frahm added, "The number one thing I would tell women is that there is hope. There is no type of cancer out there that someone hasn't overcome."

Another area of advice centered around individuality. Many of the women recommended developing a program based on each person's individual needs and desires. For example, to some extent the trade-off between conventional and alternative therapies involves different valuations of risk and benefit. Conventional therapies offer more certain statistical predictions of survival benefit, but in many cases the additional benefit can be very low in comparison with no therapy. Likewise, conventional therapies tend to be disfiguring or toxic and may lead to long-term conditions such as lymphedema or more virulent recurrences. Alternative and complementary therapies have much less data in their support, and therefore they are riskier in terms of potential survival benefit, but they are less toxic and, according to the experience of some of the women such as Soffa, the recurrences may be less virulent. Therefore, the package of therapies needs to be related to a woman's own concerns with issues such as survival, disfigurement, and toxicity. Only the patient can decide for herself what combination of risks, disfigurement, and toxicity is right for her.

Many of the women had unsatisfactory experiences with support groups. Cathy Hitchcock, Anne Frahm, Alice Cedillo, and Gayle Black had similar experiences of attending support groups that were oriented toward conventional therapies and only increased their sense of isolation. Anne Frahm noted that in one support group a lawyer explained how to make out a will, and in another one a dietitian explained how to make Jell-O. It is possible that the conventional orientation of the support groups is not shared by many of the women who attend them. In other words, there is a widespread interest in alternative and complementary approaches, but women may not feel comfortable talking about them in support groups that are hosted by conventional organizations. For example, in one case when the facilitator of the group was not present, the women were all talking about diet and alternatives; then when the facilitator returned, they resumed discussing conventional therapies. Rather than rely on official support groups, the women we interviewed tended to depend more on family, friends, and religion. They also emphasized getting out of bad relationships and mending broken ones as important pieces in their recovery program.

A Cautionary Note

The women interviewed here are all courageous leaders who, we believe, are helping to lead the way to a new framework for cancer therapy that offers patients informed choices from the best of conventional and alternative/complementary therapies. They deserve to be congratulated and honored. Nevertheless, they are not, with a few exceptions, scientists or clinicians. No matter what advice individual interviewees give in this book, it is our advice to cancer patients who read this book that they do not attempt to use supplements, diet, or any other form of less toxic therapeutic intervention on their own. Even something as apparently innocuous as a vitamin supplement can be dangerous if taken in the wrong dose or in combination with other substances; for that reason it is always important to pursue such therapeutic approaches with the guidance of a competent doctor or team of health care providers that includes persons knowledgeable about oncology and nutritional science.

Furthermore, some of the vocabulary used and causal inferences drawn in the interviews should be taken with a grain of salt. For example, many researchers prefer to speak in terms of remission rather than cure. Some also speak of a long-term survival benefit (five or ten years) or a quality-of-life benefit that is afforded by a given therapy. At a certain point, of course, a woman who has had no sign of cancer for many years would be justified in using the word *cure*.

Another problem is the difficulty of drawing causal inferences from case studies. The cases presented here are not meant to be medical case histories; they are meant instead to document the experiences of certain women patients, how they make decisions about conventional or alternative/complementary therapies, and the policy implications of the dilemmas and problems they face. It is almost impossible to draw a causal inference from a case history that is as complicated as most of those presented in this book, because the patients used multiple therapies, often both conventional and alternative/complementary, and often used them at the same time or in close sequence. Patients may intuitively feel that one particular intervention allowed them to turn the corner, but that intuition needs to be distinguished from scientific evidence.

From the viewpoint of scientific inference of clinical causality, about the only conclusion that can be drawn from the interviews is that there is a pocket of women who used alternative or complementary therapies, and they seem to have benefited. Only formal epidemiological or clinical studies could make it possible to put forward a stronger scientific claim. The main conclusion of this book is policy-oriented rather than clinically oriented: there needs to be a substantial change in research agendas, regulatory policy, and curricula to open up the doors for the evaluation and careful, experimental, clinical use of less toxic cancer therapies. Although some of the women strongly endorse alternative cancer therapies instead of conventional cancer treatments, many suggest instead that conventional medicine needs to relax and open up to less toxic alternatives. As statistical surveys show, patients are going to be using alternative and complementary therapies anyway (Eisenberg et al. 1993, McGinnis 1991). It is time that health care practitioners, the cancer research organizations, and regulatory bodies begin to address policies that allow the evaluation and clinical use of alternative and complementary cancer therapies.

Opinions of Publicly Supported Cancer Organizations

There was widespread skepticism of national organizations, both public and private, that are dedicated to conventional cancer research and therapies. Most of the women were well aware of the size of the cancer industry, and they were skeptical that the money was being spent in the best interests of patients. Alice Epstein mentioned one reason why she prefers to work with local organizations: "With local organizations, you know that they are not collecting money for maintaining their bureaucracies." Likewise, Sharon Batt advised that people work at the local level but maintain connections at the national and international levels.

Regarding national organizations, opinions of the National Cancer Institute varied. Gayle Black called the NCI hot-line, 1-800-FOR-CANCER, to get information on clinical trials and found that source of information helpful. Black also thought that the PDQ (physician's desk query) for lymphedema at the NCI provides much good information: <gopher:// gopher.nih.gov...o/supportive/lymphedema>. Susan Holloran and Virginia Soffa discussed the organization less in terms of its value as a resource and more in terms of its research priorities. Holloran expressed concern that the NCI criticizes ACCTs as unproven but does not provide funding to evaluate them. She also explained how the creation of the Office of Alternative Medicine was a very superficial attempt to respond to increasing consumer demand for alternative therapies. She pointed out that politically the decision to situate research on alternative and complementary therapies within the NIH allows the cancer research establishment to limit and control the research.

Likewise, when Soffa met with the NCI and criticized their approach, she noticed that some of the researchers were agreeing with her. She said, "If you guys agree with this, why the heck are you doing what you're doing? Why were you offering these treatments?" She was also very critical of their research on preventive medicine. "They call tamoxifen prevention. This is a total joke. I mean, let's give people another type of cancer. That's what I called it when I was there. I said, 'This is disease substitution.' This is not okay." Ann Fonfa suggested that the NCI start to run trials of matched groups of conventionally treated patients and those using nontoxic methods. In general, a changed research agenda so that nontoxic alternatives are evaluated fairly is likely to become the key policy issue for cancer activists. Intervention via congressional mandate will be necessary, and in turn a great deal of work by cancer activists will be needed to develop the political will for that intervention.

There were similar criticisms of the American Cancer Society. Myrna Gene mentioned the organization's investment in chemotherapy via its ownership of a patent on a chemotherapy drug, and Pat Fogderud's request for information about the late Harold Manner, Ph.D., met with the typical response that he is a quack. The organization offered to provide Kimberly Eckley with a wig, a level of help that she found almost ridiculous. However, Cathy Hitchcock commented that the organization was a good resource for questions about conventional therapies, and Gayle Black praised its support groups for husbands. It seems that the organization can be helpful once its limitations are understood.

Several of the interviewees attended the annual convention of the Cancer Control Society, or they used its lists of patients who were undergoing nontoxic treatment. Hess has attended two of the annual conventions, which are held annually in Pasadena, California. The information can be helpful to a novice patient, but there is also very little screening of health claims, so as in many other major consumer purchases, caveat emptor. Hess's sibling book *Evaluating Alternative Cancer Therapies* includes interviews with leading clinicians, researchers, and heads of referral and support organizations in the ACCT field, as well as a discussion of criteria for making a decision about purchasing information-providing services that are available from some of the organizations. In general, patients are warned to check out the financial interests and credentials of any organization that provides information.

Gayle Black mentioned the hot-line of the National Lymphedema Network at 1-800-541-3259 as a good resource for women with lymphedema, and she also found the lectures at SHARE, a nonprofit organization in New York, to be helpful. Likewise, Charlotte Louise mentioned that SHARE was one of the organizations, if the not the only one, that she contacted initially in New York that was open to alternatives. She served on a panel of long-term ovarian cancer survivors that SHARE put together, and it turned out that they had all used alternative or complementary therapies. Ann Fonfa chairs the Alternative/Whole Health Committee of SHARE. She is an activist among activists: she is among the women who are leading the way within the women's health movement and breast cancer activism to bring about a change in medical practice that will allow more choices for women cancer patients. Whereas many of the organizations in the breast cancer movement are funded by and to some extent co-opted by the cancer industry, Ann Fonfa is among the leaders of the movement for a different type of women's cancer activism that will open the door to less toxic therapies and diagnostic procedures. For example, she helped to circulate a petition at the National Breast Cancer Coalition (NBCC) conference that brought Wayne Jonas, M.D., of the Office of Alternative Medicine to the floor of the conference in 1997. Virginia Soffa pointed out that the large breast cancer organizations are oriented toward conventional therapies, and Wooddell noticed that the plenary sessions of the 1997 annual meeting of the NBCC were still directed toward changes within the arena of conventional therapies. With the work of activists like Ann Fonfa and other women leaders interviewed in this book, breast cancer activists may soon be more aware of the potential benefit of ACCTs. When that happens, the political context for cancer research as a whole will never be the same. In other words, we believe that the breast cancer activists may hold the key to reforming cancer research as a whole.

In addition to reforming the research agenda for cancer, several of the women pointed to needed reforms in regulatory policy. Perhaps one of the most poignant commentaries on the role of the Food and Drug Administration in limiting the access of patients to nontoxic therapies is the case of Kimberly Eckley's petition to be allowed to use antineoplastons for herself. That petition was denied; the agency thought she would do "just fine" on chemotherapy. "Who is the government to limit my choices?" she asked. The political situation is almost uncanny: a regulatory agency is making medical decisions about what type of therapeutic approach would either prevent recurrence or treat a specific cancer. Eckley commented, "I believe it's my body and it should be my decision for choosing among the various therapies." Likewise, Burzynski patient Teresa Kennett commented, "As Americans, I think that we should have access to promising nontoxic treatments for supposedly incurable diseases."

Eckley also mentioned the Access to Medical Treatments bill, which has been before the U.S. Congress for several years. Similar bills have already passed legislatures in several states. The federal law would allow doctors and patients to work together on programs of safe, experimental therapies. Passage of the federal legislation should considerably lower the risk of lawsuits and loss of license that doctors have faced when they have integrated nontoxic therapies into conventional cancer treatment. The bill may contribute to a shift in the balance of power in evaluation from the expensive and politically charged methods of randomized, clinical trials to the smaller-scale, patient-sensitive methods of clinical case reviews and outcomes assessments.

The current regulatory climate means that some cancer patients have had to go to foreign countries to obtain the care they want. Myrna Gene commented, "I think it's very sad that we have to go somewhere else when it's known that effective therapies do exist." Furthermore, as Charlotte Louise pointed out, it also means that the price of ACCTs within the United States often puts them beyond the reach of many patients. Insurance companies often do not cover experimental therapies, and in other cases doctors are forced to charge more because they have to pay legal fees to defend themselves in court.

To date, cancer patients have tended to organize around prostate cancer and breast cancer. Women and men who have other types of cancer may find themselves even more isolated, and there is a need for organizations focused on other types of cancer. However, we think that the main source of publicly led political change is likely to come from breast cancer patients. In the past, women have been very successful in developing public recognition of breast cancer as a high-priority research area. In 1995 the *New York Times* called breast cancer the charity of the year. Funding priorities have changed substantially so that breast cancer now receives the second highest total funding of all diseases researched by the NIH (Walker 1997). Yet, as Susan Holloran commented, breast cancer activism has tended to promote the status quo in the research agenda.

One of the conclusions that we draw from the interviews in this book is that more money for cancer research—for both women and men—is only the first step toward solving the problem. Surveys indicate that 10 to 50 percent of all cancer patients are using alternative therapies, often as adjuvant modalities. When one considers that well over a million people per year are diagnosed with cancer, there is a tremendous political potential for organizing a reform of the research and regulatory agenda. The women we interviewed represent only some of the most articulate leaders. Their ideas, work, and experience suggest that women's health organizations take a second step now that breast cancer research has been recognized as a high-priority issue. The next step is to restructure research priorities so that more money is spent on evaluating alternative and complementary therapies for all types of cancer. Multiple methods are needed: outcomes assessments, case study reviews, and clinical trials that compare alternative therapies with conventional therapies. Women need this information so that they can make better decisions, and policy reforms are needed so that they have the right to follow through on their decisions. Let us hope that they can achieve the political clout to make the next step a reality.

References

Austin, Steve
  1996 "When Is Allopathic Medicine Useful in the Treatment of Invasive Breast Cancer?" *Journal of Naturopathic Medicine* 6 (1): 44–48.
Block, Keith
  1997 "The Role of the Self in Health Cancer Survivorship: A View From the Front Lines of Treating Cancer." *Advances* 13 (1): 6–26.
Early Breast Cancer Trialists' Collaborative Group
  1992 "Systematic Treatment of Early Breast Cancer by Hormonal, Cytotoxic, or Immune Therapy." *Lancet* 339: 1–15.
Eisenberg, David, Ronald Kessler, Cindy Foster, Frances Norlock, David Calkins, and Thomas Delbanco
  1993 "Unconventional Medicine in the United States." *New England Journal of Medicine* 328 (4): 246–52.
Fisher, Bernard, S. Anderson, C. K. Redmond, et al.
  1995 "Reanalysis and Results after 12 Years of Follow-Up in a Randomized Clinical Trial Comparing Total Mastectomy with Lumpectomy with or without Irradiation in the Treatment of Breast Cancer." *New England Journal of Medicine* 333: 456–61.
Hess, David
  1999 *Evaluating Alternative Cancer Therapies: A Guide to the Science and Politics of an Emerging Medical Field.* New Brunswick, N.J.: Rutgers University Press.

Hildenbrand, Gar, L. Christeene Hildenbrand, Karen Bradford, Dan E. Rogers, Charlotte Gerson Strauss, and Shirley Cavin
    1996 "The Role of Follow-up and Retrospective Data Analysis in Alternative Cancer Management: The Gerson Experience." *Journal of Naturopathic Medicine* 6 (1): 49–56.
Houston, Robert
    1997 Personal correspondence. Letter of November 16.
LeShan, Lawrence
    1994 *Cancer as a Turning Point.* New York: Plume.
McGinnis, Lamar
    1991 "Alternative Therapies, 1990. An Overview." *Cancer* 67 (6 Supp.): 1788–92.
Moss, Ralph
    1995 *Questioning Chemotherapy.* New York: Equinox Press.
Overgaard, Marie, Per Hansen, et al. for the Danish Breast Cancer Cooperative Group
    1997 "Postoperative Radiotherapy in High-Risk Premenopausal Women with Breast Cancer Who Receive Adjuvant Chemotherapy." *New England Journal of Medicine* 337 (14): 949–55.
Ragaz, Joseph, Steward Jackson, et al.
    1997 "Adjuvant Radiotherapy and Chemotherapy in Node-Positive Premenopausal Women with Breast Cancer." *New England Journal of Medicine* 337 (14): 956–62.
Reed, Alison, Nicholas James, and Karol Sikora
    1990 "Mexico: Juices, Coffee Enemas, and Cancer." *Lancet* 336: 676–77.
Walker, Paulette
    1997 "Lawmakers Push NIH to Spend More on the Most Prevalent Diseases." *Chronicle of Higher Education,* April 18, A34.

Index

About the Authors

David J. Hess, Ph.D., is a cultural/medical anthropologist and professor of science and technology studies at Rensselaer Polytechnic Institute. He is the author of nine other books on science and the public, including theoretical books on the sociology and anthropology of science, technology, and medicine, such as *Science and Technology in a Multicultural World* (Columbia University Press) and *Science Studies: An Advanced Introduction* (NYU Press). He has written on popular medicine in Brazil in *Spirits and Scientists* (Penn State University Press) and numerous peer-reviewed publications, and he currently works on the politics and social aspects of alternative cancer therapies in the United States. His research includes a book on the controversial research tradition on bacteria as possible agents in cancer causation (*Can Bacteria Cause Cancer?*, NYU Press) and a collection of interviews with opinion leaders of the alternative/complementary cancer therapy community (*Evaluating Alternative Cancer Therapies*, Rutgers University Press).

The chair of the Committee on the Anthropology of Science, Technology, and Computing of the American Anthropological Association from 1996 to 1998, he has been a leader in the application of anthropological theory and methods to the social studies of science. He is the recipient of various grants and awards, including two Fulbrights and a National Science Foundation grant in the public understanding of science in the alternative cancer therapy movement. He has published in many peer-reviewed journals, including *Social Studies of Science, Cultural Anthropology, Medical Anthropology Quarterly,* and *Luso-Brazilian Review.*

Margaret J. Wooddell is a doctoral student in the science and technology studies department at Rensselaer Polytechnic Institute. A graduate of the University of Pittsburgh, she received her master's degree from North Carolina State University at Raleigh.

Prior to her doctoral studies, she was project coordinator, regulatory compliance auditor, and research scientist for a major pharmaceutical house in the pharmaceutical industry. While attending Rensselaer Polytechnic Institute, she has had several internships with the National Science Foundation.